VLISP
A Verified Implementation of Scheme

edited by

Joshua D. Guttman
The MITRE Corporation

Mitchell Wand
Northeastern University

A Special Issue of
Lisp and Symbolic Computation, An International Journal
Vol. 8, Nos. 1 & 2
March 1995

SPRINGER SCIENCE+BUSINESS MEDIA, LLC

CONTENTS

ISBN 978-0-7923-9566-9 ISBN 978-1-4615-2339-0 (eBook)
DOI 10.1007/978-1-4615-2339-0

Library of Congress Cataloging-in-Publication Data

A C.I.P. Catalogue record for this book is available
from the Library of Congress.

Printed on acid-free paper.

LISP AND SYMBOLIC COMPUTATION: An International Journal, 8, 3–4 (1995)

Preface

The VLISP project undertook to verify rigorously the implementation of a programming language. The project began at The MITRE Corporation in late 1989, under the company's Technology Program; the work was supervised by the Rome Laboratory of the United States Air Force. Northeastern University became involved a year later.

We particularly aimed at realism and at comprehensiveness. The goal of realism showed itself in the choice of a widely used programming language, namely Scheme, and in the choice of an implementation strategy that is flexible and reasonably efficient. The goal of comprehensiveness showed itself in the broad range of implementation steps that we undertook to verify. These steps lead from the abstract syntax of a high level programming language, equipped with a continuation-style denotational semantics, down to an abstract assembly language, equipped with a concrete operational semantics.

Our primary motivation was to add to the modest number of cases in which formal methods had been brought to bear on a real implementation. When we started the work, there was certainly a substantial amount of work on formal specification methods and proof methods for programs; there were a reasonable number of specification exercises, and proofs that a specification would meet a formally stated requirement; and of course there was a large body of proofs of correctness for individual algorithms. But only a few efforts had faced the issues of scale and detail that arise in establishing rigorously that a useful implementation meets its requirements. Modularization is needed to control the complexity of the task; contrasting specification methods may be needed at different levels of abstraction; and correctness conditions crucial at some levels may not even be statable at different levels. We aimed to show that these problems could be solved, and selected a Scheme language implementation as our testing ground.

We have tried to extract reusable conclusions from our problem. These are at two quite different levels. First, there are general approaches to organizing the work that we found to be beneficial and recommend to others. We have discussed them in the first paper, "VLISP: A Verified Implementation of Scheme," and summarized them at the end. We believe that they help to make formal methods more pragmatically effective. Second, there are four main verification techniques that we applied in the proof process. They are introduced in the first paper and then illustrated in detail in the following papers. We believe that they are widely reusable because we were able to use them repeatedly in VLISP, and have found new uses for them in other work since. This relatively small collection of techniques, none of them particularly arcane, allowed us to carry out a large verification. The identification of such reusable parts bodes well for the increased use of formal methods in compiler construction.

Acknowledgments. We are deeply indebted to our colleagues in the VLISP effort. Three of them joined us in preparing the papers that make up this issue, namely John D. Ramsdell and Vipin Swarup of The MITRE Corporation, and Dino P. Oliva, then a doctoral student at Northeastern University and now at the Oregon Graduate Institute. Two other important contributors to VLISP were William M. Farmer and Leonard G. Monk of MITRE.

We are grateful to Dr. Northrup Fowler III of the United States Air Force's Rome Laboratory, who oversaw the work as it was being done. The research would have been impossible without the personal commitment of Ronald Haggarty and Edward Lafferty of MITRE. MITRE kindly supplied additional funds after the end of the project itself, to enable us to prepare the papers published here.

Electronic versions of technical reports. The papers in this issue summarize, in updated and much improved form, a set of technical reports. More detailed information may be retrieved from the original technical reports, which are available electronically from the Scheme Repository using Universal Resource Locator

`ftp://ftp.cs.indiana.edu/pub/scheme-repository/doc/pubs/vlisp/`

The repository contains citations [7, 8, 10, 11, 12, 22, 23, 25, 29, 30] in the references to the introductory paper, pp. 30–32 below. Printed copies may be obtained from the authors.

Joshua D. Guttman and Mitchell Wand, January 1995

LISP AND SYMBOLIC COMPUTATION: An International Journal, 8, 5–32 (1995)

VLISP: A Verified Implementation of Scheme*

JOSHUA D. GUTTMAN guttman@mitre.org
JOHN D. RAMSDELL ramsdell@mitre.org
The MITRE Corporation
202 Burlington Road
Bedford, MA 01730-1420

MITCHELL WAND wand@ccs.neu.edu
College of Computer Science
161 Cullinane Hall
Northeastern University
Boston, MA 02115

Editors: Joshua D. Guttman and Mitchell Wand

Abstract. The VLISP project showed how to produce a comprehensively verified implementation for a programming language, namely Scheme. This paper introduces two more detailed studies on VLISP [13, 21]. It summarizes the basic techniques that were used repeatedly throughout the effort. It presents scientific conclusions about the applicability of the these techniques as well as engineering conclusions about the crucial choices that allowed the verification to succeed.

Keywords: verified, programming languages, Scheme, compiler

Table of Contents

* The work reported here was carried out as part of The MITRE Corporation's Technology Program, under funding from Rome Laboratory, Electronic Systems Command, United States Air Force, through contract F19628-89-C-0001. Preparation of this paper was generously supported by The MITRE Corporation. Mitchell Wand's participation was partly supported by NSF and DARPA under NSF grants CCR-9002253 and CCR-9014603.

1. Introduction

The VLISP project showed how to produce a comprehensively verified implementation for a programming language, namely Scheme [4, 15]. Some of the major elements in this verification were:

- The proof was based on the Clinger-Rees denotational semantics of Scheme given in [15]. Our goal was to produce a "warts-and-all" verification of a real language. With very few exceptions, we constrained ourselves to use the semantic specification as published.

  The verification was intended to be rigorous, but not completely formal, much in the style of ordinary mathematical discourse. Our goal was to verify the algorithms and data types used in the implementation, not their embodiment in code. See Section 2 for a more complete discussion of these issues.

  Our decision to be faithful to the published semantic specification led to the most difficult portions of the proofs; these are discussed in [13, Section 2.3–2.4].

- Our implementation was based on the Scheme48 implementation of Kelsey and Rees [17]. This implementation translates Scheme into an intermediate-level "byte code" language, which is interpreted by a virtual machine. The virtual machine is written in a subset of Scheme called PreScheme.

  The implementation is sufficiently complete and efficient to allow it to bootstrap itself. We believe that this is the first verified language implementation with these properties.

- The proof followed the structure of the Scheme48 implementation. It is organized into more than a dozen separable components, each of which presents an independent verification problem. This elaborate division was crucial to arriving at a tractable verification task.

  However, the proof used only a small collection of basic techniques:

  1. Semantics-preserving source-to-source transformations.
  2. Structural inductions using the denotational semantics, in the fashion of Wand and Clinger [31, 3].
  3. Verification of representations and refinements using operational semantics and the method of storage layout relations [32].
  4. The gap between denotational and operational semantics is bridged by soundness or faithfulness proofs; for the PreScheme compiler an adequacy result was achieved as well.

  Because of this small repertoire of basic techniques, we believe that the proof is accessible to readers without advanced mathematical background. With a very few exceptions, it does not require knowledge of domain theory, category theory, etc.

> We believe that this proof architecture can form a basis for other language-implementation proofs, as it uses both operational and denotational techniques to their best advantage.

The project involved 4 senior researchers and 1 Ph.D. student, with significant contributions by others, during a 3 year period from October 1989 until September 1992, when the verified system bootstrapped. The total effort was about 10 person-years. The present papers were written in 1993 and revised in 1994, with a small amount of additional funding. The specifications and proofs total about 600 pages of technical reports. The final implementation, as used in the bootstrap process, consists of about 10,000 lines of Scheme and 166 lines of C.

The techniques used in the proofs are described in detail in [13, 21]. In this paper, we discuss those aspects of the project that go beyond the individual proofs. In Section 2, we discuss the crucial choices that allowed the verification to succeed, and especially the degree of rigor we have aimed for. In Section 3, we discuss the implementation in more detail and present the results of the bootstrapping experiment. In Section 4, we discuss the structure of the proof in more detail, and introduce the small collection of basic techniques that were used repeatedly in the verification process. In Section 5, we assess the strengths and weaknesses of operational and denotational styles in various stages of the verification. In Section 6 we discuss the implications of our work for other language-verification efforts.

One basic condition of our success was to embark on a reasonably well specified task. An effort on this scale would have been hopeless without there already being a fairly well polished formal semantics for the language to be implemented. The official Scheme semantics [15, Appendix A] has been stable for several years, and it has already served as the basis for substantial work, for instance [3]. To face the modeling issues of how to formalize the semantics at the same time that one is trying to develop verification proof techniques would be very difficult indeed.

We also chose to base our implementation on the well thought out design that Kelsey and Rees used in Scheme48 [17]. Scheme48 is divided into three major parts. The first is a compiler stage, which translates Scheme source programs to an intermediate level "byte code" language. The second stage is an interpreter to execute the complex instructions of the intermediate level language. The interpreter is written in PreScheme, which may be considered as a highly restricted sub-language of Scheme. The third portion is a compiler to translate PreScheme programs, the interpreter in particular, into runnable code. VLISP has adhered not only to this overall structure, but also to many specific choices made in Scheme48.

1.1. What is Scheme?

The Scheme programming language, "an UnCommon Lisp," is defined by the language Report (currently in its fourth revision [4]), and by an IEEE standard [15]. We have taken [15] as our definition.

However, the definition consists, for our purposes, of two radically different parts. The first and much larger part provides a carefully written but non-rigorous description of the lexical and syntactic structure of the language, and of its standard procedures and data structures. Many of the standard procedures are conceptually complex; they are generally implemented in Scheme itself, using a smaller set of procedures as data manipulation primitives.

The short, second portion consists of Appendix A, which provides an abstract syntax and a formal denotational semantics for the phrases in that syntax. The semantics is concise and relatively abstract; however, for this reason, it provides only a loose specification for the implementer. Most of the standard procedures, even the data manipulation primitives, correspond to nothing in the denotational semantics; the denotations of constants are mostly unspecified; moreover, the semantics contains no treatment of ports and I/O.

The VLISP verification has taken Appendix A, in the slightly modified form given in [10], as its starting point. We have therefore concentrated on verifying those aspects of the language that it characterizes; some other aspects—especially the finiteness of address spaces—have only been introduced into our specifications at lower levels in the process of specifying and verifying our implementation.

2. Rigor and Prototyping

In this section we will discuss our approach to achieving rigor, and how we exploited non-rigorous, empirical kinds of evidence.

2.1. The Emphasis on Rigor

Rigor is not identical with formality. A formal theory is always expressed in a fully defined logical theory, with a precise syntax and semantics; formal proofs in the theory are carried out using a particular deductive system that is sound for it. There must be a syntactic decision procedure to establish whether a given purported proof is in fact a formal derivation in the system.

Full formalization is certainly a way of achieving rigor, but not the only way. Rigor has also been achieved when we know how to complete a formalization, even though a substantial amount of skilled labor may be needed to carry it out.

In our view, formality is only a means: the goal is rigorous understanding. We have chosen to emphasize the latter over the former because of our view of the purpose of verification.

Perhaps the most obvious view is that the point of verification is to eliminate all sources of error, or if that is beyond human powers, as many sources of error as possible. That is not our view.

We believe that the point is to provide *insight* into the structure of an implementation and the reasons for its correctness. We believe that several benefits follow from the mathematical insight that rigor produces:

Less Likelihood of Abuse When the intended behavior of software is rigorously described, it is less likely to be subtly misunderstood and put to uses for which it is intrinsically not suited.

Increased Reliability Errors are likely to be dramatically less frequent. Moreover, when they are found, they are likely to be matters of detail rather than fundamental design flaws.

Easier Correction of Errors When errors are encountered, they are apt to be far more easily understood, localized, and fixed.

Greater Adaptability Because of the rigorous specifications of the different portions of the system, those portions are easier to combine with new pieces in a predictable way. New but related functionality is easier to introduce without destroying old functionality.

Because these practical advantages are essentially by-products of rigorous mathematical insight, we have tried to organize the project to emphasize humanly understandable rigor rather than complete machine-checkable formality.

There are two reasons why there is a potential conflict between aiming for rigor and aiming for formality:

- Fully formalized specifications and proofs require great effort, particularly in the case of a project spanning contrasting semantic styles and covering a large implementation in detail. There is a risk that the attempt to achieve full formality would prevent covering large portions of the implementation with any acceptable degree of rigor.

- Full formality requires choices on many details that every logician knows can be handled in a variety of acceptable ways. As a consequence, the proportion of informative content in the total written specification decreases. It may be just as difficult for a human being to extract a rigorous insight into a system from a full formalization of it than it would have been starting from a non-rigorous engineering description. Similarly, fully formalized or mechanized proofs may focus attention on the need to manipulate a particular theorem-proving system at the expense of acquiring and recording an insight into the reasons why the theorems are true and the system correct.

We motivate two practical decisions from this emphasis on rigorous insight. First, we have expressed our specifications in what we believe to be a lucid and reliable form, but without the syntactic constraints of a formalized specification language. Second, we have decided to focus our verification specifically on the algorithms used throughout the implementation, rather than on their concrete embodiment in code. Our division of the proof into a large number of separately understandable verifications was also partly motivated by a desire to make each separate proof surveyable as a whole.

2.1.1. Rigorous, but Not Completely Formal Specifications

VLISP required three main different kinds of languages for specification. In no case did we completely formalize the notation, although there are no interesting mathematical problems that would have to be faced to do so. The first of these rigorous but informal specification languages is the familiar mathematical notation for denotational semantics. The second is a notation for expressing algorithms; for this purpose we have used predominantly the applicative sub-language of Scheme. There are a variety of conventions needed to interrelate these two language, such as conventions relating **cons** and the other Scheme list primitives to the denotational notations for mathematical pairs and sequences. Finally, a language was introduced to present state machine transition functions.

At several points formality might have helped us to save labor, had we had sufficiently flexible mechanized theorem proving support. These were situations in which many detailed cases had to checked, for instance, those described in [13, Sections 3.2 and 6.2]. However, tool flexibility is crucial; these situations involve quite different semantic contexts.

2.1.2. Algorithm-Level Verification.

There are several different levels at which formal methods can be applied to software. Ranged by their rough intuitive distance from the final executable image, among them are:

- Formalization of system correctness requirements;
- Verification of a high-level design specification against formalized correctness requirements;
- Verification of algorithms and data types;
- Verification of concrete program text;
- Verification of the (compiled) object code itself, as illustrated by Boyer and Yu's work [2].

Broadly speaking, the higher up a particular verification is in this list, the more there is that can go wrong between the verification process and the actual behavior of the program on a particular computer. On the other hand, if the verification is lower in the list, the mass of detail is much greater, creating a tradeoff in the informativeness and even reliability of the verification. As the amount of detail rises, and the proportion of it that is intuitively understandable goes down, we are less likely to verify exactly the properties we care about, and more likely to introduce mathematical flaws into our proofs. We have focused on the algorithm level. We have found that our algorithmic verification was an effective way to ease the development of correct software. Very few bugs emerged in software we wrote based on algorithmic specifications, as opposed to our more exploratory prototype programming. Those we did find were easy to correct, with one notable exception.

Indeed, our most difficult bug, which was very hard to isolate, generally confirms our decision. The problem concerned garbage collection. It arose precisely where we took a shortcut not reflected in the specification, for the sake of efficiency. We omitted the memory operations to ensure that newly allocated memory locations would contain a distinctive value *empty*, since we were sure the program would initialize the memory to the correct useful value before the garbage collector could be called. In this we departed from our specification, which assumed that newly allocated memory contained *empty*. But the garbage collector could in fact be called before the initialization. Hence the garbage collector would follow bit-patterns in the newly allocated memory that happened to look like pointers. Later, however, we specified a version of allocation and garbage collection which does not require the initialization to *empty*; this we successfully verified and implemented.

The algorithmic level of verification was particularly appropriate for our work. This is because we were able to arrange our code so that the great majority of it took on certain special forms. Thus, we could reason about the algorithms in a tractable way, and convince ourselves informally that these abstract algorithms matched the behavior of the code. We used three primary techniques for this purpose.

- Whenever possible we used applicative programs. As a consequence, we could regard the very same text as specifying the abstract algorithm and also as providing its implementation. In reasoning about the abstract algorithm, we used forms of reasoning such as β-reduction freely, which are not valid for all Scheme programs. However, to convince ourselves that the reasoning was a reliable prediction of the behavior of the actual Scheme code, we needed only to check that the procedures did not use state-changing primitives, I/O, or `call/cc`, and that they would terminate for all values of the parameters.

- In many other cases, we organized programs to implement a state machine. This design abstraction uses a dispatch procedure to select one of a set of transformation procedures. Each transformation procedure performs a relatively simple state transformation before tail recursively invoking the dispatch procedure. This is an organization that is very natural for a byte code interpreter in any case. Moreover, it is easy to match a short piece of non-applicative code with the specification for these simple transformation procedures.

- In the case of the PreScheme Front End, we organized the program using a set of *rules* and a control structure. Each rule specifies a simple syntactic transformation on expressions matching a particular pattern. These transformations are proved to preserve the semantics of the source program being compiled. However, the choice of whether actually to apply a rule and the choice of the order to apply rules throughout the source program is made by code implementing a control structure that need not be verified at all. This control code may freely apply the rules in any way that seems heuristically useful in optimizing the source program; since no individual rule can alter the semantics of the source program, any *finite* sequence of rule applications whatever will be safe.

However, the Front End does not terminate for all inputs. Indeed the question whether, for a given PreScheme program P, there exists a finite sequence of rule applications that transforms P to an acceptable output form appears to be algorithmically undecidable. Thus, we could not reasonably demand a terminating control structure for the Front End.

2.2. "Prototype but Verify"

A traditional view of program verification envisages first designing, developing, and debugging the programs, and then proving that the programs meet their specifications. A contrasting approach [6, 9] is that programs and their proofs should be developed hand-in-hand, with proof ideas leading the way. Our experience with the VLISP project suggests that an intermediate approach is preferable for developing *large* verified programs.

Our approach was to develop initial executable prototypes of the desired programs, using normal software engineering techniques such as modular design and type-checking. We then used proof ideas to *refine* these programs to a form amenable to verification proofs. The programs were partitioned into about a dozen components, each of which presented an independent verification problem. Each component had a clear purpose embodied in the interface specification of the component. We then used programming ideas to *optimize* the algorithms to achieve desired performance characteristics. We continued using proof ideas to refine the algorithms to achieve, or restore, clarity and correctness. Optimizations often made the intended correctness proofs much harder, so we used the prototype to estimate performance improvements to decide whether the benefits were worth the costs.

Thus, we found it indispensable to have running prototypes of portions of the system being verified, and eventually of the entire integrated system. Portions of the prototype were gradually replaced by rigorously verified code as it was developed.

3. The VLISP Implementation

Although the VLISP implementation is similar to Scheme48, the two systems differ in three main ways:

- Scheme48 uses a real stack, unlike VLISP, which stores the corresponding information in the heap. The Scheme48 stack is a fairly complex data structure, and it is not clear what invariants it maintains during execution. The Scheme48 stack also necessitates a more complex garbage collector.

- Scheme48 adds a variety of additional byte codes to speed execution of common patterns. Although most of them would not have called for changes of method, they would have added to the bulk of the verification, both in the extended compiler and in the virtual machine.

- Scheme48 handles interrupts, such as the user typing control-C at the keyboard to interrupt a long-running procedure. It was not clear how to formalize this.

Scheme48 was under active development as we were working. Moreover, its code is sparsely commented, so the easiest way to get a deep understanding of the code we were to verify was to write it ourselves.

3.1. The VLISP Bootstrap Process

We believe that VLISP is the only verified programming language implementation that has been used to bootstrap itself.

One cycle in the bootstrap process produces new versions of two binary files by executing old versions of those files. One of these binary files contains an executable version of the VLISP VM; we call this file **vvm**. The other contains a particular byte code program that the VM will execute, namely the byte code image of the VLISP byte code compiler itself. We call this file **old-vscm.image**.

The process requires five main steps; in each step another source file is used as input. In each of these five steps, in addition to the input file, there are two other ingredients. These are the executable version of the VLISP VM, and some byte code image that the VM can run. In the first step, this byte code image is **old-vscm.image**. The five steps are:

1. Produce **vscm.image** from input file **vscm.scm** using **vvm** as virtual machine and **old-vscm.image** as the byte code program. **vscm.scm** is the Scheme source for the VLISP byte code compiler. This step reconstructs the first of the two binary files. The remaining steps are all devoted to reconstructing the other, namely the executable **vvm**.

2. Produce **vps.image** from input file **vps.scm** using **vvm** as virtual machine and **vscm.image** as the byte code program. The input **vps.scm** is the Scheme source for the VLISP PreScheme Front End program, and **vps.image** is a byte code image of it.

3. Produce **pps.image** from input file **pps.scm** using **vvm** as virtual machine and **vscm.image** as the byte code program. The input file **pps.scm** is the source of the Pure PreScheme compiler, and **pps.image** is its compiled byte code image.

4. Produce **vvm.pps** from input file **vvm.scm** using **vvm** as virtual machine and **vps.image** as the byte code program. The input file **vvm.scm** is the VLISP PreScheme source of the virtual machine, and the output **vvm.pps** is the translation of it into Pure PreScheme produced by running the Front End. We always give files containing VLISP PreScheme a filename extension of **.scm**, because they are in fact Scheme programs, even though they are of a very special kind that can also be executed in a different way.

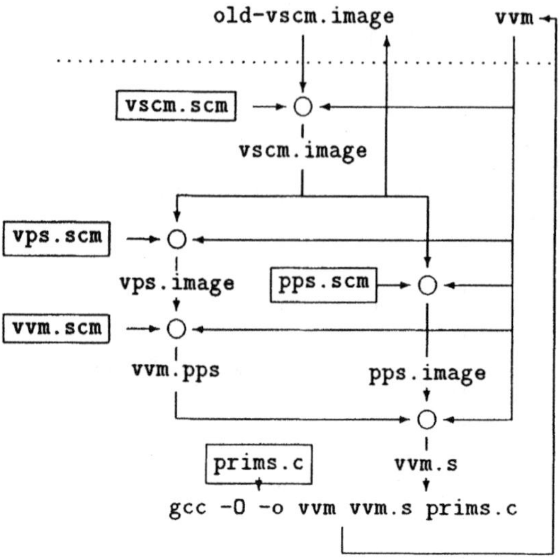

Figure 1. VLISP Bootstrap Process

5. Produce **vvm.s** from input file **vvm.pps** using **vvm** as virtual machine and the file **pps.image** as the byte code program. The output is the assembly language version of the new VLISP VM.

To create the new **vvm** executable, we then use **gcc** to link **vvm.s** with the C code for the primitives that call the operating system, and to assemble the results:

```
gcc -O -o vvm vvm.s prims.c
```

Since I/O primitives simply call the operating system, and since we are not in a position to prove anything about the effect of a call to the operating system, we did not consider it worth the trouble to code the I/O primitives directly in assembly language. Apart from compiling these C-coded primitives, the only task of the **gcc** C compiler is to combine the result with the assembly language output **vvm.s**, and to call the assembler and linker. The structure of this process is expressed in Figure 1. In this figure, the left, top and right in-arrows are always the input file, the byte code image, and the virtual machine executable, respectively.

Two initial executable versions **vvm** and **cvm** for the VM were constructed.

vvm We compiled the VLISP VM using the VLISP Front End and the Pure PreScheme compiler. These in turn had been compiled using Scheme->C [1].

cvm This VM was constructed by directly implementing the VM algorithms in C.

Table 1. Bootstrap Run Times in Minutes, using **vvm**

Input	Byte Code Image	Output	Sun4	Sun3
vscm.scm	old-vscm.image	vscm.image	26	262
vps.scm	vscm.image	vps.image	34	352
pps.scm	vscm.image	pps.image	19	192
vvm.scm	vps.image	vvm.pps	196	
vvm.pps	pps.image	vvm.s	13	

Two versions of the initial image **old-vscm.image** of the Scheme to Byte Code compiler were also constructed.

- The Scheme to Byte Code compiler source was compiled using Scheme->C, and this executable was used to compile the same source to a byte code image.
- Another image was constructed using Scheme48 [17] to run the Scheme to Byte Code compiler on itself as input.

The bootstrap process was almost completely unaffected by the choice of initial image or VM. The only difference concerned the default case of the Scheme reader. When the system is bootstrapped from an implementation that reads symbols in a particular case by default, the resulting image retains the property. We found this behavior necessary in order to allow VLISP to be bootstrapped starting with any Scheme implementation, regardless of its default case. When we modified Scheme48 to cause its reader to prefer upper case, we obtained exactly the same results as from Scheme->C.

After the first bootstrap cycle, the assembly source for the VM is unchanged by any succeeding bootstrap cycle. Because of a peculiarity in the way symbols are generated, the image of the Scheme to Byte Code compiler is unchanged by a pair of *two* bootstrap cycles.

3.2. VLISP Virtual Machine Performance

Table 1 presents the time required for each step when run on a Sun SPARCStation 10.

In order to estimate the efficiency of our interpreter program, as compiled by the VLISP PreScheme Front End and the Pure PreScheme compiler, we have also compared it with **cvm**, the C implementation of the algorithms.

cvm was carefully optimized to ensure that it achieved the maximum performance possible with the type of interpreter we implemented. For instance, we scrutinized the Sun 4 assembly code produced by the gcc C compiler with its optimizing flag -O to ensure that registers were effectively used, and that memory references into arrays were optimal. Timings are indicated in Table 2.

Table 2. Bootstrap Run Times in Minutes, using `cvm`

Input	Byte Code Image	Output	Sun4	Sun3
`vscm.scm`	`old-vscm.image`	`vscm.image`	4.3	78.8
`vps.scm`	`vscm.image`	`vps.image`	5.5	87.6
`pps.scm`	`vscm.image`	`pps.image`	3.2	49.9
`vvm.scm`	`vps.image`	`vvm.pps`	33.8	
`vvm.pps`	`pps.image`	`vvm.s`	2.3	

Differences in performance are due to three main sources. First, `cvm` was programmed to keep certain crucial global variables in machine registers. The PreScheme compiler currently does not put any global variables into machine registers. Second, we structured the virtual machine program to facilitate our verification. In particular, we used abstractions to encapsulate successive refinement layers in the machine. We also have many run-time checks in the code. They ensure that the conditions for application of the formally specified rules are in fact met as the interpreter executes. Finally, `gcc` has sophisticated optimizations, for which there is nothing comparable in the Pure PreScheme compiler.

Nevertheless, the ratio of the speed of `cvm` to the speed of the VLISP virtual machine, when run on a Sun 3, is between 3 and 4. On the Sun 4, it is about 6. The ratio is higher on the Sun 4 partly because `gcc` makes very good use of the large Sun 4 register set. Also, `gcc` does instruction scheduling to keep the Sun 4 instruction pipeline full when possible. Finally, some optimizations to primitives in the PreScheme compiler have been implemented in the Sun 3 version, but not yet in the newer Sun 4 version.

We consider these numbers reasonably good, particularly because there are many additional optimizations that could be verified and implemented for the PreScheme compiler. Indeed, more recent variants of the PreScheme implementation seem to perform much better.

4. Structure of the Proof

The Vlisp implementation is organized into more than a dozen separable components, each of which presents an independent verification problem. This division was crucial to arriving at a soluble verification task.

4.1. Refinement Layers

The proof steps are grouped into three major parts, corresponding to the major parts of the implementation. The first half dozen are devoted to the compiler stage, which translates Scheme source programs to byte code. A second group of three main verifications justify the interpreter that runs the resulting byte code programs. We frequently refer to the interpreter program as the VLISP Virtual Machine or VM. The interpreter is written in VLISP's variant of PreScheme. The compiler for VLISP PreScheme also required several verification steps.

Each of the proofs connects one programming language equipped with a semantics with another, although in some steps only the semantics may differ. We always provide the semantics either in the form of a standard denotational theory or in the form of a state machine. Thus the natural interfaces between the independent components are always a language equipped with a semantics. Each component is justified by showing the component exhibits the semantics required for its upper interface assuming its lower interface meets its semantic definition.

The large number of components was crucial to achieving a tractable and understandable verification. The sharply defined interfaces allowed division of labor. We could undoubtedly have worked far more efficiently if we had defined these interfaces earlier in our work, instead of trying to make do with a smaller number of less closely spaced interfaces.

4.2. The Main Techniques

The VLISP project turned out to require only a relatively small collection of techniques, several of which we were able to use repeatedly in different portions of the verification. We consider this a lucky outcome, as we think that these techniques can be made routine and applied in a variety of projects.

In this section we will summarize the main techniques used in the project. More detailed descriptions are spread out in [13, 21]. They play specific roles in the architecture that we have developed.

The VLISP Architecture. The VLISP Scheme and PreScheme implementations share a common structure. Each may be divided into three main sections:

1. A stage of source-to-source transformations. In the VLISP Scheme implementation this consists merely of expanding defined syntax, and since the latter has no role in the formal semantics, the verification process begins only after the stage.

   By contrast, this is a major element in the PreScheme implementation, comprising the Front End [21, Section 3]. The front end does a wide range of transformations designed to bring the source PreScheme code to a very special syntactic form that can be compiled more easily to efficient code. Each of these transformations is proved to preserve the denotation of the program.

   The same transformational approach can be used to justify many source-to-source optimizations in other programming languages, including Scheme itself [27, 18, 16].

2. A syntax-directed compiler in the Wand-Clinger style [31, 3]. Its purpose is to analyze the procedural structure of its source code. The compilation algorithms

use recursive descent, and the proof of correctness is a corresponding structural induction on the syntax of the source code. The proof establishes an equality (or a strong equivalence) between the denotations of its input and output.

3. A succession of representation decisions and optimizations. These steps are justified by reference to an operational semantics, by supplying proofs that one state machine *refines* another. For this we have repeatedly used the method of storage layout relations [32, 13, Section 4.2]. Here the main proof technique is induction on the sequence of computation steps that the state machines take.

Between the denotational methods of steps 1 and 2 and the operational methods of step 3, there is needed a proof of "faithfulness." This proof is needed to show that the first operational semantics is a sound reflection of the last denotational semantics, or, in essence, that answers computed by the state machine are those predicted by the denotational semantics.

We will briefly discuss techniques for the three steps above as well as for the proof of faithfulness.

4.2.1. Transformational Compilation

The front end of the VLISP PreScheme compiler implemented a significant number of optimizations as source-to-source transformations. The optimizations implemented include constant propagation and folding, procedure inlining (substituting the body of a procedure at a call site), and β-conversion. These optimizations allow one to write programs using meaningful abstractions without loss of efficiency.

These transformations were justified relative to the formal semantics VLISP PreScheme. Each transformation T is meaning-refining, by which we mean that, for any program P, if the semantics predict that executing P will produce a non-bottom answer, then

$$\mathcal{P}[\![P]\!] = \mathcal{P}[\![T(P)]\!],$$

where $\mathcal{P}$ is the semantic function for PreScheme programs.

The correctness proofs were made possible by carefully designing the VLISP PreScheme semantics as well as the form of each transformation rule. Three differences from the Scheme semantics greatly facilitate the justification of transformations that involve considerable code motion.

- A `lambda`-bound variable is immutable and no location is allocated for it.

- A procedure has no location associated with it, so its meaning depends only on the environment in which it was defined, and does not depend on the store as it is when the procedure is defined.

- The semantics of a `letrec` expression was defined in a fashion that ensured that the meaning of its bindings also depend only on the environment in which it is defined.

Many of the transformation rules looked unusual. For example, a set of interacting rules was used to implement β-conversion. The most significant contribution of the work on the front end is the identification of a collection of transformation rules that can both be verified relative to the formal semantics of the source language, and can also form the basis of a practical optimizing compiler.

The Front End itself uses a sophisticated control structure to apply the rules in an efficient way. In some cases the algorithm refrains from applying a rule to a phrase to which it is validly applicable, for instance, if the resulting code would become too large. However, since every change to the program is in fact carried out by applying the rules, the correctness of the rules guarantees that there is no issue of correctness for the heuristics embodied in the control structure.

4.2.2. Wand-Clinger style Compiler Proof

The Wand-Clinger style [31, 3] of compiler proof is designed to prove the correctness of a compiler phase that takes a source language to a tree-structured intermediate code. In the forms that we use, it distinguishes tail recursive and non-tail recursive calls and arranges the evaluation of arguments to procedure calls. It is also responsible for analyzing conditional expressions, and for replacing lexical variable names with numerical lexical addresses that reference the run-time environment structure. It does not analyze the primitive data structures supported by the programming language at all.

One of the ideas of [31] was to define the semantics of the target language using the same semantic domains as the source language. Thus, the correctness of the compiler could be stated as the assertion that the denotation of the output code (possibly when supplied some initial parameters) is equal to the denotation of the source code. The Wand-Clinger style correctness theorem for PreScheme [21, Theorem 4] takes just this form. Although the corresponding theorem for the Scheme implementation [13, Theorem 12] is more complex, it is still a strong form of equivalence of denotation.

The compiler algorithm is a straightforward recursive descent: to compile (e.g.) a lambda expression, one compiles its body and prefixes some additional code to it, which will place the arguments to the call in a run-time environment display rib. Similarly, to compile a conditional, one compiles the test, consequent and alternative, and then joins the resulting pieces together with some additional code to make the selection based on the value computed by the test code. In each case, the results of the recursive calls are combined according to some simple recipe.

Because the algorithm is a recursive descent and the correctness condition is (in the simplest versions) an equality of denotation, a natural form of proof suggests itself, namely an induction on the syntax of the source code. Each inductive case uses the hypothesis that all subexpressions will be correctly compiled to target code with the same denotation. Thus, in effect the content of each inductive case is to show that way the target code combines the results of its recursive calls matches

Table 3. Denotational and operational treatments of **make-cont**

$$\begin{array}{l} \mathit{make\_cont} : \mathsf{P} \rightarrow \mathbf{N} \rightarrow \mathsf{P} \rightarrow \mathsf{P} \\ \mathit{make\_cont} = \lambda\pi'\nu\pi\,.\,\lambda\epsilon\epsilon^*\rho_R\psi\,.\,\#\epsilon^* = \nu \rightarrow \pi\epsilon\langle\rangle\rho_R(\lambda\epsilon\,.\,\pi'\epsilon\epsilon^*\rho_R\psi), \\ \qquad\qquad\qquad\qquad\qquad\qquad \mathit{wrong}\ \text{"bad stack"} \end{array}$$

Rule 1: **Make Continuation**
Domain conditions: $b = \langle \texttt{make-cont}\ b_1\ \#a \rangle :: b_2$
Changes: $b' = b_2$; $a' = \langle\rangle$; $k' = \langle \mathrm{CONT}\ t\ b_1\ a\ u\ k \rangle$

the way that the semantics of the source language combines the denotations of its subexpressions.

Naturally, in practice the situation is somewhat more complex. There may be several different syntactic classes of phrases in the programming language (as there are in the PreScheme verification, for instance), and each of these will furnish a differently stated induction hypothesis. There may also be different recipes depending on syntactic features, for instance whether a procedure call is tail recursive or not. These also lead to distinct induction hypotheses. Moreover, the algorithm must pass some additional parameters, most importantly a "compile-time environment" which specifies how occurrences of lexical variables are to be translated into references to the run-time environment structure. The induction hyptheses, which are based on [3], spell out how this data is to be used.

4.2.3. Faithfulness of an Operational Semantics

An essential ingredient in the effectiveness of the Wand-Clinger style of compiler proof is that it should be relatively easy to give an operational interpretation as well as a denotational interpretation to the target code. We accomplish this by selecting a target code with a very regular denotational semantics. In the Scheme byte compiler, for instance, we follow Clinger [3] in giving each instruction a denotation that may be regarded as acting on four registers together with a store; in most cases, the denotation of an instruction invokes the code that follows it with different values for some registers or the store. As a consequence of this regularity, it is fairly straightforward to write down a corresponding set of operational rules for a state machine.

A Simple Example. Let us compare the clause specifying the denotation of a **make-cont** instruction, which builds a continuation preparatory to making a procedure call in non-tail recursive position, with the operational rule for the same instruction. They are presented in Table 3.

In the denotational clause, π' refers to the code to be executed after the next return, while π refers to the code to be executed immediately after this instruction. The ν is an integer representing the compiler's expectation about the height of the argument stack at execution time. The second block of λ-bound variables represent the register values when the instruction is executed.

In the operational rule, b represents the current code, a represents the argument stack, and k represents the continuation register; a machine state takes the form $\langle t,\ b,\ v,\ a,\ u,\ k,\ s\rangle$. In place of the denotational version's explicit conditional testing $\#\epsilon^* = \nu$, the operational rule is applicable only if $\#a$ appears as argument to the instruction. There is simply no rule covering the other case, so that if the equality fails, then the operational semantics predicts that the state machine will not advance past its current non-halt state.

Primed variables in the *Changes* section represent the values of the registers after the state transition, and registers for which no primed value appear are left unchanged in the transition; so the rule can be written more explicitly as:

$$\begin{array}{l}\langle t,\ \langle \texttt{make-cont}\ b_1\ \#a\rangle :: b_2,\ v,\ a,\ u,\ k,\ s\rangle \\ \qquad \Longrightarrow \langle t,\ b_2,\ v,\ \langle\rangle,\ u,\ \langle \text{CONT}\ t\ b_1\ a\ u\ k\rangle,\ s\rangle\end{array}$$

Just as ϵ and ρ_R appear unaltered as arguments to π in the consequent of the conditional, v' and u' do not appear in the *Changes* section of the rule. The compound term $\langle \text{CONT}\ t\ b_1\ a\ u\ k\rangle$ codes the same information as the denotational continuation $(\lambda\epsilon\ .\ \pi'\epsilon\epsilon^*\rho_R\psi)$, and the two treatments of the `return` instruction, which may eventually invoke the continuation, arranges to treat them in parallel ways.

Form of the Faithfulness Proof. The main idea of the Scheme faithfulness proof is to associate to each state in the oeprational semantics a denotation in the domain **A** of answers. If Σ is an initial state, then the denotation of Σ agrees with the denotational value of of the program that it contains, when applied to the initial parameters used in the compiler proof. For a halt state Σ, the denotation is the number contained in its value register (accumulator), and the bottom answer $\bot_{\mathbf{A}}$ if the value register does not contain a number. This choice must be compatible with the initial continuation selected to supplement the official denotational semantics.

Moreover, for each rule, it is proved that when that rule is applicable, the denotation of the resulting state is equal to the denotation of the preceeding state.

Thus in effect the denotation of an initial state equals the expected denotational answer of running the program on suitable parameters, and the process of execution leaves the value unchanged. If a final state is reached, then since the operational answer function *ans* is compatible with the initial continuation, the computational answer matches the denotational answer, so that faithfulness is assured.

In many cases, more can also be proved. For instance, Theorem 9 of [21] establishes the *adequacy* of an operational semantics. By an adequacy theorem we mean a converse to the faithfulness theorem, showing that the operational semantics will achieve a final state when the denotational semantics predicts a non-$\bot$, non-erroneous answer.

4.2.4. Refinement via Storage-Layout Relations

After the switch from the denotational framework to the operational one, many aspects of the implementations had still to be verified. These aspects were responsible for linearizing code, for implementing the primitive data structures of the languages, for representing the stack and environment structures, for introducing garbage collection in Scheme, and for omitting type tags in PreScheme.

To justify these steps we repeatedly proved *state machine refinement* theorems in both the Scheme and the PreScheme verifications. State machine refinement allows us to substitute a more easily implemented state machine (a more "concrete" machine) in place of another (a more "abstract" machine), when we already know that the latter would be acceptable for some class of computations. To justify the replacement, we must show that the former computes the same ultimate answer value as the latter when started in a corresponding initial state. As described in more detail in [13, Section 4.2], we have developed the technique of *storage layout relations* [32] to prove these refinement theorems. A storage layout relation is a relation of correspondence between the states of the concrete and abstract machines such that:

1. A concrete initial state corresponds to each abstract initial state;

2. As computation proceeds, the correspondence is maintained;

3. If either of a pair of corresponding states is a halt state, then so is the other, and moreover the two states deliver the same value as computational answer.

A storage layout relation thus establishes that the concrete machine simulates the abstract machine in a sense. The advantage of the storage layout relation as a method of proving refinement is that in establishing clause 2, which generally requires the bulk of the effort, only states linked immediately by the transition relation need be compared.

A Simple, Inductive Form of Definition. In many cases, the machine states (and their components) may be regarded in a natural way as syntactic objects, i.e. as terms in a language defined by a BNF. Then a principle of inductive definition is valid for these objects. A property of the terms (representing states and state components) may be defined in terms of the form of the term together with the value of the property for its immediate subterms. Storage layout relations defined in this way are suited for many purposes; all but two of the storage layout relations used were of this kind.

This approach to defining a storage layout relation is used when two conditions are met:

- For atomic terms in the two state machines, we can tell immediately whether they represent the same abstract computational object; and

- For compound terms, we can tell whether they represent the same abstract computational object if we know their structure and whether this correspondence holds of their immediate subterms respectively.

This approach can be made to work when the objects are not finite, but are rational trees [5], as in the proof of the linear-data machine in the PreScheme compiler [21, Section 6]. However, on this approach, when a stored object contains a reference to another store location then generally the pointers must point to the *same* location. Thus for instance, suppose a cell c stores a pair that contains a pointer to a location ℓ in which another pair is stored. Then another cell c' could correspond to c only if it too stores a pair with a pointer to ℓ. This inductive form of definition is not suitable when one wants to allow the second pointer to reference ℓ', so long as ℓ' contains appropriate objects.

This is the situation in justifying garbage collection: the structural similarity of the stored objects should suffice, without their needing to be stored in the same locations. In these cases, where the instructions of the machine create and modify structures with cyclic sequences of references, a different form of definition must be used.

Cyclic Structures: A Second-order Form of Definition. What is involved in proving a result like the correctness of garbage collection? In our formulation, there is an abstract machine with an unbounded store, in which objects are never relocated, and there is a concrete machine with a store consisting of two heaps. A copying garbage collector periodically relocates objects in these heaps.

In essence, we would like to "guess" a one-to-one correlation $\ell^C \sim \ell^A$ between a concrete store location ℓ^C and the abstract store location ℓ^A that it represents, if any. Thus it will relate some of the locations in the active heap of the concrete machine and some of the abstract store locations, presumably including all the computationally live ones. We can extend the location correlation $\sim$ by an explicit definition to a correspondence $\simeq$ between all terms representing states or their constituents. If we guessed $\sim$ correctly, then corresponding state components should:

1. Contain equal values, when either contain an concrete atomic value;
2. Reference correlated locations, when either contains a pointer;
3. Be built from corresponding subterms using the same constructor, otherwise.

This train of thought suggests defining a storage layout relation using an existential quantifier over location correlations. A concrete machine state Σ^C represents an abstract machine state Σ^A, which we will write $\Sigma^C \cong \Sigma^A$, if there exists a location correlation $\sim$ which extends to a correspondence $\simeq$ such that:

- $\simeq$ has properties 1–3; and
- $\Sigma^C \simeq \Sigma^A$.

Since $\sim$ is a relation between locations, the existential quantifier here is a second order quantifier.

There are now two main theorems that must be proved to justify a garbage collected implementation.

- First, that $\cong$ is a storage layout relation between the abstract and concrete machines. This establishes that garbage collection is a valid implementation strategy from the abstract machine at all. By contrast, it is also possible that a machine's computations depend directly on the particular locations in which data objects have been stored. This is certainly the case if it is possible to treat a pointer as an integer and apply arithmetic operations to it.

- Second, that a particular garbage collection algorithm preserves $\cong$. If the garbage collector is a function G on concrete states, then for all abstract states Σ^A and concrete states Σ^C, we must show

$$\Sigma^C \cong \Sigma^A \Rightarrow G(\Sigma^C) \cong \Sigma^A.$$

  This amounts to showing that the garbage collector simply replaces one acceptable $\sim$ with another. It establishes that the particular algorithm G is a valid way to implement garbage collection.

We have used this form of definition not only for justifying garbage collection [13, Section 6.2], but also in one other proof in VLISP where circular structures were at issue.

5. Styles of Semantics

VLISP has extensively used two semantic techniques. The first of these is the denotational approach, in which the meaning of each phrase is given by providing a denotation in a Scott domain [28, 26]. The official Scheme semantics as presented in [15, Appendix A] is of this kind.

Our operational alternative is to define a state machine, in which one state component is the code to be executed. The state machine transition function is defined by cases on the first instruction in that code. The semantics of a program is defined in terms of the computational answer ultimately produced if computation should ever terminate, when the machine is started in a state with that program as the code to be executed. The other components of the initial state are in effect parameters to the semantics.

5.1. Advantages of the Denotational Approach

The main general advantages cited for denotational semantics are:

- Its compositionality;

- Its independence of a particular execution model;
- Its neutrality with respect to different implementation strategies;
- The usefulness of induction on the syntax of expressions to prove assertions about their denotations, and of fixed point induction to prove assertions about particular values.

These advantages proved genuine in reasoning about our main compilation steps. These large transformations, which embody a procedural analysis of the source code, seem to require the freedom of the denotational semantics. We would consider it a difficult challenge to verify the PreScheme Front End, for instance, using the operational style of the Piton compiler proof [20].

5.2. Disadvantages of the Denotational Approach

There are however some serious limitations to the denotational approach in the traditional form embodied in the official Scheme semantics.

At the prosaic end of this spectrum, there is of course the fact that in some cases one must reason about the "physical" properties of code, for instance in computing offsets for branches in linearizing conditional code. In this case, the meaning of the resulting code depends not only on the meanings of its syntactic constituents, but also on their *widths* in bytes. The denotational approach seems unnatural here.

5.2.1. The Scheme Denotational Semantics

Some of our less shallow objections concern the specifics of the official Scheme semantics, while others are more general objections to the approach as traditionally practiced.

Memory Exhaustion. The official semantics always tests whether the store is out of memory (fully allocated) before it allocates a new location. We removed these tests and introduced the assumption that the store is infinite, and we understand that this change is under consideration for the next (fifth) revision of the Report on Scheme. We made the change for two main reasons:

- Any implementation must use its memory for various purposes that are not visible in the official denotational semantics. Thus, the denotational semantics cannot give a reliable prediction about when an implementation will run out of memory.
- It simplifies reasoning to treat all possible memory exhaustion problems uniformly at a low level in the refinement process.

We have chosen to specify the finiteness of memory only at the very lowest level in the refinement of the virtual machine. At this level all sources of memory exhaustion are finally visible. Moreover, many proofs at earlier stages were made more tractable by abstracting from the question of memory exhaustion.

Semantics of Constants. The official Scheme semantics contains a semantic function $\mathcal{K}$ which maps constants—certain expressions in the abstract syntax—to denotational values. But $\mathcal{K}$'s definition is "intentionally omitted." In some cases, its behavior seems straighforward: for instance, its behavior for numerals. It is however far from clear how one would define $\mathcal{K}$ for constants that require storage. We have had to treat $\mathcal{K}$ as a parameter to the semantics, and we needed to introduce axiomatic constraints governing it [13, Section 2.1].

Semantics of Primitives. Although the official Scheme semantics contains some auxiliary functions with suggestive names such as *cons*, *add*, and so on, it gives no explicit account of the meaning of identifiers such as `cons` or `+` in the standard initial environment. Apparently the framers of the semantics had it in mind that the initial store σ might contain procedure values defined in terms of the auxiliary functions such as *cons*, while programs would be evaluated with respect to an environment ρ that maps identifiers such as `cons` to the locations storing these values.

However, this presupposes a particular, implementation-dependent model of how a Scheme program starts up, namely that it should start in a store that already contains many interesting expressed values. But for our purposes it was more comprehensible to have the program start up with a relatively bare store. In the VLISP implementation, the byte code program itself is responsible for stocking the store with standard procedures. These standard procedures are represented by short pieces of byte code that contain special instructions to invoke the data manipulation primitives of the virtual machine. The initialization code to stock the store with these primitives makes up a standard prelude: The byte code compiler emits the initialization code before the application code generated from the user's program.

Input and Output. The official Scheme semantics is silent on I/O, and in the Scheme paper [13], we have followed it in ignoring I/O. In the PreScheme paper [21], however, we have included a placeholder in the semantics to model I/O, and more recent work on PreScheme has treated it in detail. Our view is that I/O is straightforward to handle, both in the operational and in the denotational framework. This is not to say that it is necessarily easy to prove that particular programs have the intended I/O behavior; rather, the language semantics is easy to characterize. Moreover, a compiler can be proved correct relative to the semantics with I/O without deep changes to the structure of the proofs as presented here.

Tags on Procedure Values. A procedure object is treated in the semantics as a pair, consisting of a store location and a functional value. The latter represents the behavior of the procedure, taking the sequence of actual parameters, an expression continuation, and a store as its arguments, and returning a computational answer. The location is used as a tag, in order to decide whether two procedure objects are equivalent in the sense of the Scheme standard procedure `eqv?`. The exact tag associated with a procedure value depends on the exact order of events when it was created. Similarly, the locations of other objects will depend on whether a location was previously allocated to serve as the tag for a procedure object. As a consequence, many natural Scheme optimizations are difficult or impossible to verify, as they change the order in which procedure tags are allocated, or make it unnecessary to allocate some of the tags.

In our PreScheme semantics, by contrast, we have avoided tagging procedures. The verification of the PreScheme Front End would have been out of the question otherwise.

Artificial Signature for Expression Continuations. The semantics specifies the type for expression continuations as $\mathtt{E}^* \rightarrow \mathtt{C}$, which means that evaluating a Scheme expression may (in theory) pass a finite sequence of "return values," as well as a modified store, to its continuation.

In fact, every expression in IEEE standard Scheme that invokes its continuation at all uses a sequence of length 1. This suggests that, in some intuitive sense, an implementation for Scheme, conforming to the IEEE standard, need not make provision for procedures returning other than a single value.

However, as a consequence, in the most literal sense, an implementation is unfaithful to the formal semantics as written if it makes no provision for multiple-value returners. A considerable amount of effort [13, Sections 2.3–2.4] was devoted to developing a semantic theory that would justify the obvious intuitive implementation.

The situation here may change in the fifth revision to the Report on Scheme. A way for the programmer to construct procedures returning zero or several values is under consideration. The Scheme48/VLISP implementation approach would need to be modified in order to provide, for this new aspect of the language, an implementation more efficient than representing multiple values by building lists.

5.2.2. The Denotational Method more Generally

One more general objection to the denotational method as practiced in the tradition exemplified by Stoy [28] is that the denotational domains are too large. Although any actual implementation represents only recursive functions manipulating a countable class of data objects, the semantic domains are uncountable in the usual approaches to constructing them. Thus, in the most obvious sense, almost all of the denotational objects are not represented in an implementation. Moreover, it is difficult to characterize smaller domains axiomatically, as a class of objects all of which have some property, while ensuring the existence of the fixed points needed to model recursion.

As a consequence, the unrepresented domain elements mean that the denotational theory makes distinctions that cannot be observed in the behavior of the implementation. This phenomenon is called a failure of *full abstraction* [24, 14, 19]. The issue about multiple value returns just mentioned may be regarded as an instance, although we showed how to repair it.

Another familiar example, related to the issues discussed in [19], would be garbage collection. As others have observed, if one takes the official Scheme semantics in the most literal way, garbage collection is a demonstrably unacceptable implementation strategy. Many command continuations, which is to say elements of the domain $\mathtt{C} = \mathtt{S} \to \mathtt{A}$, are not invariant under garbage collection: for instance, the function which returns one value if location 64 has a cons cell in it and a different value if location 64 has a vector. Thus, we get a different computational result if the implementation garbage collects, and relocates a vector where a cons cell would otherwise have been. However, in any reasonable Scheme implementation, none of these "monstrous" objects is represented; all represented objects are in fact invariant under garbage collection.

Although it is conceivable that one might be able to repair this failure of full abstraction also, the graph isomorphism property that a garbage collector must establish is complex. It would be particularly difficult to state and to reason about, because the denotational theory does not offer logical resources such as the quantifiers that would normally be used in such a definition.

Thus the correctness of a garbage-collected implementation can be stated and proved, as far as we know, only within the operational framework.

A related issue is the difficulty of stating normalcy requirements in the denotational manner (again see [14]). Consider a Scheme program fragment using a global variable `x`:

```
(let ((y (cons 1 2)))
  (set! x 4)
  (car y))
```

We have a right to expect this to return 1. That is, we have a right to expect that the storage allocated for a pair will be disjoint from the storage allocated for a global variable. However, nothing in the official semantics ensures that this will be the case. The association between identifiers, such as `x`, and the locations in which their contents are kept, is established by an "environment" ρ. But ρ is simply a free variable of type $\mathrm{Ide} \to \mathtt{L}$. Thus, the semantics makes no distinction between the environments that respect data structures in the heap and those that do not. In proving the faithfulness of the operational semantics [13, Section 3.2], we needed to introduce a comprehensive list of these "normalcy conditions."

It is not clear how to express the constraints interrelating different denotational domains—in this case, store and environment—in order to define the class of tuples that may reasonably be used together in the semantics.

There are also some intuitive requirements on the implementor that seem difficult or impossible to specify in the denotational style. For instance, the Scheme standard [15] requires that implementations of Scheme be properly tail recursive. But no plausible denotational definition of this specification has been proposed.

5.3. Advantages of the Operational Approach

We would give two main reasons why the operational approach may be uniquely appropriate in some cases.

Stating Special Requirements. Sometimes it is more convenient to use an operational style to specify particular primitives for manipulating data, such as input and output operations. A notorious puzzle is how to express denotationally the stipulation that tail recursion be handled correctly. Complexity constraints are also more naturally expressed in an operational framework.

For these reasons, we do not consider the Scheme denotational semantics suitable for framing an all-encompassing definition of the adequacy of a Scheme implementation. Some aspects of adequacy are more natural to express at a lower level of abstraction, and in a more operational style, than others.

Induction on Computational Steps. Many of the operational proofs we carried out are essentially proofs by induction on the number of computational steps that a state machines takes. The faithfulness theorem [13, Theorem 6] is a paradigm case of this. It is difficult to simulate this kind of reasoning denotationally. The traditional approach of using inclusive predicates [28] is notoriously cumbersome.

6. Conclusion

The VLISP work has been divided between a scientific portion and an engineering portion. Some of the scientific issues have been summarized in Sections 4.2 and 5. However, to apply those methods effectively on a bulky and complicated program, it was necessary to control them using a number of engineering ideas.

We focused the verification on a mathematically tractable presentation of the algorithm—rather than on concrete program text, interpreted in accordance with the semantics of its programming language—so as to ensure that the rigorous analysis was concentrated on the level at which errors are most likely to occur and can be most effectively found.

We also set out with a sharply defined initial target. Scheme's well thought out semantic definition was a necessary condition, as was the carefully organized Scheme48 implementation that served us as a design model. We found it particularly important to intersperse the formal development with a number of prototype versions of the program; we also came to use a surprising number of separate refinement steps, connected by rigidly defined interfaces.

These are essentially engineering considerations, unlike for instance the choice of refinement methods or of different semantic styles for different portions of the work.

The Main Lessons We would like to emphasize six lessons from our discussion.

Algorithm-Level Verification Algorithms form a suitable level for rigorous verification (see Section 2.1.2). In particular, they are concrete enough to ensure that the verification will exclude the main sources of error, while being abstract enough to allow requirements to be stated in an understandable way. In addition, rigorous reasoning is fairly tractable. We consider the decision to focus on algorithm-level verification as crucial to our having been able to verify a system as complex as the VLISP implementation.

Prototype but Verify Interleaving the development of prototypes with verification of the algorithms is highly effective (see Section 2.2). The two activities provide different types of information, and together they yield effective and reliable results.

Choice of Semantic Style There are different areas where denotational and operational styles of semantics are appropriate (see Section 5). The two methods can be combined in a single rigorous development using (for instance) the methods of 4.2.3.

Requirements at Several Levels Some requirements cannot be stated at the level of abstraction appropriate for others. For instance, it is not clear how to give a satisfactory specification of being properly tail-recursive in the top-level Scheme denotational semantics. It is more natural to represent these requirements lower down, in an operational framework.

Small Refinement Steps The VLISP proofs separate out a very large number of independent refinement steps. In our experience, this was crucial in order to get the insight into the reasons for correctness. That insight is in turn a strict prerequisite for rigorous verification.

Finiteness Introduced Late In our case it was crucial to model the fact that the final concrete computer has finite word size, and can thus address only a finite amount of virtual memory. However, this property is certainly not accurately expressible at the level of the denotational semantics. Moreover, it complicates many sorts of reasoning. We benefited from delaying this issue until the very last stage, so that all of our proofs (except the last) could use the simpler abstraction.

We believe that these elements have allowed us to carry out a particularly substantial rigorous verification.

References

1. Joel F. Bartlett. Scheme->C: A portable Scheme-to-C compiler. WRL 89/1, Digital Equipment Corporation Western Research Laboratory, January 1989.
2. Robert S. Boyer and Yuan Yu. Automated correctness proofs of machine code programs for a commercial microprocessor. In D. Kapur, editor, *Automated Deduction — CADE-11*, pages 416–430. 11th International Conference on Automated Deduction, Springer Verlag, 1992.
3. William Clinger. The Scheme 311 compiler: An exercise in denotational semantics. In *1984 ACM Symposium on Lisp and Functional Programming*, pages 356–364, New York, August 1984. The Association for Computing Machinery, Inc.

4. William Clinger and Jonathan A. Rees (eds.). Revised[4] report on the algorithmic language Scheme. Technical Report CIS-TR-90-02, University of Oregon, 1990.
5. Bruno Courcelle. Fundamental properties of infinite trees. *Theoretical Computer Science*, 25:95–169, 1983.
6. Edsger W. Dijkstra. *A Discipline of Programming*. Prentice-Hall, Englewood Cliffs, 1976.
7. William M. Farmer, Joshua D. Guttman, Leonard G. Monk, John D. Ramsdell, and Vipin Swarup. The faithfulness of the VLISP operational semantics. M 92B093, The MITRE Corporation, September 1992.
8. William M. Farmer, Joshua D. Guttman, Leonard G. Monk, John D. Ramsdell, and Vipin Swarup. The VLISP linker. M 92B095, The MITRE Corporation, September 1992.
9. David Gries. *The Science of Programming*. Springer-Verlag, 1981.
10. Joshua D. Guttman, Leonard G. Monk, William M. Farmer, John D. Ramsdell, and Vipin Swarup. The VLISP byte-code compiler. M 92B092, The MITRE Corporation, September 1992.
11. Joshua D. Guttman, Leonard G. Monk, William M. Farmer, John D. Ramsdell, and Vipin Swarup. The VLISP flattener. M 92B094, The MITRE Corporation, 1992.
12. Joshua D. Guttman, Leonard G. Monk, John D. Ramsdell, William M. Farmer, and Vipin Swarup. A guide to VLISP, a verified programming language implementation. M 92B091, The MITRE Corporation, September 1992.
13. Joshua D. Guttman, John D. Ramsdell, and Vipin Swarup. The VLISP verified Scheme system. *Lisp and Symbolic Computation*, 8(1/2):33–110, 1995.
14. Joseph Y. Halpern, Albert R. Meyer, and Boris A. Trakhtenbrot. The semantics of local storage, or what makes the free-list free? In *Conference Record of the Eleventh Annual ACM Symposium on the Principles of Programming Languages*, pages 245–257, 1984.
15. IEEE Std 1178-1990. *IEEE Standard for the Scheme Programming Language*. Institute of Electrical and Electronic Engineers, Inc., New York, NY, 1991.
16. Richard A. Kelsey. Realistic compilation by program transformation. In *Conf. Rec. 16th Ann. ACM Symp. on Principles of Programming Languages*. ACM, 1989.
17. Richard A. Kelsey and Jonathan A. Rees. A tractable Scheme implementation. *Lisp and Symbolic Computation*, 7(4):315–335, 1994.
18. David Kranz, Richard A. Kelsey, Jonathan A. Rees, Paul Hudak, Jim Philbin, and Norman I. Adams. Orbit: An optimizing compiler for Scheme. *SIGPLAN Notices*, 21(7):219–233, June 1986. Proceedings of the '86 Symposium on Compiler Construction.
19. Albert R. Meyer and Kurt Sieber. Towards fully abstract semantics for local variables: Preliminary report. In *Conference Record of the Fifteenth Annual ACM Symposium on the Principles of Programming Languages*, pages 191–203, 1988.
20. J Strother Moore. Piton: A verified assembly-level language. Technical Report 22, Computational Logic, Inc., Austin, Texas, 1988.
21. Dino P. Oliva, John D. Ramsdell, and Mitchell Wand. The VLISP verified PreScheme compiler. *Lisp and Symbolic Computation*, 8(1/2):111–182, 1995.
22. Dino P. Oliva and Mitchell Wand. A verified compiler for pure PreScheme. Technical Report NU-CCS-92-5, Northeastern University College of Computer Science, February 1992.
23. Dino P. Oliva and Mitchell Wand. A verified runtime structure for pure PreScheme. Technical Report NU-CCS-92-27, Northeastern University College of Computer Science, September 1992.
24. Gordon D. Plotkin. LCF considered as a programming language. *Theoretical Computer Science*, 5:223–256, 1977.
25. John D. Ramsdell, William M. Farmer, Joshua D. Guttman, Leonard G. Monk, and Vipin Swarup. The VLISP PreScheme front end. M 92B098, The MITRE Corporation, September 1992.
26. David A. Schmidt. *Denotational Semantics: A Methodology for Language Development*. Wm. C. Brown, Dubuque, IA, 1986.
27. Guy L. Steele. Rabbit: A compiler for Scheme. Technical Report 474, MIT AI Laboratory, 1978.

28. Joseph E. Stoy. *Denotational Semantics: The Scott-Strachey Approach to Programming Language Theory.* MIT Press, Cambridge, MA, 1977.
29. Vipin Swarup, William M. Farmer, Joshua D. Guttman, Leonard G. Monk, and John D. Ramsdell. The VLISP image builder. M 92B096, The MITRE Corporation, September 1992.
30. Vipin Swarup, William M. Farmer, Joshua D. Guttman, Leonard G. Monk, and John D. Ramsdell. The VLISP byte-code interpreter. M 92B097, The MITRE Corporation, September 1992.
31. Mitchell Wand. Semantics-directed machine architecture. In *Conf. Rec. 9th ACM Symp. on Principles of Prog. Lang.*, pages 234–241, 1982.
32. Mitchell Wand and Dino P. Oliva. Proving the correctness of storage representations. In *Proceedings of the 1992 ACM Conference on Lisp and Functional Programming*, pages 151–160, New York, 1992. ACM Press.

LISP AND SYMBOLIC COMPUTATION: An International Journal, 8, 33–110 (1995)

The VLISP Verified Scheme System*

JOSHUA D. GUTTMAN guttman@mitre.org
JOHN D. RAMSDELL ramsdell@mitre.org
VIPIN SWARUP swarup@mitre.org
The MITRE Corporation
202 Burlington Road
Bedford, MA 01730-1420

Editors: Joshua D. Guttman and Mitchell Wand

Abstract. The VLISP project has produced a rigorously verified compiler from Scheme to byte codes, and a verified interpreter for the resulting byte codes. The official denotational semantics for Scheme provides the main criterion of correctness. The Wand-Clinger technique was used to prove correctness of the primary compiler step. Then a state machine operational semantics is proved to be faithful to the denotational semantics. The remainder of the implementation is verified by a succession of state machine refinement proofs. These include proofs that garbage collection is a sound implementation strategy, and that a particular garbage collection algorithm is correct.

Keywords: Scheme, verified, compiler, interpreter, denotational semantics, operational semantics, refinement, garbage collection

Table of Contents

* The work reported here was carried out as part of The MITRE Corporation's Technology Program, under funding from Rome Laboratory, Electronic Systems Command, United States Air Force, through contract F19628-89-C-0001. Preparation of this paper was generously supported by The MITRE Corporation.

1. Introduction

The primary goal of the VLISP project was to produce a rigorously verified implementation of the Scheme programming language.

An implementation for a programming language may be a compiler, which translates programs in the given language to programs in a lower level language; or it may be an interpreter, which is a program that executes the higher level language directly; or it may be a combination of the two. The VLISP implementation, being modeled on Scheme48 [11], is of this mixed type. It consists of:

- A simple compiler that translates programs in the source language to target programs in an intermediate level byte code language;
- An interpreter (written in a systems-programming oriented dialect called PreScheme [11]) to execute the resulting byte code programs;
- A second compiler to translate the PreScheme code of the interpreter into assembly language code for a commercial workstation.

This paper focuses on the first two items, which make up the implementation of Scheme. The third item, which implements PreScheme, is discussed in the accompanying paper [13]. An introductory paper [7] discusses the goals and methods of the effort as a whole. The present paper is intended to serve two main purposes:

- To provide a detailed account of the techniques used in the VLISP Scheme verification; and
- To show the decomposition of layers that made the verification process tractable, that is, to display the "formal methods engineering" decisions we have made.

The VLISP effort has focused on algorithm-level rigorous verification. By this we mean to emphasize two things.

First, the proofs we have produced are about algorithms, not about concrete program text. We have carefully constructed the actual program text so that it will be a transparently faithful embodiment of the algorithm. Reasoning directly about the concrete program text (under its formal semantics) is considerably more cumbersome. The mass of detail involved in verifying concrete programs frequently obscures the essential reasons why the program is correct.

Second, our proofs are rigorous mathematical arguments, i.e., what most mathematicians mean by proofs. We have not produced derivations in a particular formal deductive system. Formal derivations, possibly assisted by mechanical proof tools, might well provide less real insight than mathematical proofs, unless the derivations were accompanied by carefully written, humanly understandable mathematical proofs. We discuss this point further in [7].

1.1. Structure of the VLISP Implementation

The VLISP Scheme implementation derives from Scheme48 [11], and is thus a byte-coded implementation. That is, a compiler phase transforms Scheme source programs into an intermediate level language; the resulting target programs are executed by an interpreter, which we refer to as the "virtual machine" VM. The compiler phase is coded in Scheme, while the interpreter is coded in PreScheme.

1.1.1. The Compiler Stages

The compiler stages act on source programs in the Scheme language, taking as its input abstract syntax trees in a format only slightly different from the format used in the Scheme Standard [9]. The ultimate output is in a linearized, binary format byte code suitable for execution in the VM. We will refer to the composite of the compiler stages as the "extended compiler."

The extended compiler consists of a sequence of procedures which rewrite the original source program in a succession of intermediate languages. Of these, we will discuss two in this paper:

- The **byte code compiler** [5] rewrites the Scheme source code into a tree-structured byte code based on Clinger's target language [1]. We will refer to this tree-structured byte code as the **basic byte code** or BBC. The BBC makes the flow of control in the Scheme program explicit, including procedure call and return, the order of argument evaluation, and the operations involved in building environment structures for local variables. BBC uses nested subtrees to represent constants, nested lambda expressions, conditionals, and procedure calls (when not in tail recursive position) in the source code. Successive phases of the compiler eliminate these nested structures in favor of linear layouts.

- The **flattener** [6] uses branch instructions to linearize conditional code and code to be executed after a procedure call returns. We call the output language of the linearizer the **flattened byte code** (FBC).

The other layers omitted from this description do not raise significant new verification issues. Their purpose is to apply other transformations needed to produce a binary image format that we call **Stored Byte Code** or SBC [17]. This is the form that is loaded and executed by the VLISP Virtual Machine.

1.1.2. The Virtual Machine

Unlike the compiler phase, which consists of a sequence of essentially separate algorithms, the interpreter comprises a single program. However, the interpreter design is built up by a succession of implementation steps.

These steps are designed to display the successive implementation decisions in a sort of rational reconstruction of the Scheme48 virtual machine. At each stage it must be shown that the new implementation decisions provide a state machine faithful to the behavior of the previous machine.

The successive abstract machines are all visible in the code of the VLISP VM. The primitive notions of each machine are shown as procedures or constants, which are in turn implemented in terms of the primitives of the next machine (or primitives of PreScheme, in the case of the last). Thus, each state machine in the sequence of refinements corresponds closely to the program text above a particular abstraction barrier.

There are three implementation steps. They involve the following three machines, of which the first provides the operational semantics for the output of the extended compiler, and of which the last is implemented directly using the PreScheme primitives.

- The **stored byte code machine**, or SBCM, which executes the byte code images produced by the compiler stages;
- The **garbage-collected state machine**, or GCSM, which may stop and copy its live data to a fresh heap non-deterministically. The heaps of this state machine (and its predecessor) are of unbounded size, and each location may store an unbounded integer or pointer (among other objects);
- The **finite stored byte code state machine**, or FSBCM, which has heaps of bounded size and has a bound on the width of an integer or pointer.

The first step defines the state transitions of the SBCM in terms of programs that manipulate the atomic components of its state. The second step demonstrates that the GCSM is a faithful refinement of the SBCM. The third step justifies the use of a finite state machine. The FSBCM cannot carry out all of the computations of the GCSM; it is correct only in the sense that when it does compute an answer, that is the same value that the GCSM would have computed. This is a sort of partial correctness.

Table 1. VLISP Verification Steps

Proof Step	Languages	Machines	Section
Byte Code Compiler	Scheme, BBC	—	2
Faithfulness	BBC	BBCM	3
Flattener	BBC, FBC	BBCM, FBCM	5
Procedural Instantiation	SBC	SBCM	6.2
Garbage Collector	"	SBCM, GCSM	6.3
Finiteness	"	GCSM, FSBCM	6.5

1.2. Structure of the Verification

The full VLISP Scheme verification is a succession of nine subverifications. Five of these justify successive compiler stages. Three justify the implementation steps embedded in the VM. The remaining subverification justifies the switch from the denotational style of semantics to an operational style. It thus provides a link between, on the one hand, the proofs of the first two compiler stages and, on the other hand, the proofs of the remaining compiler stages and all of the VM proofs.

1.2.1. Main Techniques

In this paper we will describe in detail instances of three of the four main techniques sketched in the introductory paper [7]. They include a Wand-Clinger style denotational compiler proof (Section 2); a proof that an operational semantics is faithful to a denotational semantics (Section 3); and two proofs of state machine refinement using storage layout relations (Sections 5 and 6). Of these, the first uses a simple, inductive form of definition to define the storage layout relation. The second, the garbage collection proof, must contend with cyclic structures, and therefore uses a second-order form of definition. The VLISP Scheme implementation does not use transformational compilation, which is discussed in [13].

Not all the steps in the VLISP Scheme verification are discussed in this paper. In particular, the compiler stages include a tabulator, a linker, and an image builder that do not require new techniques.

We have ordered the material to reflect a top-down view of the implementation. Within the VM, the focus will be on the garbage collection proof.

The next five subsections describe the remainder of this paper, with Subsection 1.2.*n* devoted to Section *n* of the paper. Table 1 summarizes the main VLISP verification steps discussed in this paper.

1.2.2. The Byte Code Compiler

Section 2 describes the byte code compiler, the first of the compiler stages mentioned in Section 1.1.1. It presents a proof that the byte code compiler preserves the semantics of the Scheme source code. The proof itself is adapted from Clinger's compiler proof [1], which in turn elaborates an approach derived from Wand [18]. In this approach, the source and target languages are both given denotational definitions using the same domains; thus, one can stipulate that the compiler is correct if the denotation of its output code is the same as the denotation of its input.

The denotational semantics for Scheme and for the byte code target language occupy Sections 2.1 and 2.2. We then turn to the main impediment to adapting Clinger's proof. The problem is that the official Scheme semantics makes theoretical provision for procedures that may return multiple values. However, IEEE standard Scheme offers no way of constructing such procedures, and an implementation need not support them, as VLISP does not. This contrast between the official semantics and the expressive resources of the language in its current state required us to develop (in Sections 2.3–2.4) a denotational theory interrelating procedure objects and the single-valued procedures that approximate them.

The section, thus, provides an illustration of "real-life" formal methods, in which the specification to be established may not reach the verifier in a convenient form. We encountered a mismatch between the given specification and the intended implementation and proof technique.

With the alternative semantics in hand, we carry out a Clinger-style proof in 2.5.

1.2.3. Faithfulness of an Operational Semantics

Later portions of the implementation were justified using an operational semantics based on state machines. Section 3 is devoted to justifying the transition from the denotational semantics of Section 2.2 to a corresponding state machine semantics. We show that the state machine semantics is *faithful* to the denotational semantics. By this we mean that when the state machine, starting with a program p, computes a final answer, then that is the answer predicted by the denotational semantics for p. To prove this, we use the denotational semantics to attach an answer to each state, and we prove that the transitions of the state machine leave the answer unchanged. Thus, faithfulness reduces to observing that *initial* states faithfully embed the semantics of the program to be executed, and that *final* states deliver their answers correctly.

The approach is conceptually simple and eminently suited to mechanization. However, it does not establish the converse: namely, when the denotational semantics predicts that p will evaluate to a particular answer, then the state machine actually delivers it. The method of [13, Section 5] can be used to establish this.

1.2.4. State Machine Refinement

The remainder of the paper consists of a sequence of state machine implementation steps. These steps are of two kinds, which we call refinement steps and instantiation steps. Section 4 sets up a general framework for the refinement steps.

A more concrete machine *refines* a more abstract machine when the former can compute the same final answers as the latter, when started in corresponding initial states. This idea is formalized in Definition 9. In order to prove that this relation holds, it is convenient to have a relation between states of the two machines. As the machines compute, the relation should be preserved, and if they reach final states, the relation should entail that the answers achieved are equal. Following [19], we call such a relation a ***storage layout relation***. We formalize this notion in Definition 11; we prove in Theorem 6 that a storage layout relation guarantees that refinement holds. The theorem justifies a general method that in [19] is presented only by means of an example.

In some cases we use state machine refinement to justify a translation between two different programming languages. In these cases, we exhibit a storage layout relation $\sim$ between the two state machines that give semantics for the languages. We also show that the translation function F ***establishes*** the relation $\sim$. Typically, one state component contains the program to be executed, so that establishing the relation $\sim$ means showing that $\Sigma' \sim \Sigma$, where Σ' is the concrete state that results from Σ by replacing its program p by $F(p)$.

An ***instantiation step*** replaces a declarative specification of a transition relation by a procedural specification of it. Thus, the state space of the machine is unchanged in an instantiation step. In fact, the transition relation may also be left unchanged in an instantiation step, or alternatively the degree of non-determinism in the transition relation may be reduced. What changes is the *form of description* of the transition relation. In place of a declarative description of the transition relation, we substitute a procedural description instead. To justify an instantiation step, we must show that whenever a state Σ is in the domain of the original transition relation Tr, then the procedure being introduced, when started in state Σ, terminates in some state Σ', and moreover $Tr(\Sigma, \Sigma')$.

We have not emphasized instantiation as a separate major technique. As we use it, either the justification requires only simple Hoare-style reasoning, as in Section 6.2; or else the justification centers on a relation much like a storage layout relation, as in Section 6.4.

1.2.5. The Flattener

The primary purpose of this section is to illustrate storage layout relations as a way to justify a language translation F. The translation F is the VLISP algorithm for linearizing code.

After some syntactic preliminaries (Section 5.1) we present the operational semantics of the target language in Section 5.2. The flattener algorithm itself is described in Section 5.3. The main content of the assertion that the flattener F establishes $\sim$ is presented in Section 5.4, Theorem 7. In Section 5.5 we then show that $\sim$ really is a storage layout relation.

1.2.6. The Virtual Machine

In Section 6, we describe the implementation steps used within the virtual machine. In this section there are no further changes in the programming language being executed; this is in all cases the binary stored byte code SBC. By contrast, the notion of execution is successively refined.

Section 6.2 shows how to instantiate the SBCM state machine using very simple operations. These operations are divided into *state observers* and *state modifiers.* The state observers are functions that return the value of one ultimate (atomic) constituent of the state; for instance, the value stored at a particular location in the store. State modifiers return an altered state by changing the contents of one atomic ultimate constituent of the state. To implement the declaratively defined "macro-level" instructions of the SBCM, we give a short program that executes observers and modifiers. Very few of these programs require iteration, so the simplest Hoare-style program verification suffices for ensuring them correct.

Section 6.3, on garbage collection, makes up the bulk of the discussion of the VM. There are two main facts to be established. The first, which is the subject of Section 6.3.2, is that garbage collection is a legitimate implementation strategy for the SBCM. There are many state machines for which this would not be the case; for instance, machines that allow pointer arithmetic. To establish the legitimacy of garbage collection for the SBCM, we specify the state machine GCSM, but without defining a specific garbage collection algorithm. We then exhibit a storage layout relation to establish state machine refinement.

The primary interest in this portion lies in how the storage layout relation is defined. The possibility of circular data structures means that the inductive form of definition used in the flattener proof is not available. We use instead a second order existential quantifier to assert the existence of a function correlating store locations within the GCSM and SBCM states.

The second main fact to be established is that a particular copying garbage collection algorithm does indeed respect the storage layout relation, and this instantiation step is the content of Section 6.4.

The brief Section 6.5 justifies the transition to the state machine FSBCM. This state machine has as its states a subset of those of the GCSM, in which state components are of bounded size. Its transition relation is the restriction of the transition relation of GCSM to the smaller set of states. Therefore it is clearly correct as an implementation of the GCSM, at least in the sense that when it computes an answer a, then the GCSM could also compute the same answer.

Table 2. Scheme Abstract Syntax

e	$::=$	$i \mid c_{sq} \mid \langle\texttt{quote}\ c\rangle \mid e^{+} \mid \langle\texttt{begin}\rangle^\frown e^{+}$
	$\mid$	$\langle\texttt{lambda}\ i^{*}\ e\rangle \mid \langle\texttt{dotted\_lambda}\ i^{+}\ e\rangle$
	$\mid$	$\langle\texttt{if}\ e_1\ e_2\ e_3\rangle \mid \langle\texttt{if}\ e_1\ e_2\rangle \mid \langle\texttt{set!}\ i\ e\rangle$
c	$::=$	c_{pr} | strings | lists, dotted lists, and vectors of c
c_{pr}	$::=$	numbers, booleans, characters, symbols and nil
c_{sq}	$::=$	numbers, booleans, characters and strings
i	$::=$	identifiers (variables)
Γ	$::=$	e (commands)

1.3. How to Read This Paper

Many portions of this paper can be read independently. Section 2 can be read on its own; it describes the denotational methods we used in VLISP. Section 3 relies on Sections 2.1–2.2, but not on the remainder of Section 2. Sections 5 and 6 both depend on Section 4, which justifies the storage layout method in general terms. However, their dependence on earlier material—and on each other—is limited to the BNF presentations of syntax.

We have gathered presentations of syntax, declarations of semantic functions and representative semantic clauses, and similar material into tables. For ease of reference, a list of tables appears on page 109 at the end of the paper.

2. The Byte-Code Compiler

The VLISP implementation is a byte-coded one, and the task of the compiler is to produce byte codes from a Scheme source program. The denotation of the resulting byte code program is equivalent to the denotation of the Scheme source program in a sense made precise in Section 2.5.

The byte code compiler itself is based on algorithms used by Clinger [1] and Kelsey and Rees [11]. Its purpose is to analyze the procedural structure of the source code. It distinguishes tail-recursive procedure calls from non-tail-recursive ones; it puts conditional expressions into a more explicit procedural form; and it calculates two-dimensional $\langle over, down\rangle$ lexical addresses for lexical variables, which it distinguishes from global variables.

The compiler algorithm itself is a syntax-directed recursive descent, based on the abstract syntax shown in Table 2. We regard this BNF as determining a set of tree-like abstract syntax objects, rather than as recognising a set of flat character strings. The tree-like abstract syntax objects are represented by nested sequences.

Thus for instance, a concrete program of the form (`lambda (x . y)` *body*) has as its abstract syntax:

$\langle$**dotted_lambda** $\langle$**x y**$\rangle$ $e\rangle$

where e represents the abstract syntax of the body. This abstract syntax is only slightly more abstract than the result of the normal Scheme reader, when lists are regarded as representing mathematical sequences. Dotted lambda forms are the main case in which the abstract syntax differs.

In this and subsequent BNF presentations, we regard the label on the left hand side, such as e and c, both as a typical variable ranging over the syntax class being defined, and also as symbol naming the class, in this case the Scheme expressions and constants, respectively. Thus, we will write the type of a function f taking arguments from e and yielding values in a class C in the form $f : e \rightarrow C$.

The compiler's target language is the Basic Byte Code language (BBC). Expressions of BBC are nested sequences constructed ultimately from natural numbers, Scheme identifiers, Scheme constants, and the keywords shown. We will use n-like variables for natural numbers, i-like variables for identifiers, and c-like variables for constants. Similarly for the classes defined by the grammar, with

- t for *templates*, representing procedures, which consist of the keyword `lap` followed by a constant, which annotates the name of the procedure, and the code of the procedure;
- b for *closed instruction lists* or blocks, in which execution eventually encounters a *call* or *return* instruction;
- y for *open instruction lists*, in which execution eventually runs off the end;
- z for *neutral instructions* that may occur in either closed or open instruction lists; and
- w for (general) *instruction lists*, the union of the open and closed lists.

This syntax as defined in Table 3 is more complex than might have been expected. The distinction between open and closed instruction lists captures a pattern in the code produced by the compiler, and this pattern is crucial to the correctness of the flattener (Section 5). When a conditional expression is the last Scheme expression in the block being compiled, the compiler can emit a closed instruction list in which the code of each branch will contain a `call` or `return` instruction. There need be no common code to be executed after either branch has completed. On the other hand, when the conditional expression is not the last Scheme expression in the block, the compiler emits an open instruction list in which neither branch is terminated by a `call` or `return`. Thus, execution "drops into" the following code when the selected branch is completed. The flattener algorithm uses this distinction between open and closed instruction lists systematically. Its semantic significance is summarized in Lemmas 15 and 16.

After taking cases based on the abstract syntax class of the expression being compiled, the compiler algorithm combines the code produced by its recursive calls with some additional instructions. The main dispatch and one typical case, which

Table 3. Grammar for the Basic Byte Code

t	$::=$	$\langle \mathtt{lap}\ c\ b \rangle$
b	$::=$	$\langle\langle \mathtt{return} \rangle\rangle \mid \langle\langle \mathtt{call}\ n \rangle\rangle \mid \langle\langle \mathtt{unless\text{-}false}\ b_1\ b_2 \rangle\rangle$
	$\mid$	$\langle \mathtt{make\text{-}cont}\ b_1\ n \rangle :: b_2 \mid z :: b_1$
y	$::=$	$\langle \mathtt{make\text{-}cont}\ y_1\ n \rangle :: b \mid \langle \mathtt{make\text{-}cont}\ \langle\rangle\ n \rangle :: b \mid z :: y_1 \mid \langle z \rangle$
z	$::=$	$\langle \mathtt{unless\text{-}false}\ y_1\ y_2 \rangle$
	$\mid$	$\langle \mathtt{literal}\ c \rangle \mid \langle \mathtt{closure}\ t \rangle$
	$\mid$	$\langle \mathtt{global}\ i \rangle \mid \langle \mathtt{local}\ n_1\ n_2 \rangle$
	$\mid$	$\langle \mathtt{set\text{-}global!}\ i \rangle \mid \langle \mathtt{set\text{-}local!}\ n_1\ n_2 \rangle$
	$\mid$	$\langle \mathtt{push} \rangle \mid \langle \mathtt{make\text{-}env}\ n \rangle$
	$\mid$	$\langle \mathtt{make\text{-}rest\text{-}list}\ n \rangle \mid \langle \mathtt{unspecified} \rangle$
	$\mid$	$\langle \mathtt{checkargs{=}}\ n \rangle \mid \langle \mathtt{checkargs{>}{=}}\ n \rangle$
	$\mid$	$\langle i \rangle$
w	$::=$	$b \mid y$

compiles an application, are shown in slightly simplified form in Figure 1. The remaining cases are not presented here. The parameters are:

- The expression being compiled;
- A "compile-time environment," which associates identifiers serving as lexical variables with their lexical addresses. It is enriched when the algorithm traverses a `lambda`;
- The "after code," a BBC instruction list. It is the result of a recursive call to the main dispatch to compile the portion of the procedure after the expression currently being compiled. It will be attached at the end of the code generated from the current expression.

The Scheme code implementing the algorithm can be safely regarded as a presentation of a mathematical algorithm. It is purely applicative; it makes no use of `call/cc`; and it has the form of a primitive recursion on its expression argument, so that it is guaranteed to terminate.

Syntactic correctness. If e is a Scheme expression, then $C(e, \rho_C, w)$ will refer to the result of calling the procedure `comp` on e together with the compile-time environment ρ_C and the after-code w (assumed to be a BBC instruction sequence). We will also use $C(e)$ to refer to the result of calling the procedure `comp` on e with the initial values of ρ_C and w, which are the empty compile-time environment and code consisting of a bare `return` respectively.

THEOREM 1 **(Compiler syntactic correctness)**
For any Scheme expression e, compile-time environemnt ρ_C, BBC closed instruction sequence b_0, and BBC open instruction sequence y_0,

```
(define (comp exp cenv after)
  (cond ((id? exp)
         (compile-id exp cenv after))
        ((self-quoting-constant? exp)
         (compile-constant exp cenv after))
        ((pair? exp)
         (case (car exp)
           ((lambda) (compile-lambda exp cenv after))
           ((if) (compile-if exp cenv after))
           ...
           (else
            (compile-application exp cenv after))))
        (else (compiler-error ...))))

(define (compile-application exp cenv after)
  (if (return? after)
      (let* ((proc (car exp))
             (args (cdr exp))
             (nargs (length args)))
        (comp-args args cenv
                   (comp proc cenv
                         (instruction->code-sequence
                          (make-instruction 'call nargs)))))
      (compiler-prepend-instruction
       (make-instruction 'make-cont after)
       (compile-application exp cenv return-code))))

(define (comp-args args cenv after)
  (if (null? args)
      after
      (comp (car args) cenv
            (compiler-prepend-instruction
             (make-instruction 'push)
             (comp-args (cdr args) cenv after)))))
```

Figure 1. Compiler Dispatch Procedure, and case for Procedure Call.

1. $C(e)$ is a BBC *template;*

2. $C(e, \rho_C, b_0)$ is a BBC *closed instruction sequence;*

3. $C(e, \rho_C, y_0)$ is a BBC *open instruction sequence;*

4. $C(e, \rho_C, \langle\rangle)$ is a BBC *open instruction sequence.*

The proof is a bulky but routine simultaneous structural induction on the Scheme syntax.

Since the algorithm is so straightforward a recursive descent, it is natural to use induction on the structure of expressions as a proof technique for semantic correctness. In order to carry out this idea, we will need to describe the formal semantics of the Scheme and of the byte code.

2.1. The Scheme Semantics

In this section we will briefly describe the official Scheme semantics, in the slightly modified form we have used in the VLISP project. See [16] for a description of the underlying approach, and [5] for additional details; we have summarized some notation in Table 4. Apart from a few cosmetic changes of notation, our version differs from the standard in three ways.

- The domains have been made somewhat more concrete. In particular, the domian of locations L has been identified with rthe natural numbers N, and consequently S, the domain of stores, has been identified with E^*. This formalizes our decision to regard memory as unbounded, at this level of the verification.

- We have removed tests from the semantics to check whether a new storage location can be allocated in S. The official Scheme semantics uses conditionals that raise an "out of memory" error if there is no unallocated location; when memory is conceived as unbounded, this situation will not arise. Moreover, it does not seem that all situations in which a real Scheme interpreter can run out of memory are represented in the official semantics, for instance, overflowing the stack by too many nested, non-tail-recursive procedure calls. Thus, we have chosen to represent all memory exhaustion errors uniformly at a much lower level in the formal specification.

- The constraints on $\mathcal{K}$ given in the section on Semantics of Constants have been added. It was needed to prove that an operational semantics for the BBC is faithful to its denotational semantics.

Perhaps the main cosmetic change is that we regard sequences as partial functions from natural numbers to values. To project the ith element from a sequence s, we write the function application $s\,i$. We treat pairs similarly.

Table 4. Some Notation

$\langle \ldots \rangle$	finite sequence formation, commas optional
$\#s$	length of sequence s
$\langle x \ldots \rangle$	sequence s with $s(0) = x$
$\langle \ldots x \rangle$	sequence s with $s(\#s - 1) = x$
$a :: s$	prepend (cons) a before s
$p\,0, \quad p\,1$	left and right components (resp) of a pair p of type $D_0 \times D_1$
$rev\ s$	reverse of the sequence s
$s \frown t$	concatenation of sequences s and t
$s \dagger k$	drop the first k members of sequence s
$s \ddagger k$	the sequence of only the first k members of s
$p \rightarrow a, b$	if p then a else b
$\rho[x/i]$	the function which is the same as ρ except that it takes the value x at i
x in D	injection of x into domain D
$x \mid D$	projection of x to domain D
$x, y, \ldots : D$	true if the type of $x, y, \ldots$ is a disjoint sum and $x, y, \ldots$ are injected from elements of D

Table 5. Domains for the Semantics of Scheme

$\nu \in \mathtt{N}$		natural numbers
$\alpha \in \mathrm{L}$	$= \mathtt{N}$	locations
$\rho \in \mathrm{U}$	$= i \rightarrow \mathrm{L}$	environments
T	$= \{\mathit{false}, \mathit{true}\}$	booleans
$\mathrm{T_L}$	$= \{\mathit{mutable}, \mathit{immutable}\}$	mutability flags
$\mathtt{Q}$		symbols
$\mathtt{H}$		characters
$\mathtt{R}$		numbers
$\mathrm{E_p}$	$= \mathrm{L} \times \mathrm{L} \times \mathrm{T_L}$	pairs
$\mathrm{E_v}$	$= \mathrm{L}^* \times \mathrm{T_L}$	vectors
$\mathrm{E_s}$	$= \mathrm{L}^* \times \mathrm{T_L}$	strings
$\mathtt{M}$	$= \mathrm{T} + \mathrm{T_L} + \{\mathit{null}, \mathit{empty}, \mathit{unspecified}\}$	miscellaneous
$\phi \in \mathrm{F}$	$= \mathrm{L} \times (\mathtt{E}^* \rightarrow \mathtt{K} \rightarrow \mathtt{C})$	procedure values
$\epsilon \in \mathrm{E}$	$\cong \mathtt{Q} + \mathtt{H} + \mathtt{R} + \mathrm{E_p} + \mathrm{E_v} + \mathrm{E_s} + \mathtt{M} + \mathrm{F}$	expressed values
$\sigma \in \mathrm{S}$	$= \mathtt{E}^*$	stores
$\theta \in \mathtt{C}$	$= \mathrm{S} \rightarrow \mathtt{A}$	command continuations
$\kappa \in \mathtt{K}$	$= \mathtt{E}^* \rightarrow \mathtt{C}$	expression continuations
$\mathtt{A}$		answers

Table 6. Scheme Semantic Functions

$\mathcal{K} : c \rightarrow \mathtt{E}$
$\mathcal{E} : e \rightarrow \mathtt{U} \rightarrow \mathtt{K} \rightarrow \mathtt{C}$
$\mathcal{E}^* : e^* \rightarrow \mathtt{U} \rightarrow \mathtt{K} \rightarrow \mathtt{C}$
$\mathcal{C} : \Gamma^* \rightarrow \mathtt{U} \rightarrow \mathtt{C} \rightarrow \mathtt{C}$

The domains used in the denotational semantics of Scheme are presented in Table 5. Exactly one "domain equation" is actually not an equation. It implicitly introduces an isomorphism $\psi_{\mathtt{E}}$ between $\mathtt{E}$ and a disjoint sum domain, $\mathtt{E}_\Sigma = \mathtt{Q} + \mathtt{H} + \mathtt{R} + \ldots$ Although $\mathtt{A}$ is not explicitly defined, we will stipulate throughout the remainder of this paper that it is some domain containing a $\perp$ and also numbers, but not involving $\mathtt{E}$.

The semantic domains are given in Table 6. They are not disjoint from the syntactic domains of the abstract syntax of Scheme as given in Table 2, because a Scheme constant c may be a number, boolean, ..., or else a list, dotted list, or vector of other constants. These are members of the domains $\mathtt{R}$, $\mathtt{T}$, ..., or else $\mathtt{E}_\mathrm{p}$ or $\mathtt{E}_\mathrm{v}$. In this second group of cases, the Scheme definition stipulates that the pair or vector be immutable, in contrast to the objects produced by calling cons or `make-vector`, which may be side-effected.

Semantics of Constants. The semantics of constants, given by a function $\mathcal{K}$, is "intentionally undefined" in [9]. Although we will not define a particular choice of $\mathcal{K}$, we will need to give some constraints that it must satisfy. In essence, we consider its actual value to be a parameter to the semantics of Scheme. We do, however, explicitly define its behavior on primitive constants, i.e. constants not requiring storage at run-time.

$c \in \mathtt{Q} \vee c \in \mathtt{H} \vee c \in \mathtt{R} \Rightarrow \mathcal{K}[\![c]\!] = c \text{ in } \mathtt{E}$

$\mathcal{K}[\![\text{NIL}]\!] = \mathit{null} \text{ in } \mathtt{E}$; $\mathcal{K}[\![\#\text{F}]\!] = \mathit{false} \text{ in } \mathtt{E}$; and $\mathcal{K}[\![\#\text{T}]\!] = \mathit{true} \text{ in } \mathtt{E}$

In addition, we constrain its behavior on those objects that do require storage and can be named by constants. These are strings, vectors, and pairs. We stipulate three conditions:

1. The immutability bit is set: if c is a string or vector, and $\mathcal{K}[\![c]\!]$ is a non-bottom value ϵ, then $(\epsilon \mid \mathtt{D})\ 1 = \mathit{immutable}$, where $\mathtt{D}$ is either $\mathtt{E}_\mathrm{s}$ or $\mathtt{E}_\mathrm{v}$. Similarly, if c is a pair, and $\mathcal{K}[\![c]\!]$ is a non-bottom value ϵ, then $(\epsilon \mid \mathtt{E}_\mathrm{p})\ 2 = \mathit{immutable}$.

   From this it follows that types are correct: if c is a string, vector, or pair, then $\mathcal{K}[\![c]\!] : \mathtt{D}$ where $\mathtt{D}$ is $\mathtt{E}_\mathrm{s}$, $\mathtt{E}_\mathrm{v}$, or $\mathtt{E}_\mathrm{p}$, respectively.

2. Lengths are correct:

   (A) Suppose c is a vector of length n, and $\mathcal{K}[\![c]\!]$ is a non-bottom value ϵ; then the length of its left component is n, i.e. $\#((\epsilon \mid \mathtt{E}_\mathrm{v})\ 0) = n$.

Table 7. Scheme Semantics: Some Semantic Clauses

$$\mathcal{E}[\![e_0 :: e^*]\!] = \lambda\rho\kappa\,.\,\mathcal{E}^*(\mathit{permute}(\langle e_0\rangle \frown e^*))\ \rho\ (\lambda\epsilon^*\,.\,((\lambda\epsilon^*\,.\,\mathit{applicate}(\epsilon^*\,0)\,(\epsilon^* \dagger 1)\,\kappa)\ (\mathit{unpermute}\,\epsilon^*)))$$

$$\mathcal{E}^*[\![\langle\rangle]\!] = \lambda\rho\kappa\,.\,\kappa\langle\,\rangle$$

$$\mathcal{E}^*[\![e_0 :: e^*]\!] = \lambda\rho\kappa\,.\,\mathcal{E}[\![e_0]\!]\,\rho\,(\mathit{single}(\lambda\epsilon_0\,.\,\mathcal{E}^*[\![e^*]\!]\,\rho\,(\lambda\epsilon^*\,.\,\kappa\,(\langle\epsilon_0\rangle \frown \epsilon^*))))$$

$$\mathit{single} : (\mathtt{E} \to \mathtt{C}) \to \mathtt{K}$$
$$\mathit{single} = \lambda\psi\epsilon^*\,.\,\#\epsilon^* = 1 \to \psi(\epsilon^*\,0),\ \mathit{wrong}\ \text{“wrong number of return values”}$$

$$\mathit{applicate} : \mathtt{E} \to \mathtt{E}^* \to \mathtt{K} \to \mathtt{C}$$
$$\mathit{applicate} = \lambda\epsilon\epsilon^*\kappa\,.\,\epsilon : \mathtt{F} \to ((\epsilon \mid \mathtt{F})\,1)\epsilon^*\kappa,\ \mathit{wrong}\ \text{“bad procedure”}$$

(B) Suppose c is a string of length n, and $\mathcal{K}[\![c]\!]$ is a non-bottom value ϵ; then $\#((\epsilon \mid \mathtt{E_s})\,0) = n$.

3. Subexpressions are well-defined: if c_0 is a vector or pair, and $\mathcal{K}[\![c_0]\!]$ is a non-bottom value ϵ, and c_1 is a subexpression of c_0, then $\mathcal{K}[\![c_1]\!]$ is also non-bottom.

The syntax of constants, together with the type correctness condition 1, ensures that in no case does $\mathcal{K}[\![c]\!] : \mathtt{F}$ hold. It also follows that the only real freedom in the definition of $\mathcal{K}$ concerns which locations are occupied by storage-requiring objects such as pairs and vectors.

Semantics of Expressions. In Table 7, we give the clauses—almost unchanged from [9]—associated with procedure call, as a sample of the Scheme semantics. *Permute* and *unpermute* are functions that determine the order of evaluation; they are fully specified in [5].

2.2. The Byte Code Semantics

One can understand a byte code program as operating on a state with four "registers", so to speak. These are a value register—containing an element of E—an argument stack, an environment register, and a continuation register, where the continuations here take only a single value, unlike the multiple value continuations of the official Scheme semantics. A program, when applied to values of these four

Table 8. Byte Code Semantics: Additional Domains

$\psi \in \mathtt{K}_1$	$= \mathtt{E} \rightarrow \mathtt{C}$	one argument expression continuations
$\rho_R \in \mathtt{U}_R$	$= \mathtt{N} \rightarrow \mathtt{N} \rightarrow \mathtt{L}$	runtime environments
$\pi \in \mathtt{P}$	$= \mathtt{E} \rightarrow \mathtt{E}^* \rightarrow \mathtt{U}_R \rightarrow \mathtt{K}_1 \rightarrow \mathtt{C}$	code segments

Table 9. Byte Code Semantic Functions

$$\mathcal{B} : b \cup \{\langle\rangle\} \rightarrow \mathtt{U} \rightarrow \mathtt{P}$$
$$\mathcal{Z} : z \rightarrow \mathtt{U} \rightarrow \mathtt{P} \rightarrow \mathtt{P}$$
$$\mathcal{Y} : y \cup \{\langle\rangle\} \rightarrow \mathtt{U} \rightarrow \mathtt{P} \rightarrow \mathtt{P}$$
$$\mathcal{T} : t \rightarrow \mathtt{U} \rightarrow \mathtt{P}$$

(The variable y' will range over $y \cup \{\langle\rangle\}$.)

kinds, yields a command continuation $\theta \in \mathtt{C}$. This in turn, if given a store σ, determines an answer. Thus, a code segment determines a computational answer if the contents of four registers and a store are given.

This view is expressed formally in the signature of the domain π of code segments, as it appears in Table 8. Semantic functions appear in Table 9, and representative semantic clauses stated in terms of these semantic functions are presented in Table 10. Together with similar clauses, they specify a semantics for the BBC.

The $\mathcal{B}[\![\langle\rangle]\!]$ clause for a null code sequence defines the "answer function," that is, the way that a computational answer in $\mathtt{A}$ is determined when the "program register" contains no more code and the program has thus completed execution.

The auxiliary functions (among them, those in Table 11) follow the Wand-Clinger style of byte code specification. In each case, the auxiliary function takes as arguments:

- the denotations of the operands of the instruction (if necessary);
- the denotation of the code following the current instruction;
- a sequence of four arguments, $\epsilon, \epsilon^*, \rho_R, \psi$, representing the contents of the value register, the argument stack, the environment register, and the continuation register respectively.

In typical cases, such as for instance *make_cont*, the definition returns a value of the form $\pi\epsilon'\epsilon_1{}^*\rho_R'\psi'$ for non-erroneous arguments. In effect, the instruction has invoked the remainder of the code in a new state, computed from the arguments given. Thus one may view the semantic computation of a final result as consisting of a sequence of terms of this form. The first term in the sequence is determined

Table 10. Some Byte Code Semantic Clauses

$$\mathcal{T}[\![\langle \texttt{lap}\ c\ b\rangle]\!] = \mathcal{B}[\![b]\!]$$

$$\mathcal{B}[\![\langle\rangle]\!] = \lambda\rho\epsilon\epsilon^*\rho_R\psi\sigma\ .\ \epsilon : \mathtt{R} \to \epsilon \mid \mathtt{R}\ \text{in}\ \mathtt{A}, \bot$$
$$\mathcal{B}[\![z :: b]\!] = \lambda\rho\ .\ \mathcal{Z}[\![z]\!]\rho(\mathcal{B}[\![b]\!]\rho)$$
$$\mathcal{B}[\![\langle \texttt{make-cont}\ b_1\ n\rangle :: b_2]\!] = \lambda\rho\ .\ \mathit{make\_cont}(\mathcal{B}[\![b_1]\!]\rho)n(\mathcal{B}[\![b_2]\!]\rho)$$
$$\mathcal{B}[\![\langle\langle \texttt{return}\rangle\rangle]\!] = \lambda\rho\ .\ \mathit{return}$$
$$\mathcal{B}[\![\langle\langle \texttt{call}\ n\rangle\rangle]\!] = \lambda\rho\ .\ \mathit{call}\, n$$

$$\mathcal{Y}[\![\langle \texttt{make-cont}\ y'\ n\rangle :: b]\!] = \lambda\rho\pi\ .\ \mathit{make\_cont}(\mathcal{Y}[\![y']\!]\rho\pi)\ n\ (\mathcal{B}[\![b]\!]\rho)$$
$$\mathcal{Y}[\![z :: y']\!] = \lambda\rho\pi\ .\ \mathcal{Z}[\![z]\!]\rho(\mathcal{Y}[\![y']\!]\rho\pi)$$
$$\mathcal{Y}[\![\langle\rangle]\!] = \lambda\rho\pi\ .\ \pi$$

$$\mathcal{Z}[\![\langle \text{push}\rangle]\!] = \lambda\rho\ .\ \mathit{push}$$

Table 11. Some Byte Code Auxiliary Functions

$$\mathit{make\_cont} : \mathtt{P} \to \mathtt{N} \to \mathtt{P} \to \mathtt{P}$$
$$\mathit{make\_cont} = \lambda\pi'\nu\pi\ .\ \lambda\epsilon\epsilon^*\rho_R\psi\ .\ \#\epsilon^* = \nu \to \pi\epsilon\langle\rangle\rho_R(\lambda\epsilon\ .\ \pi'\epsilon\epsilon^*\rho_R\psi),\ \mathit{wrong}\ \text{“bad stack”}$$

$$\mathit{call} : \mathtt{N} \to \mathtt{P}$$
$$\mathit{call} = \lambda\nu\ .\ \lambda\epsilon\epsilon^*\rho_R\psi\ .\ \#\epsilon^* = \nu \to \mathit{applicate}\,\epsilon\epsilon^*(\mathit{single}\,\psi),\ \mathit{wrong}\ \text{“bad stack”}$$

$$\mathit{return} : \mathtt{P}$$
$$\mathit{return} = \lambda\epsilon\epsilon^*\rho_R\psi\ .\ \psi\epsilon$$

$$\mathit{push} : \mathtt{P} \to \mathtt{P}$$
$$\mathit{push} = \lambda\pi\ .\ \lambda\epsilon\epsilon^*\rho_R\psi\ .\ \pi\epsilon(\epsilon^* \frown \langle\epsilon\rangle)\rho_R\psi$$

directly by applying the semantic clauses to the byte code program, together with some initial values. Each successive term is the result of expanding the definition for the auxiliary function used in the head instruction, followed by β-reductions and evaluations of conditionals.

Some auxiliaries, such as *return*, by contrast, do not take this form. However, if the continuation argument ψ has been created by a *make_cont*, then ψ has the form $(\lambda\epsilon\,.\,\pi'\epsilon\epsilon^*\rho_R\psi')$, so that $\psi\epsilon$ will β-reduce to a term of the requisite form $\pi'\epsilon\epsilon^*\rho_R\psi'$. A similar relation links *call* to the auxiliary *closure*, which creates procedure values.

These observations were a basic part of the motivation for the Wand-Clinger approach, and they served to motivate our approach to proving the faithfulness of the operational semantics. They can also serve as the basis for a proof of adequacy, such as is given in [13, Theorem 9], which would establish that an operational semantics computes all the non-erroneous, non-bottom answers predicted by the denotational semantics.

2.3. Multiple Values in the Scheme Semantics

The official semantics for Scheme allows a procedure to return several values to its caller, as would be needed to model the Common Lisp **values** construct or the **T** [15] **return** form. However, IEEE standard Scheme has no construct that allows a programmer to construct a procedure that would return more than one value. Assuming that a program is started with an initial store that hides no "multiple value returners," then an implementation may assume that there will never be any in the course of execution. So, many implementations of Scheme, among them VLISP, do not support multiple return values. This contrast may be seen at the formal level in the contrast between the domain of expression continuations K, as used in Scheme semantics, and the domain of one argument expression continuations K_1 which plays a corresponding role in the semantics of the byte code.

However, in the most literal sense, an implementation is unfaithful to the formal semantics as written if it makes no provision for multiple-value returners. We can make this point clear with an example. Consider the program `(F)`, which calls a procedure with no arguments. Given the following association of values, the semantics predicts that the correct computational answer from the program is 3:

Variable	Value
ρ	$\mathtt{F} \mapsto \ell_1$
σ	$\ell_1 \mapsto \phi_1;\ \ell_2 \mapsto$ *unspecified*
κ_0	$\lambda\epsilon^*\sigma\,.\,\#\epsilon^*$
ϕ_1	$\langle\ell_2, \lambda\epsilon^*\kappa_0\sigma\,.\,\kappa\langle 1,2,3\rangle\rangle$

When the program `(F)` is executed, the procedure value stored in location ℓ_1 is retrieved, and its second component, ϕ_1 is invoked with no arguments. It in turn applies the continuation κ_0 to the sequence $\langle 1,2,3\rangle$, which should then return the computational answer 3. However, if an implementation makes no provision for

Table 12. Pure Procedure Objects

ϕ_p	$\in$	$\mathtt{F}_p$	$=$	$\mathtt{E}^* \to \mathtt{K} \to \mathtt{C}$	pure (untagged) procedure values

multiple-value returners, and if κ_0 is implemented at all, then it always results in the wrong answer 1.

In the next section, we will formalize the reasoning that justifies an implementation in assuming it need implement only "single-valued" objects, and need make no provision for multiple value returners.

In essence our approach is to introduce a new semantics for Scheme. In this semantics, it is clear that there is no mechanism for multiple return values. Since this alternate semantics uses "single valued approximations" to the values used in the standard semantics, we will introduce an operator called **sva** that will transform the standard semantics $\mathcal{E}$ into an alternate semantic function $(\mathbf{sva}\,\mathcal{E})$. With the alternate semantics in place, there are two separate facts that must be proved to justify the compiler algorithm.

1. The alternate semantics is faithful to the standard semantics:

$$\mathcal{E}[\![e]\!]\rho\,\kappa\,\sigma = (\mathbf{sva}\,\mathcal{E})[\![e]\!]\rho\,\kappa\,\sigma,$$

   at least in the intended case in which the initial values κ and σ—the halt continuation and the initial store respectively—are unproblematic, single-valued objects in a sense to be defined (Theorem 2, clause 2).

2. The compiled byte code is faithful to the alternate semantics, in the sense that

$$(\mathbf{sva}\,\mathcal{E})[\![e]\!]\rho \quad \text{and} \quad (\mathbf{sva}\,\mathcal{B})[\![C(e)]\!]\rho$$

   yield the same answer when applied to suitable initial values (Theorem 4).

We will introduce for convenience a new explicitly defined domain of *pure procedure objects*. Unlike the procedure objects in $\mathtt{F}$ (which equals $\mathtt{L} \times (\mathtt{E}^* \to \mathtt{K} \to \mathtt{C})$), those in $\mathtt{F}_p$ contain only the function-like part (namely $\mathtt{E}^* \to \mathtt{K} \to \mathtt{C}$), without the location that serves as a tag (see Table 12). The location tags are used to decide whether two procedure objects are the same in the sense of the Scheme standard procedure `eqv?`. So $\mathtt{F} = \mathtt{L} \times \mathtt{F}_p$. It will also be convenient to define a few auxiliary functions:

DEFINITION 1 **(Auxiliaries)**

1. zeroth : $\mathtt{E}^* \to \mathtt{E}$ *is the strict function returning* $\bot_{\mathtt{E}}$ *if its argument* ϵ^* *is either* $\bot_{\mathtt{E}^*}$ *or* $\langle\rangle$, *and which returns* $(\epsilon^*\,0)$ *otherwise.*

2. *trunc* : $\mathtt{E}^* \to \mathtt{E}^*$ *is the non-strict function which takes its argument* ϵ^* *to* $\langle zeroth\, \epsilon^* \rangle$. *Hence*

$$trunc\, \epsilon^* = \begin{cases} \langle \bot_{\mathtt{E}^*} \rangle & \textit{if } \epsilon^* = \bot_{\mathtt{E}^*} \textit{ or } \epsilon^* = \langle\rangle \\ \langle \epsilon^*\, 0 \rangle & \textit{otherwise.} \end{cases}$$

and $\#(trunc\, \epsilon^*) = 1$, *even for* $\epsilon^* = \bot_{\mathtt{E}^*}$.

3. $one\_arg : \mathtt{K} \to \mathtt{K}_1$ *is defined to equal* $\lambda \kappa \epsilon \,.\, \kappa \langle \epsilon \rangle$

4. $multiple : \mathtt{K}_1 \to \mathtt{K}$ *is defined to equal* $\lambda \psi \epsilon^* \,.\, \psi(zeroth\, \epsilon^*)$

The auxiliaries *one_arg* and *multiple* coerce from $\mathtt{K}$ to $\mathtt{K}_1$ and back. Expanding the definitions, we have:

LEMMA 1 *1.* $one\_arg\,(multiple\, \psi) = \psi$;

2. $multiple\,(one\_arg\, \kappa) = \lambda \epsilon^* \,.\, \kappa(trunc\, \epsilon^*)$.

Recall that we write $\mathtt{E}_\Sigma$ for $\mathtt{Q} + \mathtt{H} + \mathtt{R} + \mathtt{E}_p + \mathtt{E}_v + \mathtt{E}_s + \mathtt{M} + \mathtt{F}$, and $\psi_\mathtt{E}$ for the isomorphism from $\mathtt{E}$ to $\mathtt{E}_\Sigma$.

DEFINITION 2 **(D, Ω, E-free)**
$\mathbf{D}$ *is the smallest set of domains containing:*

1. *The primitive Scheme semantic domains* $\mathtt{N}$, $\mathtt{T}$, $\mathtt{T}_\mathtt{L}$, $\mathtt{Q}$, $\mathtt{H}$, $\mathtt{R}$, $\mathtt{M}$, $\mathtt{E}$, *and* $\mathtt{A}$;

2. *The Scheme syntactic classes* e, c_{pr}, i, *and* Γ, *regarded as flat domains to which a* $\bot$ *has been added;*

3. *The byte code syntactic classes* t, b, y, z, *and* w, *also regarded as flat domains to which a* $\bot$ *has been added;*

and closed under the operations:

1. $\to$, *producing function domains (containing continuous functions);*

2. $+$, *producing disjoint union domains;*

3. *, *producing sequence domains; and*

4. $\times$, *producing product domains.*

We assume these operators are formalized so that given a domain, we can read off at most one operator and one list of argument domains that produced it; in this case we will refer to the operator *of the domain and the* arguments *of the domain. A domain not produced by one of these operators will be called an* indecomposable *domain.*

Ω *is the disjoint union of* $\mathbf{D}$ *(in some order).*

If $D \in \mathbf{D}$, *we call* D E-free *if* D *is not* $\mathtt{E}$, *and every argument of* D *is* E-*free.*

We assume **E** to be indecomposable, as opposed to $\mathbf{E}_\Sigma$, which has + as its operator.

We next define the function **sva**, which, given any object in Ω, returns the single-valued object that approximates it. As we will see, **sva** ω always belongs to the same summand of Ω as ω. Moreover, **sva** is idempotent, so that we can think of its range as determining the single-valued objects. We will extend **sva** immediately after defining it so that it may be applied to elements of the disjoint summands of Ω, in addition to the elements of Ω itself.

The heart of **sva** is its behavior on pure procedure objects ϕ_p. A pure procedure object ϕ_p is altered to another function ϕ'_p. This function ϕ'_p calls ϕ_p with a single-valued approximation to the same expressed value arguments and with the same store. The continuation argument is truncated to ensure that the modified continuation can access only one expressed value, and only a single-valued approximation to that. Crudely put, ϕ'_p cannot pass anything infected with multiple values to its continuation.

As for the uncontroversially given domains that do not involve **E**, **sva** is the identity. For all other domains, **sva** commutes in the obvious way with the operator of the domain. Thus, the only interesting case is the one for procedure objects ϕ_p.

Definition 3 (Respecting types, f^D, Single-valued approximation)
Given $f : \Omega \to \Omega$, f respects types *if f is strict, and for every D in $\mathbf{D}$ and every x in Ω such that $x : D$, we have $fx : D$.*

For each D in $\mathbf{D}$, let $f^D \in D \to D$ be defined, for $d \in D$, to be

$$f^D d = (f(d\text{in }\Omega)) \mid D.$$

sva *: $\Omega \to \Omega$ is the least fixed point of the operator $\alpha \in (\Omega \to \Omega) \to (\Omega \to \Omega)$, which is defined as follows. Let $f \in \Omega \to \Omega$ and $\omega \in \Omega$ be arbitrary. Then:*

1. *if $\omega = \bot_\Omega$, then $\alpha f \omega = \omega$;*

2. *if $\omega : D$ for an indecomposable D other than* **E**, *then $\alpha f \omega = \omega$;*

3. *if $\omega :$* **E**, *then*

$$\alpha f \omega = (\psi_{\mathbf{E}}^{-1}(f(\psi_{\mathbf{E}}(\omega \mid \mathbf{E})\text{in }\Omega) \mid \mathbf{E}_\Sigma))\text{in }\Omega;$$

4. *if $\omega : \mathbf{F}_p$, then*

$$(\lambda\epsilon^*\kappa\,.\,(\omega \mid \mathbf{F}_p)\,(f^{\mathbf{E}^*}\,\epsilon^*)\,(\lambda\epsilon^*\,.\,(f^{\mathbf{C}}(\kappa\,(trunc\,(map\,f^{\mathbf{E}}\,\epsilon^*))))))\text{in }\Omega,$$

where $(map\ f^{\mathbf{E}}\ \epsilon^*)$ is taken to be $\bot_{\mathbf{E}^*}$ for $\epsilon^* = \bot_{\mathbf{E}^*}$;

5. *if $\omega : D$ for a decomposable D other than $\mathbf{F}_p$, then associate with each argument D_i of D the functional $f^{D_i} : D_i \to D_i$, and lift these to $g : D \to D$; $\alpha f \omega = g(\omega \mid D)\text{in }\Omega$. More explicitly:*

(A) If $\omega : D_0 \to D_1$*, then* $\alpha f \omega = (\lambda y \,.\, (f^{D_1}\, ((\omega \mid (D_0 \to D_1))\, (f^{D_0}\, y))))\text{in } \Omega$*;*

(B) If $\omega : (D_0 + \ldots + D_n)$*, and comes from the ith argument* D_i *in the sense that* $(\omega \mid (D_0 + \ldots + D_n)) : D_i$*, then* $\alpha f \omega = (f^{D_i}((\omega \mid (D_0 + \ldots + D_n)) \mid D_i))\text{in } \Omega$*;*

(C) If $\omega : D^*$ *and* $\omega \mid D^* = \langle x, \ldots, y \rangle$*, then* $\alpha f \omega = \langle f^D\, x, \ldots, f^D\, y \rangle \text{in } \Omega$*;*

(D) If $\omega : D_0 \times D_1$ *and* $\omega \mid D_0 \times D_1 = \langle x, y \rangle$*, then* $\alpha f \omega = \langle f^{D_0}\, x, f^{D_1}\, y \rangle \text{in } \Omega$*.*

All of the real work of α is done by the truncation in the case 4.

If $\omega : D$, then $\alpha f \omega : D$; because in addition αf is strict, for all $f : \Omega \to \Omega$, αf respects types.

As a consequence of the definition, we may infer computational rules for manipulating expressions of the form **sva** t, depending on the type of t.

LEMMA 2 **(Rules for sva)**

1. If $D \in \mathbf{D}$ *is indecomposable and different from* $\mathtt{E}$*, then* $\mathbf{sva}^D$ *is the identity on* D*.*

2. If $D \in \mathbf{D}$ *is of the form* $D_0 \to D_1$ *and different from* $\mathtt{F}_p$*, and* $f \in D$*, then*

$$(\mathbf{sva}\, f) = \lambda y \,.\, \mathbf{sva}(f(\mathbf{sva}(y))).$$

3. If $D \in \mathbf{D}$ *is of the form* D_0^**, and* $x = \langle x_0, \ldots, x_n \rangle \in D$ *, then*

$$\mathbf{sva}\, x = \langle \mathbf{sva}\, x_0, \ldots, \mathbf{sva}\, x_n \rangle,$$

and similarly for product types.

4. If $D \in \mathbf{D}$ *is of the form* $D_0 + \ldots + D_n$*, and* $x : D_i$*, then*

$$\mathbf{sva}\, x = (\mathbf{sva}(x \mid D_i))\text{in } D.$$

Hence, if D *is* $\mathtt{E}$*-free, then* $\mathbf{sva}^D$ *is the identity on* D*.*

For $D \in \mathbf{D}$ and $d \in D$, we will abuse notation by writing **sva** d for $\mathbf{sva}^D\, d$, i.e., for $(\mathbf{sva}(d\text{in } \Omega))|D$. The following lemma provides the crucial justification for regarding **sva** as an alternative semantics.

LEMMA 3 **sva** *is idempotent.*

Proof: If we let $f_0 = \bot_{\Omega \to \Omega}$, and $f_{n+1} = \alpha f_n$, then **sva** is the supremum of the f_n for $n \in N$. Define a strict $g_0 : \Omega \to \Omega$ by letting $g_0\, \omega = \bot_D$ in Ω whenever $\omega : D$ (so each $g_0^D = \bot_{D \to D}$). Then g_0 is the least type-respecting element of $\Omega \to \Omega$. Let $g_{n+1} = \alpha g_n$. As g_1 respects types, $g_0 \sqsubseteq g_1$ and by the monotonicity of α, $g_n \sqsubseteq g_{n+1}$. Since f_1 respects types, $f_0 \sqsubseteq g_0 \sqsubseteq f_1$, so that the supremum of the g_n's is also **sva**.

For $h : \Omega \to \Omega$, let $P(h)$ mean that

(i) h respects types;
(ii) each h^D is strict; and
(iii) h is idempotent.

Since the supremum of idempotent elements of $\Omega \rightarrow \Omega$ is idempotent, and $P(g_0)$ holds, it suffices to establish that α preserves the property P. Take an arbitrary f such that $P(f)$ and let h be αf. We already know that (i) holds, and (ii) follows easily taking cases on D. For idempotence of h, pick an arbitrary $\omega \in \Omega$; the only interesting case is clause 4. Let $\omega : \mathtt{F}_p$; we must show that $(\alpha\, f)(\alpha\, f\, \omega) = (\alpha\, f\, \omega)$. By clause 4, the former (projected into $\mathtt{F}_p$ for convenience) equals:

$$\begin{aligned}
&\lambda\epsilon^*\kappa\,.\,(\lambda\epsilon^*\kappa\,.\,(\omega \mid \mathtt{F}_p)(f^{\mathtt{E}^*}\epsilon^*)(\lambda\epsilon_0{}^*\,.\,f^{\mathtt{C}}(\kappa(\mathit{trunc}(\mathit{map}\, f^{\mathtt{E}}\, \epsilon_0{}^*)))))\\
&\qquad (f^{\mathtt{E}^*}\epsilon^*)(\lambda\epsilon_1{}^*\,.\,f^{\mathtt{C}}(\kappa(\mathit{trunc}(\mathit{map}\, f^{\mathtt{E}}\, \epsilon_1{}^*))))\\
&= \lambda\epsilon^*\kappa\,.\,(\omega \mid \mathtt{F}_p)(f^{\mathtt{E}^*}(f^{\mathtt{E}^*}\epsilon^*))\\
&\qquad (\lambda\epsilon_0{}^*\,.\,f^{\mathtt{C}}(f^{\mathtt{C}}(\kappa(\mathit{trunc}(\mathit{map}\, f^{\mathtt{E}}\, (\mathit{trunc}(\mathit{map}\, f^{\mathtt{E}}\, \epsilon_0{}^*)))))))\\
&= \lambda\epsilon^*\kappa\,.\,(\omega \mid \mathtt{F}_p)(f^{\mathtt{E}^*}\epsilon^*)\\
&\qquad (\lambda\epsilon_0{}^*\,.\,f^{\mathtt{C}}(\kappa(\mathit{trunc}(\mathit{map}\, f^{\mathtt{E}}\, (\mathit{trunc}(\mathit{map}\, f^{\mathtt{E}}\, \epsilon_0{}^*)))))),
\end{aligned}$$

We have used β-reduction twice in the first step, and the idempotence of f and therefore also f^D in the second. So it suffices to prove that

$$\mathit{trunc}(\mathit{map}\, f^{\mathtt{E}}\, (\mathit{trunc}(\mathit{map}\, f^{\mathtt{E}}\, \epsilon_0{}^*))) = \mathit{trunc}(\mathit{map}\, f^{\mathtt{E}}\, \epsilon_0{}^*),$$

which follows easily taking cases on whether $0 < \#\epsilon_0{}^*$. ■

By this lemma, x is of the form **sva** y if and only if $x =$ **sva** x. We will call an object *single-valued* if it is fixed under **sva**.

Since **D** contains the syntactic classes as well as the semantic domains, it follows that **sva** may be applied to the semantic functions $\mathcal{K}$, $\mathcal{E}$, $\mathcal{E}^*$, and $\mathcal{C}$.

In particular, **sva** $c = c$; since, moreover, Scheme has no constants denoting procedure objects, the type of $\mathcal{K}[\![c]\!]$ is always $\mathtt{E}$-free. Thus,

$$(\mathbf{sva}\,\mathcal{K})[\![c]\!] = \mathbf{sva}\,(\mathcal{K}[\![\mathbf{sva}\ c]\!]) = \mathcal{K}[\![c]\!],$$

so $(\mathbf{sva}\,\mathcal{K}) = \mathcal{K}$. However, the remaining semantic functions are not unchanged under **sva**, and the alternative semantics consists in replacing them with their single-valued approximations $(\mathbf{sva}\,\mathcal{E})$, $(\mathbf{sva}\,\mathcal{E}^*)$, and $(\mathbf{sva}\,\mathcal{C})$.

2.4. Faithfulness of the Alternative Semantics

The alternative semantics is faithful in the sense that, for every Scheme expression e, it delivers the same computational answer as the official semantics, provided that a single-valued initial continuation and store are supplied. As mentioned previously, it is reasonable for a Scheme implementation to provide a single-valued store. Moreover, many natural initial continuations (which, intuitively, say how to extract the computational answer if the program finally halts) are single-valued. For instance, the VLISP operational semantics for the byte code is justified against the denotational semantics using the initial continuation:

$$halt = \lambda\epsilon^*\sigma\,.\,(\epsilon^*\,0) : \mathtt{R} \rightarrow (\epsilon^*\,0) \mid \mathtt{R} \text{ in } \mathtt{A}, \bot$$

which is single-valued.

THEOREM 2 **(Faithfulness of Alternative Semantics)**

1. *For all Scheme expressions e, environments ρ, expression continuations κ, and stores σ,*
$$(\mathbf{sva}\,\mathcal{E})[\![e]\!]\rho\,\kappa\,\sigma = \mathcal{E}[\![e]\!]\rho\,(\mathbf{sva}\,\kappa)\,(\mathbf{sva}\,\sigma)$$

2. *Suppose $\kappa = \mathbf{sva}\,\kappa$ and $\sigma = \mathbf{sva}\,\sigma$. Then $\mathcal{E}[\![e]\!]\rho\,\kappa\,\sigma = (\mathbf{sva}\,\mathcal{E})[\![e]\!]\rho\,\kappa\,\sigma$.*

Proof: The second assertion follows immediately from the first.
1. We first use Lemma 2, clause 2 repeatedly:

$$\begin{aligned}
&(\mathbf{sva}\,\mathcal{E})[\![e]\!]\rho\,\kappa\,\sigma\\
&\quad= (\mathbf{sva}(\mathcal{E}[\![\mathbf{sva}\,e]\!]))\rho\,\kappa\,\sigma\\
&\quad= (\mathbf{sva}(\mathcal{E}[\![\mathbf{sva}\,e]\!](\mathbf{sva}\,\rho)))\,\kappa\,\sigma\\
&\quad= (\mathbf{sva}(\mathcal{E}[\![\mathbf{sva}\,e]\!](\mathbf{sva}\,\rho)\,(\mathbf{sva}\,\kappa)))\,\sigma\\
&\quad= \mathbf{sva}(\mathcal{E}[\![\mathbf{sva}\,e]\!](\mathbf{sva}\,\rho)\,(\mathbf{sva}\,\kappa)\,(\mathbf{sva}\,\sigma))\\
&\quad= \mathbf{sva}(\mathcal{E}[\![\mathbf{sva}\,e]\!](\mathbf{sva}\,\rho)\,(\mathbf{sva}\,\kappa)\,(\mathbf{sva}\,\sigma))
\end{aligned}$$

However, since the domain of Scheme expressions and the domain of environments are E-free, $\mathbf{sva}\,e = e$ and $\mathbf{sva}\,\rho = \rho$. Finally, since the domain of answers is E-free, $\mathbf{sva}(\mathcal{E}[\![e]\!]\,\rho\,(\mathbf{sva}\,\kappa)\,(\mathbf{sva}\,\sigma)) = \mathcal{E}[\![e]\!]\,\rho\,(\mathbf{sva}\,\kappa)\,(\mathbf{sva}\,\sigma)$. ■

A further partial justification for the single-valued semantics that we have introduced is that it allows us to eliminate the operator *single* from the semantic clauses in which it occurs, and to truncate any continuation. These two facts are intuitively significant, as they amount to saying that the meaning of a Scheme expression, if it invokes its expression continuation at all, applies it to a sequence $\langle\epsilon\rangle$ of length 1. Hence they justify the claim that the alternate semantics ensures that procedures never return multiple values.

THEOREM 3 **(Truncate Continuations, Eliminate "Single")**

1. $(\mathbf{sva}\,\mathcal{E})[\![e]\!]\rho\,\kappa = (\mathbf{sva}\,\mathcal{E})[\![e]\!]\rho\,(\lambda\epsilon^*\,.\,\kappa\,(\mathit{trunc}\,\epsilon^*))$;

2. $(\mathbf{sva}\,\mathcal{E})[\![e]\!]\rho\,(\mathit{single}\,\psi) = (\mathbf{sva}\,\mathcal{E})[\![e]\!]\rho\,(\lambda\epsilon^*\,.\,\psi\,(\epsilon^*\,0))$.

Proof: The (very similar) proofs are by induction on e; we will show the details for clause 1.

The cases where e is a constant, an identifier, a lambda expression, a dotted lambda expression, or an assignment are immediate from the definitions of *send* and *hold*. The cases for two- and three-expression `if`, and for `begin`, are immediate from the induction hypothesis. Hence the only case of interest is for procedure call, which is as it should be. Using the semantics of procedure call, we must show

$$(\mathbf{sva}\,\mathcal{E}^*)(\mathit{permute}(\langle e_0\rangle \frown e^*))\rho\,\kappa_1 = (\mathbf{sva}\,\mathcal{E}^*)(\mathit{permute}(\langle e_0\rangle \frown e^*))\rho\,\kappa_2$$

where

$$\kappa_1 = \lambda\epsilon^* \,.\, ((\lambda\epsilon^* \,.\, \mathit{applicate}\,(\epsilon^*\,0)\,(\epsilon^* \dagger 1)\,\kappa)(\mathit{unpermute}\,\epsilon^*))$$
$$\kappa_2 = \lambda\epsilon^* \,.\, ((\lambda\epsilon^* \,.\, \mathit{applicate}\,(\epsilon^*\,0)\,(\epsilon^* \dagger 1)\,(\lambda\epsilon^* \,.\, \kappa\,(\mathit{trunc}\,\epsilon^*)))(\mathit{unpermute}\,\epsilon^*))$$

Pushing svas through κ_1, we obtain:

$$\begin{array}{l}\lambda\epsilon^* \,.\, ((\lambda\epsilon^* \,.\, \mathbf{sva}(\mathit{applicate}\,(\mathbf{sva}(\epsilon^*\,0))\,(\mathbf{sva}(\epsilon^* \dagger 1)) \\ \qquad\qquad\qquad\qquad (\lambda\epsilon^* \,.\, (\mathbf{sva}\kappa)(\mathit{trunc}\,\epsilon^*)))) \\ \qquad (\mathbf{sva}(\mathit{unpermute}\,(\mathbf{sva}\epsilon^*))))\end{array}$$

Pushing svas through κ_2 yields:

$$\begin{array}{l}\lambda\epsilon^* \,.\, ((\lambda\epsilon^* \,.\, \mathbf{sva}(\mathit{applicate}\,(\mathbf{sva}(\epsilon^*\,0))\,(\mathbf{sva}(\epsilon^* \dagger 1)) \\ \qquad\qquad\qquad\qquad (\lambda\epsilon^* \,.\, (\lambda\epsilon^* \,.\, \mathbf{sva}(\kappa\,(\mathbf{sva}(\mathit{trunc}\,\epsilon^*)))) \\ \qquad\qquad\qquad\qquad\qquad (\mathit{trunc}\,\epsilon^*)))) \\ \qquad (\mathbf{sva}(\mathit{unpermute}\,(\mathbf{sva}\,\epsilon^*)))).\end{array}$$

For these two expressions to be equal, it certainly suffices that for all κ,

$$\lambda\epsilon^* \,.\, (\mathbf{sva}\kappa)(\mathit{trunc}\,\epsilon^*) = \lambda\epsilon^* \,.\, (\lambda\epsilon^* \,.\, \mathbf{sva}(\kappa\,(\mathbf{sva}(\mathit{trunc}\,\epsilon^*))))(\mathit{trunc}\,\epsilon^*)$$

Using the definition of **sva** and the idempotence of *trunc*, we have:

$$\begin{array}{l}\lambda\epsilon^* \,.\, (\mathbf{sva}\kappa)(\mathit{trunc}\,\epsilon^*) \\ = \lambda\epsilon^* \,.\, \mathbf{sva}(\kappa\,(\mathbf{sva}(\mathit{trunc}\,\epsilon^*))) \\ = \lambda\epsilon^* \,.\, \mathbf{sva}(\kappa\,(\mathbf{sva}(\mathit{trunc}\,(\mathit{trunc}\,\epsilon^*))))\end{array}$$

■

2.5. Compiler Correctness for Single-valued Semantics

We will prove that if e is any Scheme program and b is the result of compiling it, then e and b are equivalent in that $(\mathbf{sva}\,\mathcal{E})[\![e]\!]$ and $(\mathbf{sva}\,\mathcal{B})[\![b]\!]$ deliver the same values when applied to suitable initial values. Suitable initial values for e include any environment ρ and expression continuation κ. Since the type of $(\mathbf{sva}\,\mathcal{B})[\![b]\!]$ is $\mathtt{U} \to \mathtt{E} \to \mathtt{E}^* \to \mathtt{U}_R \to \mathtt{K}_1 \to \mathtt{C}$, we use the same environment ρ as the first argument and $\mathit{one\_arg}\,\kappa$ for the last. As for the other arguments, we choose:

1. *unspecified* as the initial value in the "value register;"

2. $\langle\rangle$ as the initial "argument stack;" and

3. $\lambda \nu_1 \nu_2 \,.\, \bot$ as the initial "run-time environment."

DEFINITION 4 **(Environment Composition,** MT_C, MT_R**)** *Consider* $\rho : Ide \rightarrow \mathbf{L}$, $\rho_C : Ide \rightarrow (\mathbf{N} \times \mathbf{N} \cup \{not\_lexical\})$, *and* $\rho_R : \mathbf{N} \rightarrow \mathbf{N} \rightarrow \mathbf{L}$. *Their* environment composition $\rho \triangleleft^{\rho_R}_{\rho_C}$ *is the environment:*

$$\lambda i \,.\, \rho_C\, i = not\_lexical \rightarrow \rho\, i,\ (\lambda p \,.\, \rho_R\,(p\,0)(p\,1))(\rho_C\, i)$$

We define MT_C *to be* $\lambda i \,.\, not\_lexical$, *and* MT_R *to be* $\lambda i \,.\, \bot$.

We will refer to objects ρ_C and ρ_R as "compile-time environments" and "run-time environment" respectively. Expanding definitions and applying extensionality, we have:

LEMMA 4 $\rho \triangleleft^{\rho_R}_{\mathrm{MT}_C} = \rho$.

We return now to proving the correctness of our compiler function, namely $C(e, \rho_C, w)$, which, for the top-level call $C(e, \mathrm{MT}_C, \langle\langle \mathbf{return} \rangle\rangle)$, we abbreviate $C(e)$. We prove first that code generated by compiling a full Scheme expression (as opposed to code fragments) does not depend on the argument given for the value register. In effect, it ignores the original value in the register, and sets it before any reference to it. We use C_{args} to refer to the function implemented by `comp-args` in Table 1 on page 44.

LEMMA 5 **(Compiled expressions ignore the value register)**

1. *Let* $\pi = (\mathbf{sva}\,\mathcal{B})[\![C(e, \rho_C, b)]\!]\rho$. *For all* ϵ, ϵ', $\pi\epsilon = \pi\epsilon'$.

2. *Let* $\pi = (\mathbf{sva}\,\mathcal{Y})[\![C(e, \rho_C, y)]\!]\rho\pi_0$. *For all* ϵ, ϵ', $\pi\epsilon = \pi\epsilon'$.

3. *Let* $\pi = (\mathbf{sva}\,\mathcal{B})[\![C_{args}(e^*, \rho_C, b)]\!]\rho$, *and let* $\pi_1 = (\mathbf{sva}\,\mathcal{B})[\![b]\!]\rho$. *If for all* ϵ, ϵ', $\pi_1\epsilon = \pi_1\epsilon'$, *then for all* ϵ, ϵ', $\pi\epsilon = \pi\epsilon'$.

Proof: The proof is by simultaneous induction on e and e^*. We show one case from the (very routine) induction.

Clause 3: If $e^* = \langle\rangle$, then $C_{args}(e^*, \rho_C, b) = b$. Otherwise, it is of the form:

$$C(e, \rho_C, \langle \mathbf{push} \rangle :: C_{args}(e_1{}^*, \rho_C, b)),$$

so that the result follows by Clause 1. ■

We give next a portion of the proof of the main lemma, which is due to Will Clinger [1], for the case of the VLISP compiler.

LEMMA 6 **(Clinger's Lemma)** *Consider any Scheme expression e, BBC closed instruction list b, BBC open instruction list y, segment π, environment ρ, compile-time environment ρ_C, value sequence ϵ^*, run-time environment ρ_R, initial values ϵ, ϵ_1, and one-argument expression continuation ψ.*

1. *Let $\pi_1 = (\mathbf{sva}\,\mathcal{B})[\![b]\!]\rho$ and $\pi_2 = (\mathbf{sva}\,\mathcal{B})[\![C(e, \rho_C, b)]\!]\rho$. Then*

$$(\mathbf{sva}\,\mathcal{E})[\![e]\!]\,(\rho \triangleleft_{\rho_C}^{\rho_R})\,(\mathit{multiple}\,\lambda\epsilon\,.\,\pi_1\epsilon\epsilon^*\rho_R\psi) = \pi_2\epsilon\epsilon^*\rho_R\psi.$$

2. *Let $\pi_1 = (\mathbf{sva}\,\mathcal{Y})[\![y]\!]\rho\pi$ and $\pi_2 = (\mathbf{sva}\,\mathcal{Y})[\![C(e, \rho_C, y)]\!]\rho\pi$. Then*

$$(\mathbf{sva}\,\mathcal{E})[\![e]\!]\,(\rho \triangleleft_{\rho_C}^{\rho_R})\,(\mathit{multiple}\,\lambda\epsilon\,.\,\pi_1\epsilon\epsilon^*\rho_R\psi) = \pi_2\epsilon\epsilon^*\rho_R\psi.$$

3. *Let $\pi_1 = (\mathbf{sva}\mathcal{B})[\![b]\!]\rho$ and $\pi_2 = (\mathbf{sva}\mathcal{B})[\![C_{args}(e^*, \rho_C, b)]\!]\rho$. Suppose that the after code π_1 ignores the value register, in the sense that, for all values ϵ', $\pi_1\epsilon = \pi_1\epsilon'$. Then*

$$(\mathbf{sva}\,\mathcal{E}^*)[\![e^*]\!]\,(\rho \triangleleft_{\rho_C}^{\rho_R})\,(\lambda\epsilon_1{}^*\,.\,\pi_1\epsilon_1(\epsilon^{*\frown}\epsilon_1{}^*)\rho_R\psi) = \pi_2\epsilon\epsilon^*\rho_R\psi.$$

Proof: The proof is by a simultaneous induction on e and e^*. That is, in proving 1, we assume that 1 and 2 hold for any proper subexpression of e, and that 3 holds when each expression in e^* is a proper subexpression of e. In proving 2, we make the same assumption and also assume that 1 holds for e itself. When proving 3, we assume that 1 and 2 hold for each e occurring in e^*, and that 3 holds of any proper subsequence of e^*. To emphasize the treatment of the single-valued semantics, we give the proof of clause 3 in detail; the proofs of clauses 1 and 2 are very similar in manner to Clinger's original proof [1].

3. Here we argue by induction on e^*, assuming that 1 and 2 hold of the expressions occurring in e^*.

Base Case Suppose that $e^* = \langle\rangle$. Then, by the semantic clause for $\mathcal{E}^*$,

$$\begin{aligned}
&(\mathbf{sva}\,\mathcal{E}^*)[\![\langle\rangle]\!](\rho \triangleleft_{\rho_C}^{\rho_R})\,(\lambda\epsilon_1{}^*\,.\,\pi_1\epsilon_1(\epsilon^{*\frown}\epsilon_1{}^*)\rho_R\psi)\\
=\;& \mathbf{sva}\,((\lambda\epsilon_1{}^*\,.\,\pi_1\epsilon_1(\epsilon^{*\frown}\epsilon_1{}^*)\rho_R\psi)\langle\rangle)\\
=\;& \mathbf{sva}\,(\pi_1\epsilon_1(\epsilon^{*\frown}\langle\rangle)\rho_R\psi)\\
=\;& \mathbf{sva}\,(\pi_1\epsilon_1\epsilon^*\rho_R\psi).
\end{aligned}$$

Since π_1 is single-valued, the latter equals $\pi_1\epsilon_1\epsilon^*\rho_R\psi$. Examining the compiler's code, $C_{args}(\langle\rangle, \rho_C, b) = b$, so that $\pi_1 = \pi_2$. Since, by assumption, $\pi_1\,\epsilon = \pi_1\,\epsilon_1$, the case is complete.

Induction Step Suppose that 3 holds for e^* and and 1 holds for e, and consider $e :: e^*$. Abbreviating $\lambda\epsilon_1{}^*\,.\,\pi_1\epsilon_1(\epsilon^{*\frown}\epsilon_1{}^*)\rho_R\psi$ by κ, we may apply the semantic clause for $\mathcal{E}^*$ to put the left hand side of our goal in the form:

$$(\mathbf{sva}\,\mathcal{E})[\![e]\!]\;(\rho \triangleleft_{\rho_C}^{\rho_R})(\mathit{multiple}(\lambda\epsilon_0\,.\,(\mathbf{sva}\,\mathcal{E}^*)[\![e^*]\!]\,(\rho \triangleleft_{\rho_C}^{\rho_R})\,(\lambda\epsilon^*\,.\,\kappa\,(\langle\epsilon_0\rangle^\frown\epsilon^*))))$$

Applying κ,

$$\begin{aligned}
&(\lambda\epsilon_1{}^* \,.\, \pi_1\epsilon_1(\epsilon^{*\frown}\epsilon_1{}^*)\rho_R\psi)(\langle\epsilon_0\rangle^\frown\epsilon^*)\\
&= \pi_1\epsilon_1(\epsilon^{*\frown}(\langle\epsilon_0\rangle^\frown\epsilon^*))\rho_R\psi\\
&= \pi_1\epsilon_1((\epsilon^{*\frown}\langle\epsilon_0\rangle)^\frown\epsilon^*)\rho_R\psi
\end{aligned}$$

Hence, the left hand side equals:

$$\begin{aligned}
&(\mathbf{sva}\,\mathcal{E})[\![e]\!]\ (\rho\triangleleft^{\rho_R}_{\rho_C})(\mathit{multiple}\\
&\quad(\lambda\epsilon_0 \,.\, (\mathbf{sva}\,\mathcal{E}^*)[\![e^*]\!]\ (\rho\triangleleft^{\rho_R}_{\rho_C})\ (\lambda\epsilon^* \,.\, \pi_1\epsilon_1((\epsilon^{*\frown}\langle\epsilon_0\rangle)^\frown\epsilon^*)\rho_R\psi)))
\end{aligned}$$

Applying the induction hypothesis with $(\epsilon^{*\frown}\langle\epsilon_0\rangle)$ in place of ϵ^*, with the other variables unchanged, and letting

$$\pi_3 = (\mathbf{sva}\,\mathcal{B})[\![C_{args}(e^*, \rho_C, b)]\!]\rho,$$

we may infer:

$$(\mathbf{sva}\,\mathcal{E}^*)[\![e^*]\!]\ (\rho\triangleleft^{\rho_R}_{\rho_C})\ (\lambda\epsilon^* \,.\, \pi_1\epsilon_1((\epsilon^{*\frown}\langle\epsilon_0\rangle)^\frown\epsilon^*)\rho_R\psi) = \pi_3\ \epsilon\ (\epsilon^{*\frown}\langle\epsilon_0\rangle)\ \rho_R\ \psi$$

Plugging this in, followed by Lemma 5, then the definition of *push*, and finally the semantics of **push**, we have:

$$\begin{aligned}
&(\mathbf{sva}\,\mathcal{E})[\![e]\!]\ (\rho\triangleleft^{\rho_R}_{\rho_C})(\mathit{multiple}(\lambda\epsilon_0 \,.\, \pi_3\ \epsilon\ (\epsilon^{*\frown}\langle\epsilon_0\rangle)\ \rho_R\ \psi))\\
&= (\mathbf{sva}\,\mathcal{E})[\![e]\!]\ (\rho\triangleleft^{\rho_R}_{\rho_C})(\mathit{multiple}(\lambda\epsilon_0 \,.\, \pi_3\ \epsilon_0\ (\epsilon^{*\frown}\langle\epsilon_0\rangle)\ \rho_R\ \psi))\\
&= (\mathbf{sva}\,\mathcal{E})[\![e]\!]\ (\rho\triangleleft^{\rho_R}_{\rho_C})(\mathit{multiple}(\lambda\epsilon_0 \,.\, (\mathit{push}\ \pi_3)\ \epsilon_0\ \epsilon^*\ \rho_R\ \psi))\\
&= (\mathbf{sva}\,\mathcal{E})[\![e]\!]\ (\rho\triangleleft^{\rho_R}_{\rho_C})(\mathit{multiple}(\lambda\epsilon_0 \,.\\
&\qquad (\mathbf{sva}\,\mathcal{B})[\![\langle\mathbf{push}\rangle :: C_{args}(e^*, \rho_C, b)]\!]\rho\\
&\qquad\quad \epsilon_0\ \epsilon^*\ \rho_R\ \psi))
\end{aligned}$$

We will apply Clause 1 with

$$b = \langle\mathbf{push}\rangle :: C_{args}(e^*, \rho_C, b),$$

and thus with

$$\pi_2 = (\mathbf{sva}\,\mathcal{B})[\![C(e, \rho_C, \langle\mathbf{push}\rangle :: C_{args}(e^*, \rho_C, b))]\!]\rho.$$

Hence,

$$\begin{aligned}
&(\mathbf{sva}\,\mathcal{E})[\![e]\!]\ (\rho\triangleleft^{\rho_R}_{\rho_C})\\
&\quad(\mathit{multiple}(\lambda\epsilon_0 \,.\, (\mathbf{sva}\,\mathcal{B})[\![\langle\mathbf{push}\rangle :: C_{args}(e^*, \rho_C, b)]\!]\rho\\
&\qquad\quad \epsilon_0\ \epsilon^*\ \rho_R\ \psi))\\
&= \pi_2\ \epsilon\ \epsilon^*\ \rho_R\ \psi
\end{aligned}$$

But, by the code for C_{args}, π_2 is in fact equal to

$$(\mathbf{sva}\,\mathcal{B})[\![C_{args}(e :: e^*, \rho_C, b)]\!],$$

as the latter is the code:

$$C(e, \rho_C, \langle\mathbf{push}\rangle :: C_{args}(e^*, \rho_C, b)).$$

■

Finally, we define the appropriate notion of computational equivalence, and prove the main theorem using Clinger's lemma.

DEFINITION 5 **(Computational equivalence $\equiv$)**
A Scheme program e and a byte code program b are computationally equivalent if, for every environment ρ and expression continuation κ,

$$(\mathbf{sva}\,\mathcal{E})[\![e]\!]\rho\kappa = (\mathbf{sva}\,\mathcal{B})[\![b]\!]\rho\,\mathit{unspecified}\,\langle\rangle\,(\lambda\nu_1\nu_2\,.\,\bot)\,(\mathit{one\_arg}\,\kappa).$$

"Equivalence" is a slight abuse of language, as this is not formally an equivalence relation (its domain and codomain are disjoint). Using the rules for **sva** in Lemma 2 and also Theorem 2, we infer that the definition of $\equiv$ could equally have been stated only for *single-valued* κ:

LEMMA 7 *1.* $\mathbf{sva}\,(\mathit{one\_arg}\,\kappa) = \mathit{one\_arg}\,(\mathbf{sva}\,\kappa)$;

2. $e \equiv b$ *iff for every* ρ *and* κ *such that* $\kappa = (\mathbf{sva}\,\kappa)$,

$$(\mathbf{sva}\,\mathcal{E})[\![e]\!]\rho\kappa = (\mathbf{sva}\,\mathcal{B})[\![b]\!]\rho\,\mathit{unspecified}\,\langle\rangle\,(\lambda\nu_1\nu_2\,.\,\bot)\,(\mathit{one\_arg}\,\kappa).$$

THEOREM 4 **(Compiler semantic correctness)**
For any Scheme expression e, $e \equiv C(e)$.

Proof: The theorem is a direct consequence of Clinger's lemma, Clause 1. Let ρ be arbitrary, and let κ be single-valued. Since

$$C(e) = C(e, \mathrm{MT}_C, \langle\langle\mathtt{return}\rangle\rangle),$$

we instantiate Clause 1 by putting $(\mathbf{sva}\mathcal{B})[\![C(e)]\!]\rho = \pi_2$, and $(\mathbf{sva}\mathcal{B})[\![\langle\langle\mathtt{return}\rangle\rangle]\!]\rho = \mathbf{sva}\,\mathit{return} = \pi_1$; we also let $\psi = \mathit{one\_arg}\,\kappa$ and $\rho_R = \mathrm{MT}_R$. Substituting the other initial values in the right hand side, we infer:

$$\begin{aligned}&(\mathbf{sva}\,\mathcal{E})[\![e]\!]\,(\rho\lhd^{\mathrm{MT}_R}_{\mathrm{MT}_C})\,(\mathit{multiple}\,\lambda\epsilon\,.\,(\mathbf{sva}\,\mathit{return})\,\epsilon\langle\rangle\mathrm{MT}_R(\mathit{one\_arg}\,\kappa)) \\ &= \pi_2\,\mathit{unspecified}\,\langle\rangle\,\mathrm{MT}_R\,(\mathit{one\_arg}\,\kappa).\end{aligned} \tag{1}$$

The right hand side is already in the form we want; we need to reduce the left hand side to $(\mathbf{sva}\,\mathcal{E})[\![e]\!]\,\rho\,\kappa$. Since $\mathit{return} = \lambda\epsilon\epsilon^*\rho_R\psi\,.\,\psi\epsilon$, we may use Lemma 2, followed by Lemma 7 and the assumption that $\kappa = (\mathbf{sva}\,\kappa)$, to compute:

$$\begin{aligned}&\lambda\epsilon\,.\,(\mathbf{sva}\,\mathit{return})\,\epsilon\langle\rangle\mathrm{MT}_R(\mathit{one\_arg}\,\kappa) \\ &= \lambda\epsilon\,.\,(\mathbf{sva}\,(\mathit{one\_arg}\,\kappa))(\mathbf{sva}\,\epsilon) = \lambda\epsilon\,.\,\mathbf{sva}\,((\mathit{one\_arg}\,\kappa)(\mathbf{sva}\,(\mathbf{sva}\,\epsilon))) \\ &= \lambda\epsilon\,.\,\mathbf{sva}\,((\mathit{one\_arg}\,\kappa)(\mathbf{sva}\,\epsilon)) = \lambda\epsilon\,.\,(\mathbf{sva}\,(\mathit{one\_arg}\,\kappa))\epsilon \\ &= \lambda\epsilon\,.\,(\mathit{one\_arg}\,(\mathbf{sva}\,\kappa))\epsilon = (\mathit{one\_arg}\,\kappa).\end{aligned}$$

Hence we may rewrite Equation 1 as:

$$\begin{aligned}&(\mathbf{sva}\,\mathcal{E})[\![e]\!]\,(\rho\triangleleft^{\mathrm{MT}_R}_{\mathrm{MT}_C})\,(\mathit{multiple}\,(\mathit{one\_arg}\,\kappa))\\&=\pi_2\,\mathit{unspecified}\,\langle\rangle\,\mathrm{MT}_R\,(\mathit{one\_arg}\,\kappa).\end{aligned}$$

By Lemmas 1 and 4, the left hand side equals:

$$(\mathbf{sva}\,\mathcal{E})[\![e]\!]\,\rho\,(\lambda\epsilon^*\,.\,\kappa(\mathit{trunc}\,\epsilon^*))$$

But by Theorem 3, the latter equals $(\mathbf{sva}\,\mathcal{E})[\![e]\!]\,\rho\,\kappa$. ∎

3. Faithfulness of an Operational Semantics

With this compiler correctness result, we have completed the denotational portion of the paper. We are ready to introduce a state machine semantics for the Basic Byte Code, and to prove that the state machine semantics is faithful to the denotational one that we have been using up to now..

3.1. Operational Semantics of the Basic Byte Code

The operational semantics of the BBC is determined by a state machine. That state machine uses BBC code as well as other objects as the components of its states. We introduce an expanded syntax called the *augmented byte code* or ABC; it is a language which includes the BBC and also expressions belonging to other grammar classes. The objects from these other classes are used as state components together with code to build up the states of the machine.

The new ABC tokens are locations (which are actually the same as natural numbers, but which for clarity we indicate by l-like variables when used as locations) and the constructors appearing in small capitals in Table 13. The new ABC syntactic categories, which will be defined by BNF, are

v for *values*,
a for *argument stacks*
u for *environments*,
k for *continuations*,
s for *stores*, and
Σ for ABC *states*.

Syntactic categories from the BBC such as templates t and closed instruction lists b retain the same meaning. The additional productions do not feed back into the recursive construction of the old categories, so the productions for the old categories generate the same set of tree-like objects as they did in the BBC. The new productions are given in Table 13; the old productions, which were given in Table 3, will not be repeated here. The components of a state Σ are called, in order, its *template*, *code*, *value*, *argument stack*, *environment*, *continuation*, and

Table 13. ABC Syntactic Definition

v	::=	c | $\langle$CLOSURE $t\ u\ l\rangle$ | $\langle$ESCAPE $k\ l\rangle$
		| $\langle$MUTABLE-PAIR $l_1\ l_2\rangle$ | $\langle$STRING $l^*\rangle$ | $\langle$VECTOR $l^*\rangle$
		| UNSPECIFIED | UNDEFINED
a	::=	v^*
u	::=	EMPTY-ENV | $\langle$ENV $u\ l^*\rangle$
k	::=	HALT | $\langle$CONT $t\ b\ a\ u\ k\rangle$
s	::=	v^*
Σ	::=	$\langle t,\ b,\ v,\ a,\ u,\ k,\ s\rangle$ | $\langle t,\ \langle\rangle,\ v,\ a,\ u,\ k,\ s\rangle$

store, and we may informally speak of them as being held in registers. Strictly speaking, the template is hardly needed. It contains the name of the procedure, which is useful for debugging; moreover, its presence makes it easier to compare ABC states with the states in lower level machines, in which the template does contain crucial information. The halt states in this machine are the states such the code is $\langle\rangle$. The answer function *ans* is defined for halt states Σ by

$$ans(\langle t,\ \langle\rangle,\ v,\ a,\ u,\ k,\ s\rangle) = v : \mathtt{R} \rightarrow v \,|\, \mathtt{R},\ \bot_{\mathtt{A}}.$$

Form of the Rules. We present the machine transition relation, which we will call *acts*, as the union of subfunctions called (*action*) *rules*. The action rules are functions from disjoint subsets of *states* into *states*. Because their domains are disjoint, the union is in fact a function, and the resulting machine is deterministic.

For each rule we give a name, one or more conditions determining when the rule is applicable (and possibly introducing new locally bound variables for later use), and a specification of the new values of some state components ("registers"). Often the domain is specified by equations giving "the form" of certain registers, especially the code. In all specifications the original values of the various registers are designated by conventional variables used exactly as in the above definition of a state: t, b, v, a, u, k, and s. Call these the original register variables. The new values of the registers are indicated by the same variables with primes attached: t', b', v', a', u', k', and s'. Call these the new register variables. New register variables occur only as the left hand sides of equations specifiying new register values. Registers for which no new value is given are tacitly asserted to remain unchanged.

It may help to be more precise about the use of local bindings derived from pattern matching. The domain conditions may involve the original register variables and may introduce new variables (not among the new or old register variables). If we call these new, "auxiliary" variables $x_1, \ldots, x_j$, then the domain conditions define a relation of $j + 7$ places

(†) $R(t, b, v, a, u, k, s, x_1, \ldots, x_j)$.

Table 14. Some Operational Rules for the Basic Byte Code

Rule 1: **Return-Halt** Domain conditions: $b = \langle\langle \texttt{return} \rangle\rangle$; $k = \text{HALT}$ Changes: $b' = \langle\rangle$
Rule 2: **Return** Domain conditions: $b = \langle\langle \texttt{return} \rangle\rangle$; $k = \langle \text{CONT}\ t_1\ b_1\ a_1\ u_1\ k_1 \rangle$ Changes: $t' = t_1$ $u' = u_1$ $b' = b_1$ $k' = k_1$ $a' = a_1$
Rule 3: **Call** Domain conditions: $b = \langle\langle \texttt{call}\ \#a \rangle\rangle$; $v = \langle \text{CLOSURE}\ t_1\ u_1\ l_1 \rangle$; $t_1 = \langle \texttt{lap}\ c\ b_1 \rangle$ Changes: $t' = t_1$ $u' = u_1$ $b' = b_1$
Rule 4: **Make Continuation** Domain conditions: $b = \langle \texttt{make-cont}\ b_1\ \#a \rangle :: b_2$ Changes: $b' = b_2$ $a' = \langle\rangle$; $k' = \langle \text{CONT}\ t\ b_1\ a\ u\ k \rangle$

The domain condition really is this: the rule can be applied in a given state if there exist $x_1, \ldots, x_j$ such that (†). Furthermore, in the change specifications we assume for these auxiliary variables a local binding such that (†). Independence of the new values on the exact choice (if there is any choice) of the local bindings will be unproblematic.

Some Rules of the Basic Byte Code Machine. In Table 14, we present the rules connected with `make-cont`, `call`, and `return`. This form of presentation is more compact and convenient than the explicit form, which would write (for instance) the rule for `return` in the form:

$$\langle t,\ \langle\langle \texttt{return} \rangle\rangle,\ v,\ a,\ u,\ \langle \text{CONT}\ t_1\ b_1\ a_1\ u_1\ k_1 \rangle,\ s \rangle$$
$$\Longrightarrow \langle t_1,\ b_1,\ v,\ a,\ u_1,\ k_1,\ s \rangle$$

We will refer to all the rules R given in [6] as the ABC rules. Each of them is a partial function from states to states; the domains of the rules are pairwise disjoint; hence, they may be combined to form a unique smallest common extension function *acts*.

The full set of rules is not exhaustive, in the sense of there being a next state whenever a state s is not a halt state. On the contrary, when a state represents a program that has encountered a run-time error, the operational semantics simply provides no next state.

Table 15. Semantic Functions for the Faithfulness Proof

$\mathcal{D}_v : v \to \mathtt{E}$
$\mathcal{D}_a : v^* \to \mathtt{E}^*$
$\mathcal{D}_u : u \to \mathtt{N} \to \mathtt{N} \to \mathtt{L}$
$\mathcal{D}_k : k \to \mathtt{E} \to \mathtt{C}$
$\mathcal{D}_s : v^* \to \mathtt{E}^*$

3.2. Faithfulness: Form of the Proof

The main idea of the faithfulness proof, which is presented in full in [3], is to associate a denotation in the domain $\mathtt{A}$ with each state. If Σ is an initial state with template $t = \langle \mathtt{lap}\ c\ b \rangle$, then the denotation of Σ agrees with the denotational value of

$$\mathcal{T}[\![t]\!]\rho\ \mathit{unspecified}\ \langle\rangle\ (\lambda \nu_1 \nu_2 \,.\, \bot)\ (\mathit{one\_arg}\ \kappa_0)$$

where $\kappa_0 = \lambda \epsilon^* \,.\, (\epsilon^*\ 0) : \mathtt{R} \to (\epsilon^*\ 0) \mid \mathtt{R}$ in $\mathtt{A}, \bot$. This ensures that the denotation of an initial state containing t matches its value as used in the compiler proof. For a halt state Σ, the denotation is equal to its computational answer $ans(\Sigma)$, which has been defined to yield the same value as κ_0.

Moreover, for each rule, it is proved that when that rule is applicable, the denotation of the resulting state is equal to the denotation of the preceeding state.

Thus in effect the denotation of an initial state equals the expected denotational answer of running the program on suitable parameters, and the process of execution leaves the value unchanged. If a final state is reached, then since the *ans* function is compatible with κ_0, the computational answer matches the denotational answer, so that faithfulness is assured.

Denotational and Operational Answers. We define in this section the notions of the denotational and operational answers associated with an ABC state.

Our definition requires the new semantic functions shown in Table 15. The definitions of the functions take an additional primitive, namely a function ρ_G : Ide $\to$ L. It associates the names of global variables with the locations in which their values are stored. It is not defined, but only constrained below in the definition of *normal states*. The semantic functions are defined by the equations shown in Table 16.

DEFINITION 6 **(Denotational and Operational Answer)** *The* denotational answer *of an* ABC *state* $\Sigma = \langle t, b, v, a, u, k, s \rangle$, *denoted* $\mathcal{D}[\![\Sigma]\!]$, *is the value of*

$$\mathcal{B}[\![b]\!]\rho_G(\mathcal{D}_v[\![v]\!])(\mathcal{D}_a[\![a]\!])(\mathcal{D}_u[\![u]\!])(\mathcal{D}_k[\![k]\!])(\mathcal{D}_s[\![s]\!]).$$

The operational answer *of* Σ, *denoted* $\mathcal{O}[\![\Sigma]\!]$, *is defined inductively to be the smallest partial function such that:*

1. *If* Σ *is a halt state, then* $\mathcal{O}[\![\Sigma]\!] = ans(\Sigma)$ $[= \mathcal{D}_v[\![v]\!] | \mathtt{R}$ *in* $\mathtt{A}]$;

Table 16. Semantic Clauses for the Faithfulness Proof

$\mathcal{D}_v[\![c]\!] = \mathcal{K}[\![c]\!]$.
$\mathcal{D}_v[\![\langle \text{CLOSURE } t\ u\ l\rangle]\!] = \mathit{fix}(\lambda\epsilon.\langle l, (\lambda\epsilon^*\kappa.\mathcal{T}[\![t]\!]\rho_G\epsilon\epsilon^*\mathcal{D}_u[\![u]\!](\lambda\epsilon.\kappa\langle\epsilon\rangle))\rangle)$ in E.
$\mathcal{D}_v[\![\langle \text{ESCAPE } k\ l\rangle]\!] = \langle l, \mathit{single\_arg}(\lambda\epsilon\kappa.\mathcal{D}_k[\![k]\!]\epsilon)\rangle$ in E.
$\mathcal{D}_v[\![\langle \text{MUTABLE-PAIR } l_1\ l_2\rangle]\!] = \langle l_1, l_2, \mathit{mutable}\rangle$ in E.
$\mathcal{D}_v[\![\langle \text{STRING } l^*\rangle]\!] = \langle l^*, \mathit{mutable}\rangle$ in E.
$\mathcal{D}_v[\![\langle \text{VECTOR } l^*\rangle]\!] = \langle l^*, \mathit{mutable}\rangle$ in E.
$\mathcal{D}_v[\![\text{UNSPECIFIED}]\!] = \mathit{unspecified}$ in E.
$\mathcal{D}_v[\![\text{UNDEFINED}]\!] = \mathit{empty}$ in E.

$\mathcal{D}_a = \mathit{rev} \circ (\mathit{map}\ \mathcal{D}_v)$.

$\mathcal{D}_u[\![\text{EMPTY-ENV}]\!] = (\lambda\nu_1\nu_2.\bot)$.
$\mathcal{D}_u[\![\langle \text{ENV } u\ l^*\rangle]\!] = \mathit{extend}_R\ \mathcal{D}_u[\![u]\!](\mathit{rev}\ l^*)$.

$\mathcal{D}_k[\![\text{HALT}]\!] = (\lambda\epsilon\sigma.\epsilon : \mathtt{R} \to \epsilon|\mathtt{R} \text{ in } \mathtt{A}, \bot)$.
$\mathcal{D}_k[\![\langle \text{CONT } \langle \mathtt{lap}\ c\ b_0\rangle\ b\ a\ u\ k\rangle]\!] = \lambda\epsilon.\mathcal{B}[\![b]\!]\rho_G\epsilon\mathcal{D}_a[\![a]\!]\mathcal{D}_u[\![u]\!]\mathcal{D}_k[\![k]\!]$.

$\mathcal{D}_s = (\mathit{map}\ \mathcal{D}_v)$.

2. Otherwise, $\mathcal{O}[\![\Sigma]\!]$ *is* $\mathcal{O}[\![\mathit{acts}(\Sigma)]\!]$.

Note that, by the definition of $\mathcal{K}$ on R (see Section 2.1), if $v \in \mathtt{R}$, then $\mathcal{D}_v[\![v]\!] : \mathtt{R}$.

Let $\Sigma = \langle\langle \mathtt{lap}\ c\ b_0\rangle, b, v, a, u, k, s\rangle$ be an ABC state. The functions L_{glo}, L_{env}, L_{mp}, and L_{ip} map ABC states to finite sets of locations. The formal definitions ([3]) will not be repeated here; the functions represent respectively the sets of locations in use in Σ for global variables, local variables, mutable pairs, and immutable pairs. For instance, L_{glo} is the range of the function ρ_G.

DEFINITION 7 **(Normal States, Initial States)**
Σ is normal if the following conditions hold:

(1) $L_{\text{glo}}(\Sigma) \cup L_{\text{env}}(\Sigma) \cup L_{\text{ip}}(\Sigma) \cup L_{\text{mp}}(\Sigma) \subseteq \mathit{dom}(s)$.

(2) $L_{\text{glo}}(\Sigma)$, $L_{\text{env}}(\Sigma)$, $L_{\text{ip}}(\Sigma)$, $L_{\text{mp}}(\Sigma)$ *are pairwise disjoint.*

(3) For each immutable pair $p =$ `'(`c_1 `.` c_2`)` *occurring in* Σ, *there are* $l_1, l_2 \in \mathtt{L}$ *such that* $s(l_1) = c_1$ *and* $s(l_2) = c_2$; *and similarly for immutable vectors and strings.*

A store s is codeless if it contains no value v of the form $\langle$CLOSURE $t\ u\ l\rangle$ *or the form* $\langle$ESCAPE $k\ l\rangle$.

A initial state for a BBC *template* $t = \langle \mathtt{lap}\ c\ b\rangle$ *is any normal* ABC *state of the form*

$$\langle t, b, \text{UNSPECIFIED}, \langle\rangle, \text{EMPTY-ENV}, \text{HALT}, s\rangle$$

where s is codeless.

The restriction of initial states to those containing codeless stores plays no role in proving faithfulness, but simplifies the proof of the flattener below. The following lemmas are needed in the proof of faithfulness.

LEMMA 8 *If Σ is a normal* ABC *state, R is an* ABC *rule, and $\Sigma' = R(\Sigma)$, then Σ' is also a normal* ABC *state.*

The proof examines the individual rules.

LEMMA 9 *If $\Sigma = \langle t, \langle\rangle, v, a, u, k, s\rangle$ is a normal* ABC *state with $v \in \mathtt{R}$, then $\mathcal{D}[\![\Sigma]\!] = \mathcal{D}_v[\![v]\!]|\mathtt{R}$ in $\mathtt{A}$.*

The proof is a simple calculation.

LEMMA 10 *If Σ and Σ' are normal* ABC *states such that $\mathcal{O}[\![\Sigma]\!]$ is defined and $\Sigma' = R(\Sigma)$ for some* ABC *rule R, then $\mathcal{D}[\![\Sigma]\!] = \mathcal{D}[\![\Sigma']\!]$.*

Proof: (Selected Case) The full proof is a lengthy examination of 34 cases, one for each rule. Let Σ and Σ' be normal ABC states such that $\mathcal{O}[\![\Sigma]\!]$ is defined and $\Sigma' = R(\Sigma)$ for some special rule R. To prove Lemma 10, we must show that, for each special rule R, if Σ satisfies the domain conditions of R, then $\mathcal{D}[\![\Sigma]\!] = \mathcal{D}[\![\Sigma']\!]$.

The individual cases require, almost exclusively, definitional expansion and β-reduction. A typical case concerns the rule for a *return* instruction:

Case 2: $R =$ Return. Let $\Sigma = \langle\langle \mathtt{lap}\ c\ b\rangle, \langle\langle \mathtt{return}\rangle\rangle, v, a, u, k, s\rangle$, where $k = \langle \textsc{cont}\ t_1\ b_1\ a_1\ u_1\ k_1\rangle$ and $t_1 = \langle \mathtt{lap}\ c'\ b'\rangle$.

Then $R(\Sigma) = \Sigma' = \langle t_1, b_1, v, a_1, u_1, k_1, s\rangle$.

$$
\begin{aligned}
\mathcal{D}[\![\Sigma]\!] &= \mathcal{B}[\![\langle\langle \mathtt{return}\rangle\rangle]\!]\rho_G(\mathcal{D}_v[\![v]\!])(\mathcal{D}_a[\![a]\!])(\mathcal{D}_u[\![u]\!])(\mathcal{D}_k[\![k]\!])(\mathcal{D}_s[\![s]\!])\\
&= (\lambda\rho.\mathit{return})\rho_G(\mathcal{D}_v[\![v]\!])(\mathcal{D}_a[\![a]\!])(\mathcal{D}_u[\![u]\!])(\mathcal{D}_k[\![k]\!])(\mathcal{D}_s[\![s]\!])\\
&= \mathit{return}(\mathcal{D}_v[\![v]\!])(\mathcal{D}_a[\![a]\!])(\mathcal{D}_u[\![u]\!])(\mathcal{D}_k[\![k]\!])(\mathcal{D}_s[\![s]\!])\\
&= (\lambda\epsilon\epsilon^*\rho_R\psi.\psi\epsilon)(\mathcal{D}_v[\![v]\!])(\mathcal{D}_a[\![a]\!])(\mathcal{D}_u[\![u]\!])(\mathcal{D}_k[\![k]\!])(\mathcal{D}_s[\![s]\!])\\
&= (\mathcal{D}_k[\![k]\!])(\mathcal{D}_v[\![v]\!])(\mathcal{D}_s[\![s]\!])\\
&= (\lambda\epsilon.\mathcal{B}[\![b_1]\!]\rho_G\epsilon(\mathcal{D}_a[\![a_1]\!])(\mathcal{D}_u[\![u_1]\!])(\mathcal{D}_k[\![k_1]\!]))(\mathcal{D}_v[\![v]\!])(\mathcal{D}_s[\![s]\!])\\
&= \mathcal{B}[\![b_1]\!]\rho_G(\mathcal{D}_v[\![v]\!])(\mathcal{D}_a[\![a_1]\!])(\mathcal{D}_u[\![u_1]\!])(\mathcal{D}_k[\![k_1]\!])(\mathcal{D}_s[\![s]\!])\\
&= \mathcal{D}[\![\Sigma']\!]
\end{aligned}
$$

■

Although not all of the cases are as straightforward as this (see [3] for all the details), the proof is a perfect illustration of the observation that much formal verification requires long but *exquisitely tedious* arguments. A proof tool in which it is possible to reason effectively about denotational domains would ease the burden of constructing these proofs, and would increase confidence that no error is hidden within the bulky LaTeX source.

THEOREM 5 **(Faithfulness)** *The operational semantics for* BBC *is faithful: for all* BBC *templates t and all initial states* Σ *for t, if* $\mathcal{O}[\![\Sigma]\!]$ *is defined, then* $\mathcal{D}[\![\Sigma]\!] = \mathcal{O}[\![\Sigma]\!]$.

Proof: The proof is a straightforward induction on the length of the computation sequence determining $\mathcal{O}[\![\Sigma]\!]$, using Lemmas 8–10. ■

In fact the actual VLISP faithfulness proof as described in [3] differs from this description in several ways. First, the proof is not carried out at the level of the BBC, but rather at the level of the Tabular Byte Code introduced in [5]. This version of the byte code uses a template table to store embedded templates (representing locally introduced procedures), constants, and global variables. These are referenced by their numeric index within the table. Conceptually this makes no difference to any of the issues described here, so we have opted to avoid introducing another grammar.

Moreover, the actual proof is somewhat more complex. The operational semantics and the denotational semantics differ in the order in which they copy values from the argument stack into the store when making a new environment rib after a procedure call. One order simplified the denotational reasoning, while the other order is more natural to implement. For this reason [3] splits the faithfulness proof into two parts. The first part has exactly the form described in this section, but uses a state machine with an appropriate version of the rule to make an environment rib. The second part shows that the machine with the actual, implemented rule *refines* the one used in the first part, in the sense to be developed in the next section.

Theorem 5 is a conditional: it asserts only that *if* the machine computes an answer, then that is the correct answer. This property also holds of less useful machines than the BBCM, for instance a machine whose transition relation is empty. However, we conjecture that the technique of [13, Theorem 9] would allow us to prove the converse, which would establish the adequacy of the operational semantics. It would assert that the machine succeeds in computing an answer when the denotational semantics predicts a non-$\perp$, non-erroneous answer. The work described in this section was carried out before we became aware of that technique.

4. State Machine Refinement

In the remainder of this paper, we will show how some state machines *refine* others. Refinement allows us to substitute a more easily implemented state machine (a more "concrete" machine) in place of another (a more "abstract" machine) that we already know would be acceptable.

We consider non-deterministic machines but not I/O here. Non-deterministic machines arose naturally when we introduced garbage collection. By contrast, we avoided treating I/O. On the one hand, the official Scheme semantics does not treat I/O. On the other hand, I/O can be added, either within the denotational or the operational style, without any very serious theoretical problem, but with more notational burden.

In this section we will define a notion of state machine refinement, and we will justify a particular technique for showing that one state machine refines another. We call this technique "storage layout relations," following Wand and Oliva [19], although the underlying idea appears to be much older [8]. Wand and Oliva introduce the method by means of an example. Because VLISP used the method repeatedly, we will use this section to provide a formal definition, and to justify the method relative to a precise notion of refinement. We begin with some notation for state machines.

4.1. State Machines

There are many ways of pinning down details for state machines. Since we consider non-deterministic machines but not I/O, the following is convenient.

DEFINITION 8 **(State Machines)**
State transition machines *are 5-tuples*

$$\langle states,\ inits,\ halts,\ acts,\ ans \rangle$$

such that

(a) $inits \subseteq states$, *and* $halts \subseteq states$;

(b) $acts \subseteq states \times states$;

(c) $\Sigma \in halts$ *implies that* Σ *is not in the domain of acts; and*

(d) $ans : halts \rightarrow \mathtt{A}$.

If $\langle \Sigma, \Sigma' \rangle \in acts$, we will say that Σ *can proceed to* Σ'. A state Σ is called a *halt state* if $\Sigma \in halts$, which is equivalent to $ans(\Sigma)$ being well defined. If *acts* is actually a function, then the machine is *deterministic*.

If T is a finite or infinite sequence of states, then it is a *computation* (or a *trace*) if and only if $T(0) \in inits$ and, for every i such that $T(i+1)$ is defined, $\langle T(i), T(i+1) \rangle \in acts$.

A computation is *maximal* if it is infinite or its last state is not in the domain of *acts*. A finite, maximal computation is *successful* if its last state is a halt state; any other finite, maximal computation is *erroneous*.

A state is *accessible* if it is $T(i)$ for some computation T and integer i.

When T is a successful computation, that is, a finite computation terminating with a halt state Σ, we will write $ans(T)$ to mean $ans(\Sigma)$. Otherwise, $ans(T)$ is undefined. We will say that M *can compute* a *from* Σ if there exists a T such that $T(0) = \Sigma$ and $ans(T) = a$.

4.2. Refinement and Storage Layout Relations

In this section we will define a notion of refinement suitable for state machines without I/O. We will then introduce the notion of a *storage layout relation*, which we will show guarantees refinement.

In this section we will let M^A and M^C be state machines, which we regard as abstract and concrete respectively, and we will let decorated symbols refer to objects in these state machines. So for instance $inits^A$ is the set of initial states of M^A; the variable T^C ranges over the traces of M^C; and the variable Σ^C ranges over the states of M^C.

The reader may want to pronounce the relations $\sim_0$, $\sim$, and $\approx$ in this section using terms such as "refines" or "implements." This motivates the order of the arguments, with the more concrete argument always appearing on the left.

DEFINITION 9 **(Refinement)** *Consider a relation* $\sim_0 \subseteq inits^C \times inits^A$.

M^C weakly refines M^A via $\sim_0$ *iff, whenever* $\Sigma^C \sim_0 \Sigma^A$ *and* M^C *can compute a from* Σ^C, *then* M^A *can compute a from* Σ^A.

M^C strongly refines M^A via $\sim_0$ *iff:*

1. *Every abstract initial state corresponds to some concrete initial state:*

$$\forall \Sigma^A : inits^A \,.\, \exists \Sigma^C : inits^C \,.\, \Sigma^C \sim_0 \Sigma^A$$

2. *Whenever* $\Sigma^C \sim_0 \Sigma^A$ *and* M^C *can compute a from* Σ^C, *then* M^A *can compute a from* Σ^A;

3. *Whenever* $\Sigma^C \sim_0 \Sigma^A$ *and* M^A *can compute a from* Σ^A, *then* M^C *can compute a from* Σ^C.

Strong refinement in the sense given here is a very natural notion when state machines return information only through eventually computing an answer. As for weak refinement, it is an informative relation between state machines—it explains what behavior to expect from the concrete machine M^C—only when *enough* abstract initial states correspond to concrete initial states, and when *enough* abstract computations can be simulated on the concrete machine. As we use weak refinement, the computations that can be simulated are those in which all the values that arise can be stored in a machine word of fixed width, such as 32 bits.

Our standard approach [19] for proving that one state machine refines another is to prove that there is a *storage layout relation* between them. The definition makes use of a similarity relation on traces, induced from a similarity relation on states.

DEFINITION 10 **(Sequential extension $\approx$)** *Consider a relation*

$$\sim \subseteq states^C \times states^A.$$

Then $\approx$, *the* sequential extension *of* $\sim$, *is the relation between traces of* M^C *and traces of* M^A *such that* $T^C \approx T^A$ *iff there exists a monotonic function* f *from the domain of* T^C *onto the domain of* T^A, *such that for all* i *in the domain of* T^C,

$$T^C(i) \sim T^A(f(i)).$$

Thus, $f(i)$ tells us "where we are" in the abstract trace, when we have reached position i in the concrete trace. In some cases, however, more than one function f will meet the condition.

The following lemma is intended to bring out the operational significance of $\approx$. It holds between two traces when their successive states are related by $\sim$. Either the concrete machine can proceed by a "stuttering" transition, which corresponds to no transition in the abstract machine, or else the two machines may each perform a transition. In either case, the resulting states must still be related by $\sim$. The stuttering transition is expressed below in Clause 3, while the lockstep transition is expressed in Clause 4.

LEMMA 11 *Suppose that* $\sim \subseteq \mathit{states}^C \times \mathit{states}^A$. *Let* $\simeq$ *be the least relation between traces of* M^C *and traces of* M^A *such that:*

1. $\langle\rangle \simeq \langle\rangle$;
2. *If* Σ^C *and* Σ^A *are initial states and* $\Sigma^C \sim \Sigma^A$, *then* $\langle\Sigma^C\rangle \simeq \langle\Sigma^A\rangle$;
3. *If* Σ_0^C *can proceed to* Σ_1^C, *and* $\Sigma_1^C \sim \Sigma^A$, *then*
$$T^C \frown \langle\Sigma_0^C\rangle \simeq T^A \frown \langle\Sigma^A\rangle \quad \text{implies} \quad T^C \frown \langle\Sigma_0^C, \Sigma_1^C\rangle \simeq T^A \frown \langle\Sigma^A\rangle;$$
4. *If* Σ_0^C *can proceed to* Σ_1^C, Σ_0^A *can proceed to* Σ_1^A, *and* $\Sigma_1^C \sim \Sigma_1^A$, *then*
$$T^C \frown \langle\Sigma_0^C\rangle \simeq T^A \frown \langle\Sigma_0^A\rangle \quad \text{implies} \quad T^C \frown \langle\Sigma_0^C, \Sigma_1^C\rangle \simeq T^A \frown \langle\Sigma_0^A, \Sigma_1^A\rangle.$$

Then if T^C *and* T^A *are finite,* $T^C \simeq T^A$ *iff* $T^C \approx T^A$.

Proof: We first make a general observation. Suppose that i is in the domain of T^C, and $x = \{j \mid 0 \leq j \leq i\}$. Then, since f is monotonic and onto the domain of T^A, the image of x under f is

$$\{j \mid 0 \leq j \leq f(i)\}.$$

Letting $i = 0$, we may infer that $f(0) = 0$ unless the trace T^C is $\langle\rangle$. Similarly, we must have either $f(i+1) = f(i)$ or $f(i+1) = f(i) + 1$, whenever $i+1$ is in the domain of T^C.

$\Rightarrow$: If $T^C \simeq T^A$ by Clause 1 or 2, then the function f is the empty function or the function mapping 0 to 0 respectively.

Suppose that $T^C \frown \langle\Sigma_0^C, \Sigma_1^C\rangle \simeq T^A \frown \langle\Sigma^A\rangle$ holds by Clause 3, that the index of the last occurrence of Σ_1^C is $i+1$, and the index of the last occurrence of Σ^A

is j. Then inductively there is an acceptable f_0 mapping $\{k \mid 0 \leq k \leq i\}$ onto $\{k \mid 0 \leq k \leq j\}$. Then extending f_0 to f by stipulating $i+1 \mapsto j$, f is monotone and onto $\{k \mid 0 \leq k \leq j\}$. Moreover, by the hypothesis to Clause 3, $T^C(i+1) \sim T^A(j)$.

Suppose that $T^C \frown \langle \Sigma_0^C, \Sigma_1^C \rangle \simeq T^A \frown \langle \Sigma_0^A, \Sigma_1^A \rangle$ holds by Clause 4, where the last occurrences of Σ_1^C and Σ_1^A have indices $i+1$ and $j+1$ respectively. Then inductively there is an acceptable f_0 mapping $\{k \mid 0 \leq k \leq i\}$ onto $\{k \mid 0 \leq k \leq j\}$, which we may extend to the needed f by stipulating $i+1 \mapsto j+1$.

$\Leftarrow$: By induction on T^C. Let f be an acceptable function from the domain of T^C to the domain of T^A. The cases for $\langle\rangle$ and $\langle \Sigma^C \rangle$ are immediate from Clauses 1 and 2. Otherwise, T^C is of the form $T_0^C \frown \langle \Sigma_0^C, \Sigma_1^C \rangle$, where the last occurrence of Σ_1^C has index $i+1$. If $f(i+1) = f(i)$, then apply Clause 3; if $f(i+1) = f(i)+1$, apply Clause 4. ■

In the following definition, we use the notion of quasi-equality [2, 4], written $s == t$, meaning that s and t are equal if either of them is well defined. If $\downarrow$ means "is defined," then $s == t$ is in effect an abbreviation of $(s\downarrow \vee t\downarrow) \Rightarrow s = t$. In particular, $ans^C(\Sigma^C) == ans^A(\Sigma^A)$ implies that either both Σ^C and Σ^A are halt states, or else neither of them is.

Definition 11 (Storage layout relation) *A relation* $\sim \subseteq states^C \times states^A$ *is a* storage layout relation *for* M^C *and* M^A *iff:*

1. *Every abstract initial state corresponds to some concrete initial state:*

$$\forall \Sigma^A : inits^A \,.\, \exists \Sigma^C : inits^C \,.\, \Sigma^C \sim \Sigma^A;$$

2. *For every concrete trace, and abstract initial state* Σ^A *corresponding to its first member, some corresponding abstract trace starts from* Σ^A*:*

$$\forall T^C, \Sigma^A : inits^A \,.\, T^C(0) \sim \Sigma^A \Rightarrow \exists T^A \,.\, T^A(0) = \Sigma^A \wedge T^C \approx T^A;$$

3. *For every abstract trace, and concrete initial state* Σ^C *corresponding to its first member, some corresponding concrete trace starts from* Σ^C*:*

$$\forall T^A, \Sigma^C : inits^C \,.\, \Sigma^C \sim T^A(0) \Rightarrow \exists T^C \,.\, T^C(0) = \Sigma^C \wedge T^C \approx T^A;$$

4. *Of two corresponding states, if both are halt states, then they deliver the same answer, and otherwise neither is a halt state:*

$$\forall \Sigma^C, \Sigma^A \,.\, \Sigma^C \sim \Sigma^A \Rightarrow ans^C(\Sigma^C) == ans^A(\Sigma^A).$$

A relation $\sim \subseteq states^C \times states^A$ *is a* weak storage layout relation *for* M^C *and* M^A *iff conditions 2 and 4 above hold.*

THEOREM 6 **(Storage layout relations guarantee refinement)** *If $\sim$ is a weak storage layout relation for M^C and M^A, then M^C weakly refines M^A via the relation $\sim_0$ defined to be $\sim \cap\, inits^C \times inits^A$.*

If $\sim$ is a storage layout relation $\sim$ for M^C and M^A, then M^C strongly refines M^A via $\sim_0 = \sim \cap\, inits^C \times inits^A$.

Proof: Clause 1 of Definition 9 is immediate from Clause 1 of Definition 11.

We next argue that Clause 4 of Definition 11 implies that, when $T^C \approx T^A$,

$$ans^C(T^C) == ans^A(T^A). \qquad (\dagger)$$

On the one hand, if $ans^C(T^C)$ is well-defined, then T^C terminates in a halt state at its last index i. Moreover, $T^C(i) \sim T^A(f(i))$, so by Clause 4, $answer^C(T^C(i)) = answer^A(T^A(f(i)))$. Finally, since T^A is a trace, $f(i)$ must be its last index, and $ans^A(T^A) = answer^A(T^A(f(i)))$. On the other hand, if $ans^A(T^A)$ is well-defined, similar reasoning applies, using the fact that f is onto.

To prove Clause 2 of Definition 9, suppose that T^C computes the answer a from Σ^C. By Clause 2 of Definition 11, there is a T^A with $T^A(0) = \Sigma^A$ and $T^C \approx T^A$. By $\dagger$, $ans^A(T^A) = a$.

For Clause 3, we use Clause 3 of Definition 11 similarly. ∎

Clause 2 in Definition 11 is, in essence, a safety condition on the concrete machine, while Clause 3 is a liveness condition on it, as the following lemma suggests. In this lemma, we will use γ as a variable over sequences of states of M^C.

LEMMA 12 **(Safety and liveness conditions)** *Consider a relation $\sim \subseteq states^C \times states^A$.*

1. *(Safety) Suppose that whenever $\Sigma_0^C \sim \Sigma_0^A$ and Σ_0^C can proceed to Σ_1^C, then*
   - *(A) either $\Sigma_1^C \sim \Sigma_0^A$ (a stuttering step);*
   - *(B) or else there exists a Σ_1^A such that Σ_0^A can proceed to Σ_1^A and $\Sigma_1^C \sim \Sigma_1^A$.*

   Then Clause 2 of Definition 11 holds.

2. *(Liveness) Suppose that whenever $\Sigma_0^C \sim \Sigma_0^A$ and Σ_0^A can proceed to Σ_1^A, then there exists a γ such that:*
   - *(A) $\forall i \,.\, i < \#\gamma - 1 \Rightarrow \gamma(i) \sim \Sigma_0^A$;*
   - *(B) $\gamma(\#\gamma - 1) \sim \Sigma_1^A$; and*
   - *(C) γ is* tracelike, *in the sense that*

   $$\forall i < \#\gamma - 1 \,.\, \langle \gamma(i), \gamma(i+1) \rangle \in acts^C.$$

   With this definition, γ is a trace T^C if it is tracelike and $\gamma(0)$ is an initial state.

Then Clause 3 of Definition 11 holds.

Proof: 1. By induction on T^C. 2. By induction on T^A. ■

This lemma shows that the notion of storage layout relation is akin to the notion of a ***weak bisimulation*** (see [12, Chapter 5, Definition 5], for example). However, in our formulation, the relation is one-sided in that all the silent τ-transitions are taken by the concrete machine.

In many cases, such as the linearizer algorithm presented in Section 5, we use a storage layout relation to prove not just that one state machine refines another, but that a particular language translation F is correct. To see why that makes sense, let M^A be the state machine that gives the operational semantics for the source language, and let M^C give the operational semantics for the target language. Also, suppose that the states of M^A have the form of pairs $\langle p, \Sigma_0 \rangle$, where p is a program in the *source* language of F and Σ_0 contains the remaining state components, while the states of M^C have the form $\langle p', \Sigma'_0 \rangle$, where p' is a program in the *target* language of F. Suppose further that at least for *initial* states, the non-code portion of a state may be shared between an abstract state and a concrete state. That is,

$$\langle p, \Sigma_0 \rangle \in \mathit{inits}^A \Rightarrow \langle F(p), \Sigma_0 \rangle \in \mathit{inits}^C.$$

This was the point of the restriction to codeless stores in Definition 7.

Then we may say that F *exhibits* M^C *as a refinement of* M^A if M^C refines M^A via a relation built from projection, F, and pairing. In particular, the relation is to hold between a concrete initial state $\langle p', \Sigma'_0 \rangle$ and an abstract initial state $\langle p, \Sigma_0 \rangle$ if $p' = F(p)$ and $\Sigma'_0 = \Sigma_0$. If this relation is a refinement, then M^C computes the same answers when started in state $\langle F(\Sigma^A(0)), \Sigma^A(1) \rangle$ that M^A computes when started in state Σ^A.

How can we use the storage layout relation method to prove that F refines M^C to M^A? We must exhibit a storage layout relation $\sim$ such that F establishes $\sim$, in the sense that $\langle F(p), \Sigma_0 \rangle \sim \langle p, \Sigma_0 \rangle$, whenever the latter is an initial state of M^A.

We illustrate this method in the next section, by proving that the VLISP flattener (or code linearizer) is correct. Section 5.4 proves that the flattener establishes a relation $\sim$, which is the real content of Theorem 7. Then Theorem 8 in Section 5.5 shows that $\sim$ is in fact a storage layout relation.

5. The Flattener

The **flattener** [6] transforms byte coded procedures in the BBC into a linear rather than a tree-structured form. Conditionals are represented in a familiar way using `branch` and `branch-if-false` instructions that involve a numeric offset to the target code. Similarly, the target code to which a procedure should return is indicated by a numeric offset from the instruction. We call the output language of the flattener the **flattened byte code** (FBC).

However, before we introduce the new language, we will provide a bit more detail about the BBC and its operational semantics (Section 5.1). We will then present the FBC and give it an operational semantics (Section 5.2) in a style very similar to the presentation of the BBC semantics in Section 3.1. We will briefly describe the flattener algorithm(Section 5.3). To prove the correctness of this algorithm, we develop a correspondence relation between flattened and unflattened code, and prove that the flattener produces code bearing this relation to its input (Section 5.4). Finally, we extend the code correspondence relation to a storage layout relation between states of the newly introduced flattened byte code state machine (FBCM) and the BBCM (Section 5.5). This establishes that the FBCM is a refinement of the BBCM.

5.1. The Basic Byte Code in More Detail

In order to describe the operational semantics of conditionals in the BBCM, we will need to refer to the *open-adjoin* of an open instruction list y and any instruction list w, written $y^\smile w$ and defined as follows:

DEFINITION 12 **(Open-adjoin)**

$$\langle z\rangle^\smile w = z :: w;$$

$$(z :: y)^\smile w = z :: (y^\smile w);$$

$$(\langle \texttt{make-cont}\ y\ n\rangle :: b)^\smile w = \langle \texttt{make-cont}\ y^\smile w\ n\rangle :: b;\ \textit{and}$$

$$(\langle \texttt{make-cont}\ \langle\rangle\ n\rangle :: b)^\smile w = \langle \texttt{make-cont}\ w\ n\rangle :: b.$$

It may help to note, first, that in the grammar presented in Table 3, a closed BBC instruction list can contain (at top level) no instruction of the form $\langle$**make-cont** y $n\rangle$ or $\langle$**make-cont** $\langle\rangle$ $n\rangle$, and, hence, that an open instruction list is either a list of neutral instructions or contains exactly one instruction of this form. Open-adjoin proceeds recursively inwards from its first argument through the code lists of such instructions until it reaches one which is just a (possibly empty) list of neutral instructions and then it concatenates w to the "open" end of that list.

LEMMA 13 **(Properties of open-adjoin)** *For all y, w, y_1, and b,*

1. *$y^\smile w$ is well-defined by the above recursion and is an instruction list;*

2. *$y^\smile y_1$ is open, and $y^\smile b$ is closed; and*

3. *$y^\smile(y_1{}^\smile w) = (y^\smile y_1)^\smile w$ (associativity).*

The rules for conditionals in open instruction lists use $^\smile$, as shown in Table 17.

Table 17. BBCM Open Branch Rules

Rule 5: **Open Branch/True**	Rule 6: **Open Branch/False**
Domain conditions:	Domain conditions:
$b = \langle\texttt{unless-false}\ y_1\ y_2\rangle :: b_1$	$b = \langle\texttt{unless-false}\ y_1\ y_2\rangle :: b_1$
$v \neq \mathit{false}$	$v = \mathit{false}$
Changes:	Changes:
$b' = y_1 {}^\smile b_1$	$b' = y_2 {}^\smile b_1$

Table 18. Flattened Byte Code: Syntax

$$
\begin{array}{rcl}
t & ::= & \langle\texttt{template}\ c\ w\rangle \\
w & ::= & \langle\rangle \mid m{}^\frown w \\
m & ::= & \langle\texttt{call}\ n\rangle \mid \langle\texttt{return}\rangle \mid \langle\texttt{make-cont}\ n_0\ n_1\ n_2\rangle \mid \langle\texttt{literal}\ c\rangle \\
 & \mid & \langle\texttt{closure}\ t\rangle \mid \langle\texttt{global}\ i\rangle \mid \langle\texttt{local}\ n_0\ n_1\rangle \mid \langle\texttt{set-global!}\ i\rangle \\
 & \mid & \langle\texttt{set-local!}\ n_0\ n_1\rangle \mid \langle\texttt{push}\rangle \mid \langle\texttt{make-env}\ n\rangle \\
 & \mid & \langle\texttt{make-rest-list}\ n\rangle \mid \langle\texttt{unspecified}\rangle \mid \langle\texttt{branch}\ n_0\ n_1\rangle \\
 & \mid & \langle\texttt{branchf}\ n_0\ n_1\rangle \mid \langle\texttt{checkargs=}\ n\rangle \mid \langle\texttt{checkargs>=}\ n\rangle \mid \langle i\rangle
\end{array}
$$

5.2. Flattened Byte Code Syntax and Operational Semantics

The Flattened Byte Code (FBC) is a modification of the Basic Byte Code that uses unnested linear sequences of tokens for the code part of its templates. Instead of the BBC conditional instruction **`unless-false`**, FBC has **`branchf`** and **`branch`**, both of which take a pair of numeric operands that together indicate an offset to another location in the instruction sequence. The syntax of **`make-cont`** has been altered so that it too can use numeric offsets. The BNF definitions of these classes appear as Table 18. In this version of the syntax, the code sequences are not exclusively unnested, since the instructions $\langle\texttt{closure}\ t\rangle$ and $\langle\texttt{constant}\ c\rangle$ may have nested subexpressions. However, in the full VLISP development, this is not the case; a "tabularizer" stage had previously moved the nested values into a template table, in which they were referenced by a natural number index (cf. page 69).

FBC states—characterized in Table 19—differ from BBC states in that their templates and code belong to the FBC language rather than the BBC language. In addition, instead of having a "code register" they have a numerical "program counter," to which we will refer conventionally as n. It is interpreted as an offset into the code sequence of the template. We will use the variable w to refer to the code sequence (or just the *code*) of a state, i.e., $w = t(2)$. With our conventions, $w(n)$ is

Table 19. Flattened Byte Code State Machine: State Component Syntax

$$
\begin{aligned}
v &::= c \mid \langle \text{CLOSURE } t\ u\ l\rangle \mid \langle \text{ESCAPE } k\ l\rangle \mid \langle \text{MUTABLE-PAIR } l_1\ l_2\rangle \\
&\quad \mid \langle \text{STRING } l^*\rangle \mid \langle \text{VECTOR } l^*\rangle \mid \text{UNSPECIFIED} \mid \text{UNDEFINED} \\
a &::= v^* \\
u &::= \text{EMPTY-ENV} \mid \langle \text{ENV } u\ l^*\rangle \\
k &::= \text{HALT} \mid \langle \text{CONT } t\ b\ a\ u\ k\rangle \\
s &::= v^* \\
\Sigma &::= \langle t,\ n,\ v,\ a,\ u,\ k,\ s\rangle
\end{aligned}
$$

Table 20. Typical FBCM Rules

Rule 1: **Call**
Domain conditions: $w \dagger n = \langle \texttt{call}\ \#a\rangle ^\frown w_1$; $v = \langle \text{CLOSURE } t_1\ u_1\ l_1\rangle$
Changes: $t' = t_1$; $n' = 0$; $u' = u_1$

Rule 2: **Make Continuation**
Domain conditions: $w \dagger n = \langle \texttt{make-cont}\ n_1\ n_2\ \#a\rangle ^\frown w_1$
Changes: $n' = n + 4$; $a' = \langle\rangle$; $k' = \langle \text{CONT } t\ (n + 4 + (n_1 \oplus n_2))\ a\ u\ k\rangle$

Rule 3: **Branchf/False**
Domain conditions: $w \dagger n = \langle \texttt{branchf}\ n_1\ n_2\rangle ^\frown w_1$; $v = \mathit{false}$
Changes: $n' = n + 3 + (n_1 \oplus n_2)$

Rule 4: **Branchf/True**
Domain conditions: $w \dagger n = \langle \texttt{branchf}\ n_1\ n_2\rangle ^\frown w_1$; $v \neq \mathit{false}$
Changes: $n' = n + 3$

the first element of $w \dagger n$, if $0 \leq n < \#w$. The states in *halts* are those such that $n = \#w$ (so $w \dagger n = \langle\rangle$). The answer function, normal states, and initial states are defined as before.

The presentation of the rules for the FBC (Table 20) will use the same conventions as were used for the BBC, except that here n stands for the offset of the ingoing state, n' for the offset of the state produced, and w for $t(2)$, the code sequence of the template of the ingoing state. The operator $\oplus$ takes two integers and returns an integer representing an offset they are together coding; it is defined by the condition $n_0 \oplus n_1 = (256 * n_0) + n_1$. In the FSBCM implementation, the values of n_0 and n_1 are always stored in a single byte. The operator $\oplus$ is needed so that we can represent offsets that are larger than 255. Although large numbers may be represented in more than one way in the form $n_0 \oplus n_1$ (if n_1 may be large), this does not affect our proof.

```
(define (flatten-code code category)
  (if (null? code)
      empty-code-sequence
      (let ((instr (car code))
            (after-code (cdr code)))
        (case (operator instr)
          ((make-cont)
           (flatten-make-cont
            (rand1 instr) (rand2 instr) after-code category))
          ((unless-false) ...)
          (else
           (flatten-default instr after-code category))))))

(define (flatten-make-cont saved nargs after category)
  (let ((after-code (flatten-code after 'closed))
        (saved-code (flatten-code saved category)))
    (add-offset+byte-instruction
     'make-cont (code-length after-code) nargs
     (adjoin-code-sequences after-code saved-code))))

(define (flatten-default instr after category)
  (let ((after-code (flatten-code after category)))
    (prepend-instruction instr after-code)))
```

Figure 2. Flattener Algorithm

5.3. The Flattener

The flattener is implemented by a purely applicative Scheme program, part of which is shown in Figure 2; it is a straightforward recursive descent. It is however sensitive to the syntactic category of the code that it is flattening, whether it is a *closed* BBC instruction list b or an *open* BBC instruction list y.

An obvious induction shows that the algorithm terminates, and produces a syntactically well-formed FBC template from any BBC template.

We will use $F(w)$ to abbreviate the result of applying `flatten-code` to w and *closed*, if w is of the form b, and for the result of applying `flatten-code` to w and *open*, if w is of the form y.

In the next two subsections, we will exhibit a relation between BBCM states and FBCM. The task of the first section is to show that the flattener establishes this relation; the task of the second section is to show that the relation is in fact a storage layout relation. Thus, the two subsections together establish that flattening code leaves its computational results unchanged.

Table 21. Recursive Conditions for $\simeq$.

1. For $m = \langle \texttt{return} \rangle$ or $\langle \texttt{call}\, n \rangle$, $m^\frown w_F \simeq \langle m \rangle$.
2. $\langle \texttt{closure}\, t_F \rangle^\frown w_F \simeq \langle \texttt{closure}\, t \rangle :: m^*$ if, first, either $m^* = w_F = \langle\rangle$ or $w_F \simeq m^*$, and, second, the code correspondence holds between the code embedded within t_F and t respectively:
$$t_F(2) \simeq t(2).$$
3. For atomic z other than closure, $z^\frown w_F \simeq z :: m^*$ if either $m^* = w_F = \langle\rangle$ or $w_F \simeq m^*$.
4. $\langle \texttt{make-cont}\, n_0\, n_1\, n \rangle^\frown w_F \simeq \langle \texttt{make-cont}\, w\, n \rangle :: b$ if
$$w_F \simeq b \quad \text{and} \quad w_F \dagger (n_0 \oplus n_1) \simeq w.$$

4′. $\langle \texttt{make-cont}\, n_0\, n_1\, n \rangle^\frown w_F \simeq \langle \texttt{make-cont}\, \langle\rangle\, n \rangle :: b$ if
$$w_F \simeq b \quad \text{and} \quad w_F \dagger (n_0 \oplus n_1) = \langle\rangle.$$

5. $\langle \texttt{branchf}\, n_0\, n_1 \rangle^\frown w_F \simeq \langle\langle \texttt{unless-false}\, b_1\, b_2 \rangle\rangle$ if
$$w_F \simeq b_1 \quad \text{and} \quad w_F \dagger (n_0 \oplus n_1) \simeq b_2.$$
6. $\langle \texttt{branchf}\, n_0\, n_1 \rangle^\frown w_F \simeq \langle \texttt{unless-false}\, y_1\, y_2 \rangle :: w$ if
$$w_F \simeq y_1{}^\smile w \quad \text{and} \quad w_F \dagger (n_0 \oplus n_1) \simeq y_2{}^\smile w.$$
7. $\langle \texttt{branch}\, n_0\, n_1 \rangle^\frown w_F \simeq w$ if $w_F \dagger (n_0 \oplus n_1) \simeq w$.

5.4. Code Correspondence

We will define the storage layout relation between states justifying this refinement in terms of a preliminary "code correspondence" relation $\simeq$ holding between flattened and unflattened code. We will write $w_F \simeq w$; the main theorem of this section asserts that the flattener establishes this relation: $F(w) \simeq w$. The correspondence relation is defined as the least relation satisfying the conditions given in Table 21. One fine point in the definition concerns expressions of the form $w \dagger n$: when we make an atomic assertion about $w \dagger n$, we are implicitly asserting that it is well defined, so that $n \leq \# w$. We will repeatedly use a fact about sequences:

LEMMA 14 **(drop/adjoin)** *When $n \leq \# w_0$, $(w_0 \dagger n)^\frown w_1 = (w_0{}^\frown w_1) \dagger n$.*

For *closed* instruction lists, adding code to the end of a flattened version does not destroy the $\simeq$ relation. Since the proofs in this section are all similar, we present only the first in detail.

LEMMA 15 **($\simeq$/adjoin)** *If $w_0 \simeq b_0$, then for any w_1, $w_0{}^\frown w_1 \simeq b_0$.*

Proof: We will assume that w_0 is not of the form $\langle \mathbf{branch}\ n_0\ n_1\rangle^\frown w_2$, so that $w_0{}^\frown w_1 \simeq b_0$ is not true in virtue of clause 6. For otherwise, $w_2 \dagger (n_0 \oplus n_1) \simeq b_0$, and we may apply the lemma to infer that

$$w_2 \dagger (n_0 \oplus n_1)^\frown w_1 \simeq b_0.$$

(Naturally, $w_2 \dagger (n_0 \oplus n_1)$ might begin with a **branch**, but this may be repeated only a finite number of times.)

Since $w_2 \dagger (n_0 \oplus n_1)^\frown w_1 = w_2{}^\frown w_1 \dagger (n_0 \oplus n_1)$, we may apply clause 6 to infer:

$$\langle \mathbf{branch}\ n_0\ n_1\rangle^\frown (w_2{}^\frown w_1) \simeq b_0.$$

By the associativity of $^\frown$, the desired conclusion holds.

The proof is by induction mirroring the inductive definition of $\simeq$.

1. Suppose $b_0 = \langle m\rangle = \langle\langle \mathtt{return}\rangle\rangle$ or $\langle\langle \mathtt{call}\ n\rangle\rangle$, and $w_0 = \langle m\rangle^\frown w$. By the associativity of $^\frown$, $(\langle m\rangle^\frown w)^\frown w_1 = \langle m\rangle^\frown(w^\frown w_1)$, which is also an instance of clause 1.

2. Suppose that $b_0 = \langle \mathtt{closure}\ t\rangle :: b$ and $w_0 = \langle \mathtt{closure}\ t_1\rangle^\frown w$. Since $w_0 \simeq b_0$, we may infer from the definition of $\simeq$ that $w \simeq b$ and $t_1(2) \simeq t(2)$. Hence we may apply the induction hypothesis to infer that $w^\frown w_1 \simeq b$, and we may then apply Clause 2 to infer that $w_0{}^\frown w_1 \simeq b_0$.

3. Suppose that $b_0 = z :: b$, $w_0 = z^\frown w$, where z is not a $\mathtt{closure}$ instruction. (The syntax ensures that m^* really is of the form b.) Since, inductively, $w^\frown w_1 \simeq b$, we simply apply clause 3 to $w^\frown w_1$.

4. If $b_0 = \langle \mathtt{make\text{-}cont}\ b_1\ n\rangle :: b$, and $w_0 = \langle \mathtt{make\text{-}cont}\ n_0\ n_1\ n_2\rangle^\frown w$: Assume inductively:

$$w^\frown w_1 \simeq b \quad\text{and}\quad w \dagger (n_0 \oplus n_1)^\frown w_1 \simeq b_1.$$

By the drop/adjoin lemma, we may apply clause 4 with $w^\frown w_1$ in place of w.

4′. A closed instruction sequence b_0 is not of this form.

5, 6, 7. Similar to 4.

■

In contrast to closed instruction lists, for *open* instruction lists, adding code to the end of a flattened version corresponds to $^\smile$:

LEMMA 16 **($\simeq$/open-adjoin)** *If $w_0 \simeq y$ and $w_1 \simeq w$, then $w_0{}^\frown w_1 \simeq y^\smile w$.*

The main theorem of this section asserts that the output produced by the flattener bears the code correspondence relation $\simeq$ to its input. Its proof is similar in structure to the proof of Lemma 15.

THEOREM 7 **(Flattener establishes $\simeq$)** $F(w) \simeq w$.

Table 22. Closure Conditions for $\sim$.

1. $x \sim x$, if x is self corresponding
2. $\langle \text{CLOSURE } t_1\ u\ l \rangle \sim \langle \text{CLOSURE } t_2\ u\ l \rangle$, if $t_1 \sim t_2$
3. $\langle \text{ESCAPE } k_1\ l \rangle \sim \langle \text{ESCAPE } k_2\ l \rangle$, if $k_1 \sim k_2$
4. $v_1^* \sim v_2^*$, if $\#v_1^* = \#v_2^*$ and, for every $n < \#v_1^*$, $v_1^*(n) \sim v_2^*(n)$
5. $\langle \texttt{template}\ c\ w \rangle \sim \langle \texttt{template}\ c\ b \rangle$, if $w \simeq b$
6. $\langle \text{CONT } t_2\ n\ a_2\ u\ k_2 \rangle \sim \langle \text{CONT } t_1\ b\ a_1\ u\ k_1 \rangle$, if
   (A) $t_2(2) \dagger n \simeq b$, and
   (B) $a_2 \sim a_1$ and $k_2 \sim k_1$
7. $\langle t_2,\ n,\ v_2,\ a_2,\ u,\ k_2,\ s_2 \rangle \sim \langle t_1,\ b,\ v_1,\ a_1,\ u,\ k_1,\ s_1 \rangle$, if
   (A) $t_2(2) \dagger n \simeq b$, and
   (B) $v_2 \sim v_1$, $a_2 \sim a_1$, $k_2 \sim k_1$, and $s_2 \sim s_1$
8. $\langle t_2,\ n,\ v_2,\ a_2,\ u,\ k_2,\ s_2 \rangle \sim \langle t_1,\ b,\ v_1,\ a_1,\ u,\ k_1,\ s_1 \rangle$, if each is a halt state and $v_1 = v_2$.

5.5. State Correspondence

Based on the underlying "code correspondence" relation $\simeq$, we will define a binary "miscellaneous correspondence" relation $\sim$ between various kinds of syntactic objects of the FBCM on the left and the BBCM on the right, building up to a notion of correspondence between FBC states and BBC states that is preserved by state transitions. The main result of this section is that the state correspondence is a storage layout relation; hence by Theorem 6 the FBCM is a faithful refinement of the BBCM.

Because the two languages share some syntactic objects, we can simplify the definition. Some of the objects that are shared by the two languages are *self corresponding*, namely, the HALT continuation; all environments; UNDEFINED; UNSPECIFIED; all constants; and all values beginning with MUTABLE-PAIR, STRING, or VECTOR.

The relation $\sim$ is then defined recursively, as the least set of pairs whose right element is a member of one of the ABC classes t, v, a, u, k or s, or is an ABC state, and which satisfies the closure conditions given in Table 22. Note especially clauses 6 and 7, which reflect differences in how, and even in which registers, the two machines store "active" code. Also, clause 4 applies to both argument stacks and stores.

By this definition and Definition 7, which ensures that the stores of initial states are codeless, we may infer that if an initial BBC and an initial FBC state share the same store, then they correspond if their code corresponds. That is, suppose $t_F = \langle \texttt{template}\ c\ w \rangle$; $t = \langle \texttt{template}\ c'\ b \rangle$; and $w \simeq b$. Then

$$\langle t_F, 0, \text{UNSPECIFIED}, \langle\rangle, \text{EMPTY-ENV}, \text{HALT}, s \rangle$$

corresponds to

$$\langle t, t(2), \text{UNSPECIFIED}, \langle\rangle, \text{EMPTY-ENV}, \text{HALT}, s\rangle.$$

By Theorem 7, we can always take w to be $F(b)$, so condition 1 in Definition 11 (storage layout relations) is satisfied. Moreover, condition 4 follows immediately from clause 8 for $\sim$; hence:

LEMMA 17 *$\sim$ satisfies the initial condition (1) and the halt condition (4) for being a storage layout relation.*

The following easy lemma shortens the proof of the preservation theorem somewhat and justifies a looser way of thinking about computations of BBC and FBC state machines. One can talk about what they *do* (or *would do* under given circumstances), not just about what they *might* do.

LEMMA 18 **(Determinacy of Transitions)**
If M is either the BBCM *or the* FBCM, *and M is in state Σ, then there is at most one state Σ' such that M can proceed by one rule transition from Σ to Σ'.*

Proof: The domain conditions for the different rules (of the same machine) are pairwise mutually incompatible, as can be seen by looking just at the required form of the code register, except for a few cases when one must also consider the value register or the argument register. Given a particular rule and a state, there is always at most one way of binding the variables of the domain equations so that they are satisfied. The next state is clearly determined by the rule, the ingoing state, and these bindings. ■

For instance, the rules for primitives allocating new storage stipulate that the new locations selected lie immediately after the previously active portion of the store.

Clearly the BBC rules are closely paralleled by the FBC rules: let us say that a BBC rule A *corresponds* to an FBC rule B if A and B have the same name, also that Closed Branch/True and Open Branch/True both *correspond* to Branchf/True, and finally that Closed Branch/False and Open Branch/False both *correspond* to Branchf/False. No BBC rule corresponds to Branch. A *branch* rule means one whose name ends in /True or /False—four for BBC and two for FBC.

THEOREM 8 **(Preservation of State Correspondence)**
Let Σ be the state of the BBCM *and Σ_F the state of the* FBCM, *and assume that $\Sigma_F \sim \Sigma$. Then*

1. *if the* FBCM *proceeds by the Branch rule to state Σ'_F, then $\Sigma'_F \sim \Sigma$ and the* FBCM *cannot proceed from Σ'_F by the Branch rule;*

2. *if the* FBCM *cannot proceed by the Branch rule, then, if either machine proceeds, then the other machine proceeds by a corresponding rule, and the resulting states correspond.*

The proof consists of a careful analysis of the rules of the two machines. Using Lemma 17, Lemma 12, and Theorem 6, we can infer:

THEOREM 9 $\sim$ *is a storage layout relation for the* FBCM *and the* BBCM. *Hence, the* FBCM *refines the* BBCM.

The VLISP Scheme compiler is structured as the composition of five stages: the byte code compiler, tabulator, flattener, linker, and image builder. We have now completed our presentation of the algorithms and correctness proofs of the byte code compiler and the flattener. We have ignored the tabulator and the linker since they do not raise significant new verification issues. The image builder, which produces the final SBC program as a binary image (i.e., a flat sequence of bits), uses a storage layout relation defined in a different way. However, since this same technique is used in the more interesting proof of the garbage collector (see Section 6.3), we will not describe the image builder in this paper.

6. The Virtual Machine

The VLISP Scheme compiler translates any Scheme program p to a program *sbc* in a language called Stored Byte Code (SBC), while the VLISP Virtual Machine (VM) evaluates SBC programs to answers. Together, these evaluate Scheme programs to answers.

The semantics of SBC is given in terms of a state machine called the Stored Byte Code Machine (SBCM); the meaning of *sbc* is given by the answer computed by the SBCM when started in an initial state Σ_0 constructed from *sbc*. The correctness of the compiler as a whole asserts that if the SBCM computes an answer a when started in Σ_0, then a is the result of applying the denotation of p to suitable initial parameters $\vec{x}$.

The correctness of the VLISP Virtual Machine (VM) requires that when the VM evaluates *sbc* to an answer a, then the SBCM should compute a when started in an initial state constructed from *sbc*. In this section, we present the algorithms and correctness proofs of parts of the VLISP Virtual Machine relative to the SBCM.

There are three main reasons why the SBCM must be refined before being embodied in concrete program code. First, the size of the active store in the SBCM is unbounded in size, whereas any concrete implementation will have a limited address space. As a consequence, a garbage collector must be introduced. Second, other values are also bounded by the finite resources available to a concrete implementation. Third, the declarative specifications of some of the rules are not trivial to embody in concrete, procedural code. For this last reason, we will instantiate these rules using programs that manipulate a set of primitive operations that can be directly and reliably coded. We thus *refine* and *instantiate* the state machine description until we obtain a concrete implementation of the VM. *Refinement* is a binary relation between state machines; as formalized in Section 4, these state machines may have completely different state spaces.

Instantiation is a binary relation between machines sharing the same state space. Instantiation may reduce the non-determinism of a machine; however, it is useful even if the two state machines are identical, as is the case in Section 6.2. The reason is that the *description* of the state machine has changed; in place of the declarative rules, we have substituted algorithms calling simple primitive operations, and have thus moved closer to a concrete program.

We use refinement and instantiation in contrasting ways. We use refinement to alter the states and action rules of state machines. We use instantiation to specify algorithms that implement the action rules. In both cases, the minimal correctness criterion is that we should refine the observable behavior of the state machines, in the sense that every observable behavior of the more concrete machine should also be an observable behavior of the more abstract machine.

We will briefly describe the state machine SBCM. We proceed by alternately instantiating and refining the state machine as follows:

1. We define a collection of primitive state operations that observe and modify states. We *instantiate* the SBCM action rule descriptions by coding them in terms of these state operations. The state machine remains the same, while its description is altered (made more "concrete"). The correctness proof shows that the implementation of each action rule meets its specification; this is long and tedious.

2. We justify garbage collection in two main steps:

   (A) We *refine* the SBCM to the Garbage-Collected Stored Byte Code Machine (GCSM). This machine is similar to the SBCM except that it includes a new primitive state-modifying operation (**gc**). The refinement proof uses the storage layout relation technique to show that the GCSM refines the SBCM. The main difference between this proof and the proof of the flattener in Section 5 is in the definition of the storage layout relation.

   (B) We *instantiate* the **gc** primitive by presenting a concrete implementation that is defined in terms of the primitive state operations. The instantiation proof shows that the garbage collector meets the specification of the action rule.

3. We *weakly refine* the GCSM to a Finite, Garbage-Collected Stored Byte Code Machine (FGCSM). The FGCSM state set is a subset of the GCSM state set, namely the set of all states with components of bounded size. The length of stacks, the length of stores, and the values of registers, stack cells, and store cells receive upper bounds. The FGCSM initial states, halt states, action rules, and answer function are restrictions of the corresponding GCSM components. The proof of weak refinement is trivial.

4. We directly encode the FGCSM description in PreScheme; this is the concrete implementation of the VLISP Virtual Machine.

Our implementation also incorporates several optimizations, mentioned in Section 6.6; we have not justified these optimizations in this paper since they add complexity to the proofs but do not involve any new techniques.

6.1. Stored Byte Code and its State Machine

Stored Byte Code (SBC) language represents the image builder's output. Its operational semantics is given in terms of a deterministic state machine called the *Stored Byte Code Machine* (SBCM).

The abstract syntax of SBC is presented in Table 23. An SBC program is an SBC store together with an index into the store. A store is a sequence of cells, with each cell being one of:

1. A header $\langle$HEADER $h\ p\ m\rangle$ where h (the *header tag*) is a tag that describes the object occupying the storage that follows; p (the *mutability flag*) is a boolean value that describes whether the object is mutable; and m (the *header size*) is the number of cells in the stored object;
2. A pointer $\langle$PTR $l\rangle$ where l is an index into the store;
3. A number $\langle$FIXNUM $n\rangle$ where n is an integer;
4. An immediate value $\langle$IMM $imm\rangle$ where imm is a simple (unstructured) value such as a character, boolean, etc.
5. A byte b where b is a number that represents either a character or an instruction opcode.

A term of the form 2, 3, or 4 above is called a value descriptor. For each byte that represents an instruction opcode, we define a named constant and refer to the byte by this name, e.g., `call`, `return`, etc.

We will write a typical state of the SBCM in the form

$$\langle t, n, v, a, u, k, s, r\rangle$$

where n is a number, t, v, u, k, and r are value descriptors, a is a stack of value descriptors and s is a store. The components of the state are called, in order, its template, offset, value, argument stack, environment, continuation, store, and spare.

The stores in accessible states of the SBCM, where again by an *accessible* state we mean a state that occurs in some trace of the machine, satisfy a representation invariant, namely they contain a collection of *stored objects*. A stored object consists of a header and a tuple of values. The header contains a type tag for the stored object and the length of the tuple of values. The header and the values are stored in consecutive locations in the store. The address l at which the first value is stored is called the address of the stored object, and the term $\langle$PTR $\ell\rangle$ is called a pointer to the stored object. We name the stored object by its header tag; thus we call a stored object with header tag TEMPLATE a "template" stored object.

Table 23. **Abstract Syntax of Stored Byte Code (SBC).**

program	::=	$\langle s\ v\rangle$
s	::=	*cell**
cell	::=	*desc* | *byte*
desc	::=	$\langle$HEADER *htag bool n*$\rangle$ | *v*
v	::=	$\langle$PTR *n*$\rangle$ | $\langle$FIXNUM *n*$\rangle$ | $\langle$IMM *imm*$\rangle$
imm	::=	FALSE | TRUE | $\langle$CHAR *n*$\rangle$ | NULL | UNDEFINED
		UNSPECIFIED | EMPTY-ENV | HALT | EOF
htag	::=	*bhtag* | *dhtag*
bhtag	::=	STRING | CODEVECTOR
dhtag	::=	PAIR | SYMBOL | VECTOR | LOCATION | TEMPLATE |
		CLOSURE | PORT | CONTINUATION | ENVIRONMENT
byte	::=	*n*
a	::=	v^*
Σ	::=	$\langle v_0\ n\ v_1\ a\ v_2\ v_3\ s\ v_4\rangle$

DEFINITION 13 **(Stored Objects)** *s contains a* stored object *at ℓ (or alternatively, ℓ* is a pointer to an object in *s) if:*

1. $s(\ell-1) = \langle\text{HEADER } h\ p\ m\rangle$, *for some h, p, and m;*

2. $s(j)$ *is a well-defined non-header value for each j for* $\ell \le j < \ell + m$.

A state Σ is composed of stored objects *if, whenever* $\langle\text{PTR } \ell\rangle$ *occurs in any (transitive) component of Σ, then the store of Σ contains a stored object at location ℓ.*

If s contains a stored object at ℓ with $s(\ell-1) = \langle\text{HEADER } h\ p\ m\rangle$ *for some h, p, and m, then* $\mathcal{S}(\langle\text{PTR } l\rangle, s)$ *extracts the stored object in s at l:*

$$\mathcal{S}(\langle\text{PTR } l\rangle, s) = \langle h\ p\ \langle s(l)\ldots s(l+m-1)\rangle\rangle$$

$\mathcal{H}(\langle\text{PTR } l\rangle, s)$ *gives its header type* $h = (\mathcal{S}(\langle\text{PTR } l\rangle, s))(0)$.

DEFINITION 14 **(Current Instruction, Parameters)**
Let $\Sigma = \langle t, n, v, a, u, k, s, r\rangle$ *and let*

$$\mathcal{S}(t, s) = \langle\text{TEMPLATE FALSE } c{::}v^*\rangle$$
$$\mathcal{S}(c, s) = \langle\text{CODEVECTOR FALSE } b^*\rangle$$

for some sequences v^*, b^*. *Then,*

Table 24. Action Rule for the `call` Instruction.

Rule 0: call m Domain conditions: $current\_inst(n,t,s) = \texttt{call}$ $current\_inst\_param(n,1,t,s) = m$ $\mathcal{S}(v,s) = \langle \text{CLOSURE FALSE } \langle t_1\ u_1\ d_1\rangle\rangle$ Changes: $t' = t_1$ $n' = 0$ $u' = u_1$

$$current\_inst(n,t,s) = b^*(n)$$
$$current\_inst\_param(n,i,t,s) = b^*(n+i)$$

$current\_inst(n,t,s)$ is the current instruction, while $current\_inst\_param(n,i,t,s)$ is the ith parameter to the current instruction.

An SBCM state is initial if it is of the form

$$\langle t, 0, \langle \text{IMM UNSPECIFIED}\rangle, \langle\rangle, \langle \text{IMM EMPTY-ENV}\rangle, \langle \text{IMM HALT}\rangle, s, r\rangle$$

and satisfies the two state invariants in Lemma 19 below. A state $\langle t,n,v,a,u,k,s,r\rangle$ is a halt state if:

- $current\_inst(n,t,s) = \texttt{return}$
- $k = \langle \text{IMM HALT}\rangle$

As before, *acts* is the union of subfunctions called *(action) rules*. Table 24 presents the `call` rule as an example. As with the flattened byte code machine FBCM (Lemma 18), the SBCM is deterministic: for every state of the SBCM, there is at most one rule that can be applied in that state, and there is at most one next state that the rule may produce. Two basic invariants hold for SBCM-accessible states.

LEMMA 19 **(SBCM Invariants)** *If an accessible state Σ with store s contains a term of the form $\langle \text{PTR } \ell\rangle$, then ℓ points to an object in s.*

If $\Sigma = \langle t,n,v,a,u,k,s,r\rangle$ is accessible, then

1. $\mathcal{H}(t) = \text{TEMPLATE}$;
2. $n < \#(\mathcal{S}(c,s)(2))$, *where $c = \mathcal{S}(t,s)(2)(1)$ is the code component of the template;*
3. *either $u = \langle \text{IMM EMPTY-ENV}\rangle$ or $\mathcal{H}(u) = \text{ENVIRONMENT}$; and*
4. *either $k = \langle \text{IMM HALT}\rangle$ or $\mathcal{H}(k) = \text{CONTINUATION}$.*

Table 25. SBCM State Observers for $\Sigma = \langle t, n, v, a, u, k, s, r \rangle$.

Register Observers

`template-ref` Σ	$=$	t
`offset-ref` Σ	$=$	n
`value-ref` Σ	$=$	v
`env-ref` Σ	$=$	u
`cont-ref` Σ	$=$	k
`spare-ref` Σ	$=$	r

Stack Observers

`stack-top` Σ	$=$	$a(0)$ if $\#a > 0$
`stack-empty?` Σ	$=$	$(\#a = 0)$
`stack-length` Σ	$=$	$\#a$

Stored Object Observers

Let $d = \langle \text{PTR } l \rangle$ and $s(l-1) = \langle \text{HEADER } h\ p\ m \rangle$. Then,

`stob-ref` $d\ i\ \Sigma$	$=$	$s(l+i)$
`stob-tag` $d\ \Sigma$	$=$	h
`stob-mutable?` $d\ \Sigma$	$=$	p
`stob-size` $d\ \Sigma$	$=$	m

6.2. The Instantiated SBCM Description

The action rules of the SBCM are instantiated in terms of some primitive operations on states.

We define a set of primitive operations on the state, and we instantiate each action rule of the SBCM in terms of these operations. The state operations are presented in Tables 25 and 26. These operations are classified into two categories.

State Observers These are functions that return an atomic piece of information about the state. They may be composed when the return type of one state observer matches the type of a parameter to another observer; we will call a (well-formed) expression built from variables, constants, and names for state observers an "observer expression."

State Modifiers These are procedures that modify a component of a state. A "state modifier expression" consists of a state modifier name applied to observer expressions.

Each SBCM action rule is instantiated as a program composed from state observer and modifier expressions using the constructs **`while`**, **`if-then-else`**, and sequential composition. Tests are equations between observer expressions or boolean combinations of equations. The atomic statements are the modifier expressions. We will

Table 26. SBCM State Modifiers for $\Sigma = \langle t, n, v, a, u, k, s, r \rangle$.

Register Modifiers			
`template-set` $vd\ \Sigma$	$=$	$\Sigma[t' = vd]$	
`offset-set` $i\ \Sigma$	$=$	$\Sigma[n' = i]$	
`value-set` $vd\ \Sigma$	$=$	$\Sigma[v' = vd]$	
`env-set` $vd\ \Sigma$	$=$	$\Sigma[u' = vd]$	
`cont-set` $vd\ \Sigma$	$=$	$\Sigma[k' = vd]$	
`spare-set` $vd\ \Sigma$	$=$	$\Sigma[r' = vd]$	
Stack Modifiers			
`stack-push` $vd\ \Sigma$	$=$	$\Sigma[a' = vd :: a]$	
`stack-pop` Σ	$=$	$\Sigma[a' = a \dagger 1]$	if $\#a > 0$
`stack-clear` Σ	$=$	$\Sigma[a' = \langle\rangle]$	
Miscellaneous Modifiers			
`assert` $p\ \Sigma$	$=$	if p then Σ else **abort**	
Stored Object Modifiers			
`make-stob` $h\ p\ m\ \Sigma$	$=$		

$$\Sigma[s' = s \frown \langle \text{HEADER } h\ p\ m \rangle \frown v_1 \frown \ldots \frown v_m]$$
$$[r' = \langle \text{PTR } \#s + 1 \rangle]$$
$$\text{where } v_1 = \ldots = v_m = \langle \text{IMM UNDEFINED} \rangle$$

`stob-set` $\langle \text{PTR } l \rangle\ i\ vd\ \Sigma \;=\; \Sigma[s' = s[(l + i) \mapsto vd]]$

```
(assert (closure-stob? (value-ref))
        "op/call: value register does not contain a closure")
(template-set
 (stob-ref (value-ref) 0))     ;; Closure's template
(env-set
 (stob-ref (value-ref) 1))     ;; Closure's env
(offset-set 0)
```

Figure 3. Instantiation of the call Action Rule.

call such a program a *rule program*. We will say that a rule program is *applicable* in a state Σ if the domain conditions of the associated rule are true in Σ.

The instantiations are exceedingly simple programs. In fact, only the rule *make-rest-list*, which makes an argument list—when calling a Scheme procedure with a dotted argument list—requires the `while` construct; the others can be instantiated using only a primitive recursive `for`-loop. The majority of rules require no iteration whatever. Thus, the instantiated programs are easily verified using Hoare logic.

Figure 3 presents the instantiation of the `call` action rule. The proof of its correctness consists of simple Hoare-style reasoning about the effects of this straight-line code.

THEOREM 10 *The instantiation of the* SBCM *action rules is correct with respect to the specification of the action rules.*

The proof is simple, but highly tedious. A detailed examination of the correctness of all the action rules was carried out. This process would have been eased had we had reasonable mechanized proof support, particularly during phases of development when the rule specifications and instantiations changed.

The SBCM is deterministic, so the instantiation is identically the same state machine: it has (extensionally) the same transition relation. Although the state machine remains the same, the instantiation provides a much more informative description of it. The instantiation determines the majority of the code for the VM.

6.3. The Garbage-Collected Stored Byte Code Machine (GSBCM)

In this section we define the Garbage Collected Stored Byte Code Machine (GCSM) and prove that it is a faithful refinement of the SBCM. As a consequence, we justify adding garbage collection to the instantiated form of the GCSM.

The SBCM and GCSM share the same set of states, the same initial states, halt states, and answer function. The only difference between them is that the GCSM includes a new primitive state modifier (called **gc**). It is not fully specified, so that the GCSM is not a deterministic state machine. We will define **gc** in terms of a relation $\cong$ of similarity between GCSM states and SBCM states. We define $\cong$ in turn using a variant of the storage-layout relations approach. The treatment in [19] assumes that terms are tree-structured, and storage layout relations are defined by structural induction over such terms. However, our states can effectively contain cycles, since a Scheme program, during execution, can use operations with side-effects to construct circular data structures. A garbage collector must faithfully relocate these data structures also. Thus the storage layout relations cannot be defined by structural induction over the states regarded as terms.

Instead, we use an existential quantifier. Two states Σ and Σ^A are similar if *there exists* some correlation between locations in their respective stores, such that corresponding values can be found in correlated locations, as well as in registers. Because we formalize the correlation as a binary predicate relating concrete and abstract store locations, this is a *second-order* existential quantifier.

Our experience is that this technique is intuitively understandable and that it leads to straightforward proof obligations. By contrast, although the technique of taking *greatest fixed points* is sometimes suggested for building up a representation relation suited to circular structures, it seems not to be easily applicable to this problem. It is intuitively important that the representation relation between concrete and abstract locations should be one-one on the active parts of the stores, so that an assignment to a concrete location can match an assignment to the corresponding abstract location. There is, however, generally no single greatest relation $\sim$ between concrete and abstract store locations which is one-one on the active locations. For instance, if different locations in the abstract store contain the same values, then there are arbitrary but incompatible choices about which concrete locations should correspond to each.

6.3.1. State Similarity

We formalize locations as natural numbers, but use ℓ-like variables when we are regarding the numbers as store locations. We will typically indicate objects from the more abstract SBCM by variables with a superscript A, leaving variables representing GCSM objects unadorned. Since the SBCM and GCSM agree in their sets of states, however, as well as in their other components apart from *acts*, the objects involved are generally drawn from the same sets. The superscript only connects the object with the machine we regard it as arising in.

DEFINITION 15 **(Store Correspondence)** *Suppose $\sim$ is a binary relation on natural numbers, regarded as representing concrete and abstract store locations. Then $\sim$ is a* store correspondence between *concrete store s* and *abstract store s^A if for all values of the location variables, the following three conditions are met:*

1. *if $\ell_0 \sim \ell^A$ and $\ell_1 \sim \ell^A$, then $\ell_0 = \ell_1$;*
2. *if $\ell \sim \ell_0^A$ and $\ell \sim \ell_1^A$, then $\ell_0^A = \ell_1^A$;*
3. *if $\ell \sim \ell^A$, then ℓ and ℓ^A are in the domain of s and s^A respectively.*

An explicit condition extends a store correspondence to a correspondence between values of all kinds:

DEFINITION 16 **(Term Correspondence)** *Let $\sim$ be a store correspondence between stores s and s^A.*

The term correspondence generated by $\sim$ *is a relation $\simeq$ between cells (i.e., value descriptors or bytes)* cell *and* cell^A, *defined by taking cases on* cell^A. cell $\simeq$ cell^A *holds just in case one of the following holds:*

1. $\text{cell}^A = \langle \text{PTR}\ l^A \rangle$ *and*
   (A) $\langle \text{PTR}\ l \rangle = \text{cell}$;
   (B) $s^A(l^A - 1) = s(l-1) = \langle \text{HEADER}\ h\ p\ m \rangle$, *for some header type h, mutability bit p and stored object length m; and*
   (C) *for all* $0 \leq i < m$, $(l+i) \sim (l^A + i)$.
2. $\text{cell}^A = \langle \text{FIXNUM}\ m \rangle = \text{cell}$, *for some number m.*
3. $\text{cell}^A = imm = \text{cell}$, *for some immediate value imm.*
4. $\text{cell}^A = b = \text{cell}$, *for some byte b.*

If x and x^A are not cells, then for convenience we will say that $x \simeq x^A$ just in case $x = x^A$.

Finally, we define the state correspondence to hold if *there exists* a suitable store correspondence:

DEFINITION 17 **(State Similarity)** *Let $\sim$ be a store correspondence between concrete* GCSM *store s and abstract* SBCM *store s^A, with generated term correspondence $\simeq$.*

Σ and Σ^A, of the forms

$$\langle t, n, v, a, u, k, s, r \rangle \quad and \quad \langle t^A, n^A, v^A, a^A, u^A, k^A, s^A, r^A \rangle,$$

respectively, are similar with respect to $\sim$, *written $\Sigma \approx \Sigma^A$, just in case the invariants on* SBCM *states given in Lemma 19 hold and:*

1. $\#a^A = \#a$ *and* $\forall 0 \leq i < \#a \,.\, a(i) \simeq a^A(i)$;
2. *for all locations l^A and l,* $l \sim l^A \Rightarrow s(l) \simeq s^A(l^A)$;
3. $x \simeq x^A$, *where x and x^A are any of the pairs of state components* $\langle t, t^A \rangle$, $\langle n, n^A \rangle$, $\langle v, v^A \rangle$, $\langle u, u^A \rangle$, $\langle k, k^A \rangle$, *and* $\langle r, r^A \rangle$.

Finally, Σ and Σ^A are similar, *written $\Sigma \cong \Sigma^A$, just in case there exists a store correspondence $\sim$ such that Σ and Σ^A are similar with respect to $\sim$.*

We will slightly abuse notation by sometimes not showing $\sim$ when using $\simeq$ and $\approx$. When both $\simeq$ and $\approx$ are used in the same assertion, then we assume they are generated by the same omitted $\sim$. If Σ and Σ^A are similar with respect to $\sim$, then we will call it a *witness* for $\Sigma \cong \Sigma^A$. By inspecting the structure of states we can verify:

LEMMA 20 **(Properties of $\cong$)**

1. *$\cong$ is an equivalence relation;*

2. *$\Sigma \cong \Sigma^A \Rightarrow ans(\Sigma){=}{=}ans(\Sigma^A)$, where ans is defined as in Section 3.1, and $s{=}{=}t$ means that s and t are equal if either of them is well defined (see Section 4.2); hence,*

3. *$\Sigma \cong \Sigma^A \Rightarrow \Sigma \in halts$ iff $\Sigma^A \in halts$.*

6.3.2. Legitimacy of Garbage Collection

We now define the GCSM to be a state machine having the same states, initial states, halt states, and answer function as SBCM. It differs from the SBCM only in the tuple component *acts*. We regard any transition from Σ to Σ' where $\Sigma \cong \Sigma'$ as a potential garbage collection, and allow garbage collection to occur non-deterministically in the course of executing any rule program immediately before executing the storage-allocating modifier **make-stob**.

To formalize this idea, we add one state modifier to the ones that were used in the SBCM, and we also add one keyword to the programming language for building up rule programs. The modifier is gc. Its specification is non-deterministic: gc Σ returns some state Σ' such that $\Sigma \cong \Sigma'$. The keyword is **maybe**; if e is a modifier expression, then so is **maybe** e. It also introduces non-determinism. If the modifier expression e, executed in state Σ, may return Σ', then so may **maybe** e, and moreover **maybe** e may do nothing and return Σ unchanged.

Because $\cong$ happens to be a reflexive relation, there is in fact no difference between gc and **maybe** gc. Nevertheless, we introduce both because the two kinds of non-determinism get resolved differently. The non-determinism of gc is resolved in Section 6.4, when we select a particular garbage collection algorithm. The non-determinism introduced by the **maybe** is resolved when we pass to a finite machine in Section 6.5. At that point the stores are finite, and garbage collection can occur when they are nearly full.

The transition relation of the GCSM is defined implicitly by means of rule programs. If P is one of the rule programs of the SBCM, then P′ is defined to be the result of replacing every occurence of (**make-stob** $h\ p\ m$) by

(**maybe** (gc))
(**make-stob** $h\ p\ m$)

If P′ derives from a SBCM rule program P in this way, we will say that P′ *corresponds to* P. We define *acts* to be the set of pairs $\langle\Sigma, \Sigma'\rangle$ such that for some SBCM rule program P, P is applicable in Σ, and the corresponding program P$'$, when started in Σ, may terminate in Σ'. Thus, the domain conditions for the SBCM rules are carried over in the GCSM; the changes of state are the same, except that gc is permitted.

We want to establish that $\cong$ is a storage layout relation between SBCM and GCSM. Clause 1 of Lemma 20 implies Clause 1 of Definition 11, while Clause 2 of the lemma is the same as Clause 4 of Definition 11. By Lemma 12 and Theorem 6, to show that GCSM refines SBCM it suffices to show the safety and liveness conditions hold.

The safety condition asserts that for every pair of similar states $\Sigma \cong \Sigma^A$, if Σ can proceed to Σ_1, then either $\Sigma_1 \cong \Sigma^A$ or else Σ^A can proceed to some Σ_1^A such that $\Sigma_1 \cong \Sigma_1^A$. In fact, the latter always holds, so the liveness condition is also satisfied. To prove this, we will show

1. If $\Sigma \cong \Sigma^A$, then the domain conditions for a rule either hold in both states or else fail in both states (Theorem 11); and

2. If $\Sigma_0 \cong \Sigma_0^A$ and P$'$ corresponds to P, then either both programs fail to terminate when started in those states (respectively) or else both programs terminate, and the results satisfy $\cong$ (Theorem 12).

For both these results, the real heart of the matter is that the individual observers and modifiers are invariant under $\cong$. We will separate observers and modifiers in the following two lemmas, each of which is proved [17] by perfectly straightforward (but lengthy) applications of the definitions:

LEMMA 21 **(Observers respect $\simeq$)** *Let $\sim$ be a store correspondence, with generated term correspondence $\simeq$; let e be any of the state observers listed in Table 25, taking state parameter and possibly other parameters. Suppose:*

1. $\Sigma \approx \Sigma^A$; and

2. the respective components of $\vec{x}$ and $\vec{x}^A$ satisfy $\simeq$.

Then $e(\Sigma, \vec{x}) \simeq e(\Sigma^A, \vec{x}^A)$.

LEMMA 22 **(State modifiers preserve $\cong$)** *Let $\sim$ be a store correspondence, with generated term correspondence $\simeq$; let e be any of the state modifiers listed in Table 26, taking state parameter and possibly other parameters. Suppose:*

1. $\Sigma \approx \Sigma^A$; and

2. the respective components of $\vec{x}$ and $\vec{x}^A$ satisfy $\simeq$.

Then $e(\Sigma, \vec{x}) \cong e(\Sigma^A, \vec{x}^A)$.

In the proof of Lemma 22, the underlying store correspondence $\sim$ is used unaltered for every modifier except `make-stob`, and in this case the new correspondence $\sim'$ is the extension of $\sim$ which associates the newly allocated locations.

The following lemma ensures that test expressions in rule programs are invariant with respect to similar states:

LEMMA 23 *Let $\sim$ be a store correspondence, with generated term correspondence $\simeq$. Suppose:*

1. *e and e' are observer expressions;*

2. *$\Sigma \approx \Sigma^A$; and*

3. *the respective components of $\vec{x}$ and $\vec{x}^A$ satisfy $\simeq$;*

4. *the respective components of $\vec{y}$ and $\vec{y}^A$ satisfy $\simeq$;*

Then $e(\Sigma, \vec{x}) = e'(\Sigma, \vec{y})$ iff $e(\Sigma^A, \vec{x}^A) = e'(\Sigma^A, \vec{y}^A)$.

Proof: By structural induction on observer expressions, using Lemma 21 and the definition of $\approx$. ∎

THEOREM 11 *Let $\sim$ be a store correspondence. Suppose:*

1. *R is any* SBCM *rule (with auxiliary variables);*

2. *The domain condition for R is satisfied in Σ using the witnessing values $\vec{x}$ for the auxiliary variables;*

3. *$\Sigma \approx \Sigma^A$;*

4. *Σ consists of stored objects.*

Then there is an $\vec{x}^A$ such that:

1. *$\#\vec{x} = \#\vec{x}^A$;*

2. *$\vec{x}(i) \simeq \vec{x}^A(i)$, for each i where $0 \leq i < \#\vec{x}$;*

3. *The domain condition for R is satisfied in Σ^A using the witnessing values $\vec{x}^A$.*

Proof: Let $\vec{x}^A(i)$ be $\vec{x}(i)$ if the latter is not of the form $\langle \text{PTR } \ell \rangle$. Otherwise, let $\vec{x}^A(i)$ be $\langle \text{PTR } \ell^A \rangle$ where ℓ^A is some ℓ' such that $\ell \sim \ell'$.

On the assumption there is such an ℓ', then it follows that conditions 1 and 2 are satisfied. Condition 3 follows from Lemma 23, because the domain conditions are always equations between observer expressions.

Thus, it suffices to show that there is an ℓ' such that $\ell \sim \ell'$, whenever $\langle \text{PTR } \ell \rangle$ is a witnessing value for a domain condition auxiliary variable. By Definition 15 clause 1, there is at most one such ℓ', so $\vec{x}^A$ is actually unique.

Inspecting the domain conditions of the rules, we find three cases:

1. The value of some state register r_0 is $\langle \text{PTR } \ell \rangle$;

2. The value of some state register r_0 is $\langle \text{PTR } \ell_0 \rangle$, and $\langle \text{PTR } \ell \rangle$ is a component of the object stored at ℓ_0;

3. The value of some state register r_0 is $\langle \text{PTR } \ell_0 \rangle$; $\langle \text{PTR } \ell_1 \rangle$ is a component of the object stored at ℓ_0; and $\langle \text{PTR } \ell \rangle$ is a component of the object stored at ℓ_1.

The third case occurs in the rules to reference or set the value of a global variable, as the store location for the variable is determined from the current template table.

In the first case, we use Definition 17 clause 3 to infer that, if v is the value of r_0 in Σ^A, then $\langle \text{PTR } \ell \rangle \simeq v$. By Definition 16, v is of the form $\langle \text{PTR } \ell^A \rangle$, and by clause 1c, $\ell \sim \ell^A$. The remaining cases are similar, except that Definitions 17 and 16 must be used repeatedly. ■

THEOREM 12 **(Corresponding programs produce corresponding results)** *Suppose that $\Sigma_0 \cong \Sigma_0^A$, and that* P′ *and* P *are corresponding rule programs. Then, when* P′ *and* P *are started in states Σ_0 and Σ_0^A respectively, then either*

1. *both fail to terminate; or else*

2. *both terminate, and in states Σ_1 and Σ_1^A, respectively, such that $\Sigma_1 \cong \Sigma_1^A$.*

Proof: By induction on the sequence of states traversed as P′ and P compute, using Lemmas 22 and 23. ■

From Lemma 20 and Theorems 11 and 12, we may conclude:

THEOREM 13 *The* GCSM *refines the* SBCM.

6.4. The Instantiated GSBCM Description

We instantiate the gc primitive by a specific garbage collection algorithm *gc* and we prove that it satisfies the property that $\text{gc}(\Sigma) \cong \Sigma$. The algorithm uses a simple semi-space garbage collection technique where two stores are maintained, one active and one inactive. During garbage collection, "live" data from the active store is copied to the inactive store and then the roles of the two stores are swapped. Live data refers to data that can be accessed either directly or indirectly (via pointers) from the registers (or stack) of the state. The garbage collection algorithm is presented in Table 4. In this presentation, the new (not-yet-active) store is regarded as the set of locations beyond the end of the old (previously active) store. Thus, if s is the old store, and $\#s \leq \ell$, then $\langle \text{PTR } \ell \rangle$ points at the location $\ell - \#s$ words beyond the beginning of new space. To model the change of active store, we use the auxiliary function *shift*, a partial function from states and integers to states. It in effect translates the store to the left, adjusting all of the pointers to match.

DEFINITION 18 **(Shift_store, Shift)** *If s is a store, then*

$$\text{shift\_store}(s, j) = \lambda i. \begin{cases} \langle \text{PTR } \ell - j \rangle & \textit{if } s(j+i) = \langle \text{PTR } \ell \rangle \\ s(j+i) & \textit{otherwise} \end{cases}$$

If Σ is a state, then shift(Σ, j) *is the result of replacing the store s of Σ by* shift_store(s, j)*, and replacing every component* $\langle$PTR $\ell\rangle$ *of* Σ *with* $\langle$PTR $\ell - j\rangle$.

The result of *shift*(Σ, j) is a well-formed state if $j \leq \ell$ whenever $\langle$PTR $\ell\rangle$ is a component of Σ, and $j \leq \ell$ whenever $\langle$PTR $\ell\rangle$ occurs at a location ℓ_0 in its store such that $j \leq \ell_0$. This condition ensures that a pointer always has a nonnegative value after the translation.

The garbage collector, which implements the algorithm given in Figure 4, uses several auxiliary functions. The function *gc-convert* takes a pointer to a stored object in the active store as argument. If the object has not yet been copied from the old store to the new store, it copies the stored object and returns a pointer to the newly allocated stored object. It also replaces the header of the old stored object with a pointer to the new object, called a ***broken heart***; all other pointers to the old stored object will eventually be modified to point to the new object. If the object has already been copied to the new store, *gc-convert* returns the broken heart. The result of this function is always a pointer to an object in the new store.

The function *gc-trace* takes an arbitrary value d as argument. If the value d is not a pointer, it returns the argument value d. Otherwise it invokes *gc-convert* on the pointer d and returns the result.

The function *gc-trace-stack* successively calls *gc-trace* on each element of the argument stack a. It accumulates the result values into a new argument stack a'.

The function *gc-scan-heap* successively calls *gc-trace* on each value in the new store. Each call to *gc-trace* may potentially extend the new store by copying a stored object to it.

Finally, the function *gc* invokes *gc-trace* on all registers, on all components of the stack and on the store. All resulting pointers reference the new store, so we may apply *shift* to discard the old store.

We regard the garbage collector as an algorithm rather than simply a function. In the course of executing, the garbage collector modifies the store component of the state repeatedly. We say somewhat informally—for instance, in Lemma 25—that a store s *occurs* in a run of the garbage collection algorithm. By this we mean that *gc-trace* returns a pair $\langle d\ s\rangle$ on some "call" from gc_0, *gc-trace-stack*, or *gc-scan-heap*.

Garbage collection is indeed a non-trivial algorithm and it transforms the store through a succession of intermediate values. Therefore, the proof requires the use of a relation similar to $\cong$ to express an invariant maintained by the algorithm. This technique is used to prove that each intermediate GCSM state encountered during garbage collection is similar (by a state correspondence relation $\cong^{gc}$ still to be specified) to the GCSM state prior to garbage collection. Since $\cong^{gc}$ will be defined to coincide with $\cong$ when a store contains no broken hearts, it will follow that garbage collection preserves $\cong$.

DEFINITION 19 **(GC Term Correspondence, GC State Similarity)**
Let $\sim$ be a store correspondence between GCSM *stores s and s'.*

Let $\Sigma = \langle t, n, v, a, u, k, s, r \rangle$ be a GCSM state. Then,

$$
\begin{array}{l}
\mathit{gc\text{-}convert}(\langle \text{PTR } l \rangle, s) = \\
\quad \langle \langle \text{PTR } l' \rangle\ s \rangle \quad \text{if } s(l-1) = \langle \text{PTR } l' \rangle \quad \text{(Object already relocated)} \\
\quad \langle \langle \text{PTR } l' \rangle\ s'' \rangle \\
\qquad \text{if } s(l-1) = \langle \text{HEADER } h\ p\ m \rangle \\
\qquad \text{and } l' = \#s + 1 \\
\qquad \text{and } s' = s \frown s(l-1) \frown s(l) \frown \ldots \frown s(l+m-1) \\
\qquad \text{and } s'' = s'[l-1 \mapsto \langle \text{PTR } l' \rangle]
\end{array}
$$

$$
\mathit{gc\text{-}trace}(d, s) = \begin{cases} \mathit{gc\text{-}convert}(d, s) & \text{if } d \text{ is a pointer} \\ \langle d\ s \rangle & \text{otherwise} \end{cases}
$$

$$
\begin{array}{l}
\mathit{gc\text{-}trace\text{-}stack}(a, s) = \langle a'\ s_{\#a} \rangle \\
\quad \text{where } s_0 = s \text{ and } \mathit{gc\text{-}trace}(a(i), s_i) = \langle a'_i\ s_{i+1} \rangle \\
\qquad \text{for } 0 \leq i < \#a \\
\quad \text{and } a' = \langle a'_0\ a'_1\ \ldots a'_{\#a-1} \rangle
\end{array}
$$

$$
\begin{array}{ll}
\mathit{gc\text{-}scan\text{-}heap}(s, m) = & \\
\quad s & \text{if } m = \#s \\
\quad \mathit{gc\text{-}scan\text{-}heap}(s'[m \mapsto d], m+1), & \\
\qquad \text{where } \langle d, s' \rangle = \mathit{gc\text{-}trace}(s(m), s) & \text{otherwise}
\end{array}
$$

$$
\begin{array}{l}
\mathit{gc}_0(\Sigma, n_0) = \langle t', n, v', a', u', k', s_7, r' \rangle \\
\quad \text{where } \mathit{gc\text{-}trace}(t, s) = \langle t'\ s_1 \rangle \\
\quad \text{and } \mathit{gc\text{-}trace}(v, s_1) = \langle v'\ s_2 \rangle \\
\quad \text{and } \mathit{gc\text{-}trace}(u, s_2) = \langle u'\ s_3 \rangle \\
\quad \text{and } \mathit{gc\text{-}trace}(k, s_3) = \langle k'\ s_4 \rangle \\
\quad \text{and } \mathit{gc\text{-}trace\text{-}stack}(a, s_4) = \langle a'\ s_5 \rangle \\
\quad \text{and } \mathit{gc\text{-}trace}(r, s_5) = \langle r'\ s_6 \rangle \\
\quad \text{and } \mathit{gc\text{-}scan\text{-}heap}(s_6, n_0) = s_7
\end{array}
$$

$$
\mathit{gc}(\Sigma) = \mathit{shift}(\mathit{gc}_0(\Sigma, \#s), \#s)
$$

Figure 4. Garbage Collection Algorithm

The GC term correspondence generated by $\sim$ *is a relation* $\simeq^{gc}$ *between cells (i.e., value descriptors or bytes)* cell *and* cell$'$, *defined by taking cases on* cell$'$. cell $\simeq^{gc}$ cell$'$ *holds just in case one of the following holds:*

1. cell$' = \langle \text{PTR } l' \rangle$ *and* cell $= \langle \text{PTR } l \rangle$. *Let* l_1 *be* l *unless* $s(l-1)$ *is a broken heart* $\langle \text{PTR } l_0 \rangle$, *in which case let* l_1 *be* l_0. *Let* l_1' *be* l' *unless* $s'(l'-1)$ *is a broken heart* $\langle \text{PTR } l_0' \rangle$, *in which case let* l_1' *be* l_0'. *We require further:*
   - *(A)* $s'(l_1'-1) = s(l_1-1) = \langle \text{HEADER } h\ p\ m \rangle$, *for some header type* h, *mutability bit* p *and stored object length* m; *and*
   - *(B) for all* $0 \leq i < m$, $(l_1+i) \sim (l_1'+i)$.
2. cell$' = \langle \text{FIXNUM } m \rangle =$ cell, *for some number* m.
3. cell$' = imm =$ cell, *for some immediate value* imm.
4. cell$' = b =$ cell, *for some byte* b.

Σ *and* Σ', *of the forms* $\langle t, n, v, a, u, k, s, r \rangle$ *and* $\langle t', n', v', a', u', k', s', r' \rangle$, *respectively, are* GC-similar with respect to $\sim$, *written* $\Sigma \approx^{gc} \Sigma'$, *just in case:*

1. $\#a' = \#a$ *and* $\forall 0 \leq i < \#a \,.\, a(i) \simeq^{gc} a'(i)$;
2. *for all locations* l' *and* l, $\quad l \sim l' \Rightarrow s(l) \simeq^{gc} s'(l')$;
3. $x \simeq^{gc} x'$, *where* x *and* x' *are any of the pairs of state components* $\langle t, t' \rangle$, $\langle n, n' \rangle$, $\langle v, v' \rangle$, $\langle u, u' \rangle$, $\langle k, k' \rangle$, *and* $\langle r, r' \rangle$.

Σ *and* Σ' *are* GC-similar, *written* $\Sigma \cong^{gc} \Sigma'$, *just in case there exists a store correspondence* $\sim$ *such that* Σ *and* Σ' *are GC-similar with respect to* $\sim$.

LEMMA 24 $\cong^{gc}$ *is a transitive relation. That is,*

$$\Sigma_2 \cong^{gc} \Sigma_1 \text{ and } \Sigma_3 \cong^{gc} \Sigma_2 \Rightarrow \Sigma_3 \cong^{gc} \Sigma_1$$

Proof: Compose the witness store correspondences. ■

GC stored objects are like stored objects, except that we may dereference a broken heart for free:

DEFINITION 20 **(GC Stored Objects)** *If* $s(l-1)$ *is a broken heart* $\langle \text{PTR } l_0 \rangle$, *let* $l_1 = l_0$; *let* $l_1 = l$ *otherwise. Then* s *contains a* GC stored object *at* l *if:*

1. $s(l_1 - 1) = \langle \text{HEADER } h\ p\ m \rangle$, *for some* h, p, *and* m;
2. $s(j)$ *is a well-defined non-header value for each* j *for* $l_1 \leq j < l_1 + m$.

A state Σ consists of GC stored objects *if, whenever* $\langle \text{PTR } l \rangle$ *occurs in any (transitive) component of* Σ, *then the store of* Σ *contains a GC stored object at location* l. *Similarly, a store* s consists of GC stored objects *if, whenever* $\langle \text{PTR } l \rangle$ *occurs in a cell of* s, *then* s *contains a GC stored object at location* l.

LEMMA 25 *1. Suppose that s is a store encountered (i.e., returned by* gc-trace*) during garbage collection of a* GCSM *accessible state; then s consists of GC stored objects.*

2. If Σ consists of stored objects and $\Sigma' = \mathrm{gc}(\Sigma)$, then Σ' consists of stored objects.

Proof: 1. This holds of every accessible GCSM store prior to garbage collection. During garbage collection, all mutations of the store are made via the function *gc-trace* which preserves this property.

2. Since Σ consists of stored objects, it consists (*a fortiori*) of GC stored objects. Using part 1 inductively, the same is true of $\mathrm{gc}_0(\Sigma)$. The property of consisting of GC stored objects is preserved by *shift*, so $\Sigma' = \mathit{shift}(\mathrm{gc}_0(\Sigma), \#s)$ consists of GC stored objects. Finally, Σ' contains no broken hearts, so it also consists of stored objects. ■

This establishes that *gc* preserves the first invariant of Lemma 19; the properties given in its second clause are straightforward consequences of the algorithm.

The following key lemma asserts that the function *gc-trace* respects similarity, i.e., it maps values and states to similar values and states.

LEMMA 26 *Let s be a store encountered (i.e., returned by* gc-trace*) during garbage collection of a* GCSM *accessible state Σ, and let d be a component of Σ. Let*

$$\text{gc-trace}(d, s) = \langle d' \; s' \rangle$$

for some d', s'. Suppose d is not a pointer, or that $d = \langle \text{PTR } l \rangle$ and s contains a GC stored object at l.

Then there exists a store correspondence $\sim$ between s and s' with generated GC term correspondence $\simeq^{gc}$ such that

1. $d' \simeq^{gc} d$

2. $\langle t, n, v, a, u, k, s', r \rangle \cong^{gc} \Sigma$ with $\sim$ as the witness store correspondence.

Proof: The proof is by cases. We show the crucial case in which d is a pointer $\langle \text{PTR } l \rangle$ and $s(l-1)$ is a header, rather than a broken heart, so that the object must be copied.

Case: $d = \langle \text{PTR } l \rangle$ and $s(l-1) = \langle \text{HEADER } h \; p \; m \rangle$, so, by definition of *gc-trace*, $d' = \langle \text{PTR } l_0 \rangle$, $l_0 = \#s + 1$, and

$$\begin{aligned} s' = s&[l_0 - 1 \mapsto s(l-1)][l_0 \mapsto s(l)] \ldots [l_0 + m - 1 \mapsto s(l + m - 1)] \\ &[l - 1 \mapsto \langle \text{PTR } l_0 \rangle] \end{aligned}$$

Define $\sim$ as follows:

$$\begin{array}{rl} l_0 + i \sim l + i & \text{for } 0 \le i < m \\ x \sim x & \text{for all } x \in \mathit{dom}(s) \text{ such that } s(x) \text{ is not a header} \\ & \text{and } x \ne l + i \text{ for } 0 \le i < m. \end{array}$$

1. $s(l-1) = \langle\text{HEADER } h\ p\ m\rangle$ by case condition. $s'(l_0-1) = s(l-1) = \langle\text{HEADER } h\ p\ m\rangle$ by definition of s'. For all $0 \le i < m$, $l_0 + i \sim l + i$ holds by definition of $\sim$. Thus, by definition of $\simeq^{gc}$,

$$\langle\text{PTR } l_0\rangle \simeq^{gc} \langle\text{PTR } l\rangle.$$

2. We first show that if vd is a value in one of the registers, or a component of the stack, then $vd \simeq^{gc} vd$. First, if vd is not a pointer, $vd \simeq^{gc} vd$ holds by definition of $\simeq^{gc}$.

   Second, suppose $vd = \langle\text{PTR } y\rangle$ where $y \neq l$. Let $x = l'$ if $s(y-1)$ is a broken heart $\langle\text{PTR } l'\rangle$ and let $x = y$ otherwise. Then $s(x-1) = s'(x-1) = \langle\text{HEADER } h'\ p'\ m'\rangle$ for some h', p', m', and $x+i \sim x+i$ for all $0 \le i < m'$. Thus $\langle\text{PTR } y\rangle \simeq^{gc} \langle\text{PTR } y\rangle$ holds by definition of $\simeq^{gc}$.

   Finally, if $vd = \langle\text{PTR } l\rangle$, then we know that $s(l-1) = \langle\text{HEADER } h\ p\ m\rangle$ by the case condition. Further, $s'(l-1) = \langle\text{PTR } l_0\rangle$ and $s'(l_0-1) = \langle\text{HEADER } h\ p\ m\rangle$ by definition of s'. Finally, for all $0 \le i < m$, $l_0 + i \sim l + i$ holds by definition of $\sim$. Thus, $\langle\text{PTR } l\rangle \simeq^{gc} \langle\text{PTR } l\rangle$ holds by definition of $\simeq^{gc}$.

   To complete the proof that $\langle t, n, v, a, u, k, s', r\rangle \cong^{gc} \Sigma$, we need to show that:

$$\text{for all } x, x',\ x' \sim x \Rightarrow s'(x') \simeq^{gc} s(x)$$

   So assume $x' \sim x$.

   If $x \neq l + i$ for $0 \le i < m$, then $x = x'$ by definition of $\sim$. Since x is in the domain of $\sim$, $s(x)$ is not a header (by definition of $\sim$). Thus $x \neq l - 1$, and so $s'(x') = s'(x) = s(x)$. The result then follows since $vd \simeq^{gc} vd$ was shown above for any component of the state.

   Otherwise, $x = l + i$ for some $0 \le i < m$. Then, $x' = l_0 + i$ by definition of $\sim$. Now $s'(x') = s'(l_0 + i) = s(l + i) = s(x)$ by definition of s'. The result then follows since $vd \simeq^{gc} vd$ was shown above for any component of the state.

■

LEMMA 27 *Let s_0 and s consist of stored objects, where s_0 is a prefix of s and $\#s_0 \le l$. Let $\Sigma = \langle t, n, v, a, u, k, s, r\rangle$, and let* gc-trace$(s(l), s) = \langle d'\ s'\rangle$. *Then $\langle t, n, v, a, u, k, s'[l \mapsto d'], r\rangle \cong^{gc} \Sigma$.*

Hence, inductively, $\langle t, n, v, a, u, k,$ gc-scan-heap$(s, \#s_0), r\rangle \cong^{gc} \Sigma$.

Proof: By Lemma 26, $\langle t, n, v, a, u, k, s', r\rangle \cong^{gc} \Sigma$ with $\sim$ as the witness store correspondence. Let $\sim$ extend to the term correspondence $\simeq^{gc}$. Then, by the same lemma, $d' \simeq^{gc} s(l)$.

If $s(l)$ is not a pointer, then by definition of *gc-trace*, $s(l) = s'(l) = d'$. Thus, $s'[l \mapsto d'] = s'$ and so $\langle t, n, v, a, u, k, s'[l \mapsto d'], r\rangle \cong^{gc} \Sigma$.

If $s(l) = \langle \text{PTR } l_0 \rangle$ for some l_0, then by definition of *gc-trace*, $s(l) = s'(l) = \langle \text{PTR } l_0 \rangle$ since *gc-trace* only modifies $s(l_0 - 1)$ if it is a header and hence $l_0 - 1 \neq l$. Thus, we have that $d' \simeq^{gc} s'(l) = \langle \text{PTR } l_0 \rangle$. We show that

$$\langle t, n, v, a, u, k, s'[l \mapsto d'], r \rangle \cong^{gc} \langle t, n, v, a, u, k, s', r \rangle$$

since the result will then follow by transitivity of $\cong^{gc}$ (lemma 24).

Let $\sim$ be the identity function on all defined locations of s' that are not headers of stored objects, and generate the term correspondence $\simeq^{gc}$. We prove that $\sim$ is the witness store correspondence to the above state correspondence.

For all terms vd that are components of the state, $vd \simeq^{gc} vd$ holds. This is immediate for non-pointer values, while for pointer values $\langle \text{PTR } l_0 \rangle$ it depends on $s'(l_0 - 1)$ and $s'[l \mapsto d'](l_0 - 1)$ being the same header value. This holds since we know that $s'(l)$ is not a header and hence $l \neq l_0 - 1$.

Moreover, $s'[l \mapsto d'](l) \simeq^{gc} s'(l)$, because, as we showed above, $d' \simeq^{gc} s'(l) = \langle \text{PTR } l_0 \rangle$.

Finally, we must show that *gc-scan-heap* terminates. We assume that the original store s_0 consists of stored objects, and that s has the property that if $i < \#s_0$ and $s_0(i)$ is not a header, then $s(i) = s_0(i)$. Let $\langle d, s' \rangle = \textit{gc-trace}(s(m), s)$, let $s'' = s'[m \mapsto d]$, and let $\#s_0 \leq m$. We have:

1. s, s', and s'' all contain the same total number of headers;

2. Assuming

   $$\forall n \geq m, \forall l' \,.\, s(n) = \langle \text{PTR } l' \rangle \Rightarrow l' < \#s_0,$$

   then we may infer

   $$\forall n \geq m + 1, \forall l' \,.\, s''(n) = \langle \text{PTR } l' \rangle \Rightarrow l' < \#s_0,$$

   using the assumptions that s_0 consists of stored objects and agrees with s on non-headers.

3. If $\#s < \#s''$, then s'' has one fewer header below $\#s_0$ than did s.

■

The correctness of gc_0 now follows from Lemmas 24, 26, and 27.

LEMMA 28 *Let* $\Sigma = \langle t, n, v, a, u, k, s, r \rangle$ *and* $\Sigma' = \text{gc}_0(\Sigma, \#s)$. *Then* $\Sigma' \cong^{gc} \Sigma$.

We now justify the application of *shift*:

LEMMA 29 *Let* $\Sigma = \langle t, n, v, a, u, k, s, r \rangle$ *be a* GCSM *state and let*

$$\text{gc}_0(\Sigma) = \langle t_1, n_1, v_1, a_1, u_1, k_1, s_1, r_1 \rangle.$$

If, for some l_0, *one of* t_1, v_1, u_1, k_1, r_1, $a_1(i)$ *for* $0 \leq i < \#a$, *or* $s_1(i)$ *for* $\#s \leq i$ *is the value* $\langle \text{PTR } l_0 \rangle$, *then*

1. $l_0 \geq \#s$;

2. $s_1(l_0 - 1) = \langle\text{HEADER } h\ p\ m\rangle$ *for some* h, p, m.

Proof: By definition of *gc*, the state components t, v, u, k, r, $a(i)$, and $s(i)$ are replaced by the values of *gc-trace* applied to the components.

Let s' be a store encountered during garbage collection of Σ such that if s' contains a header of the form $\langle\text{PTR } l_0\rangle$, then $l_0 > \#s$ and $s'(l_0 - 1) = \langle\text{HEADER } h\ p\ m\rangle$ for some h, p, m. If d' is the value of a state component of Σ, and $gc\text{-}trace(d', s') = (d'', s'')$, then we prove that s'' also satisfies the above property. That is, we prove that if s'' contains a header of the form $\langle\text{PTR } l_0\rangle$, then $l_0 > \#s$ and $s'(l_0 - 1) = \langle\text{HEADER } h\ p\ m\rangle$ for some h, p, m. If s' also contains the same header $\langle\text{PTR } l_0\rangle$, this follows by induction hypothesis. Otherwise, by definition of *gc-trace*,

$$s'' = (s' \frown s'(l-1) \frown s'(l) \frown \ldots \frown s'(l+m-1))[l-1 \mapsto \langle\text{PTR } \#s' + 1\rangle]$$

where $s''(l-1) = \langle\text{PTR } \#s' + 1\rangle$ is the above mentioned header. The result follows since $\#s' + 1 > \#s$ and $s''(\#s') = s'(l-1) = \langle\text{HEADER } h\ p\ m\rangle$ for some h, p, m (by definition of *gc-trace*).

By induction, we have that all intermediate stores during garbage collection satisfy the property. But it follows from the definition of *gc-trace* that given such stores, if *gc-trace* returns a pointer $\langle\text{PTR } l_0\rangle$, then $l_0 \geq \#s$ and $s_1(l_0-1) = \langle\text{HEADER } h\ p\ m\rangle$ for some h, p, m. ■

Finally, combining Lemmas 25, 28 and 29, we have:

THEOREM 14 **(Garbage Collection preserves $\cong^{gc}$, $\cong$)** *If Σ consists of stored objects, then*

$$\text{gc}(\Sigma) \cong^{gc} \Sigma$$

and

$$\text{gc}(\Sigma) \cong \Sigma.$$

Implementation Note. Our proofs are proofs about algorithms, while of course our implementation consists of code. Thus, we have taken care to ensure that our code reflects the algorithms it implements in as lucid a way as possible. There is, however, one complication in matching the VM program to its specification. It is due to the fact that VLISP PreScheme, in the version used in this work, compiles to a language in which all procedure calls are in tail recursive position. Thus, where a procedure call is not in tail recursive position, the Front End must substitute the code for the called procedure in line. There are several instructions in the SBCM that cause memory to be allocated, and each of them, when coded in the obvious way, contains a non-tail-recursive call to an allocation routine, which in turn calls the garbage collector if the allocation would exceed a bound. These calls are not tail recursive, because the original procedure must do some initializations within the new memory object after it has been allocated. Rather than have the code for the garbage collector duplicated in line at each of the original call sites, we have programmed the calls to the allocation procedure and garbage collector in a partial continuation passing style. Because this programming decision affects only a small number of call sites, and only one subroutine, the implementation has lost only a little lucidity as a consequence of this programming approach. Our PreScheme implementation has since been improved; procedure calls in non-tail-recursive position need no longer be expanded in line [14].

6.5. The Finite Stored Byte Code Machine (FSBCM)

A finite state machine (with any fixed word size, bounded store size, and bounded stack size) cannot simulate all the computation histories of the GCSM, because there will always be computations that require more pointers than can be stored in words, stores, or stacks of the given size. We define a Finite Stored Byte Code Machine (FGCSM) and prove that it is a *weak* refinement (see Section 4) of the GCSM.

Table 27 contains the abstract syntax for the states of the FGCSM. The definition ensures that they form a proper subset of the states of SBC. The initial (halt) FGCSM states are the FGCSM states that are GCSM initial (halt) states. The FGCSM action rules are the GCSM action rules with domain and range restricted to FGCSM states. Thus, if an FGCSM action rule is defined on an FGCSM state, then its value at that state is the same as that of the corresponding GCSM action rule. The implemented values of **max-store-size** and of the upper and lower bounds for fixed point numbers reflect a 32-bit word size in which two bits are reserved for tags.

The finite machine is only partially correct. That is, any computation trace of the finite machine simulates a computation trace of the garbage collected machine. Thus, if the finite machine computes an answer, then the garbage collected machine computes the same answer. The finite machine is easily shown to be correct in this weaker sense.

THEOREM 15 *Let $\sim$ be the identity relation on* FGCSM *states. Then $\sim$ is a weak storage layout relation between* FGCSM *and* GCSM, *and* FGCSM *weakly refines* GCSM.

6.6. Concrete Virtual Machine

A concrete implementation of the Virtual Machine is obtained by directly encoding the FGCSM as a PreScheme program. The actual VLISP Virtual Machine implementation differs from the implementation described here in several ways:

1. The actual implementation is designed to run on machines with 32-bit physical memory words. Since there are fewer than 256 distinct FSBC bytes, the implementation optimizes the representations of "string" and "codevector" stored

Table 27. Abstract Syntax of Finite Stored Byte Code (FSBC).

program	::=	*term*
term	::=	⟨*store vdesc*⟩
store	::=	*cell** *with* #*cell** < `max-store-size`
stack	::=	*vdesc** *with* #*vdesc** < `max-stack-size`
cell	::=	*desc* | *byte*
desc	::=	⟨HEADER *htag bool* nat_1⟩ | *vdesc*
vdesc	::=	⟨PTR nat_2⟩ | ⟨FIXNUM *int*⟩ | ⟨IMM *imm*⟩
imm	::=	FALSE | TRUE | ⟨CHAR nat_3⟩ | NULL | UNDEFINED
		UNSPECIFIED | EMPTY-ENV | HALT | EOF
htag	::=	*bhtag* | *dhtag*
bhtag	::=	STRING | CODEVECTOR
dhtag	::=	PAIR | SYMBOL | VECTOR | LOCATION | TEMPLATE |
		CLOSURE | PORT | CONTINUATION | ENVIRONMENT
byte	::=	nat_4
nat_1	::=	0..`max-object-size`
nat_2	::=	0..`max-pointer-size`
nat_3	::=	0..127
nat_4	::=	0..255
int	::=	`min-fixnum-size`..`max-fixnum-size`

objects by packing the bytes within them; specifically, four bytes are packed into a single store cell.

2. The actual implementation represents both the argument stack and the store within a single vector (called the *heap*). The representation is non-trivial and is designed to optimize certain expensive action rules. Specifically, this optimization permits the action rules `make-env` and `make-cont` to create environment and continuation stored objects respectively, without copying the contents of the argument stack to the store. This results in a much faster interpreter.

3. The actual implementation contains two heaps, only one of which is in active use. During garbage collection, it copies the reachable contents of the active heap to the inactive heap and switches the roles of the heaps. In this paper, the state machines have a single store, and the garbage collector copies reachable objects to the end of the current store.

4. The correctness proof of the garbage collector requires that all stored objects in the store have active value fields. To meet this condition, the state operation `make-stob` is specified (see Table 26) to create a new stored object and to initialize the value fields of this object to a distinctive value (⟨IMM UNDEFINED⟩). Since this is time-consuming, the actual implementation does not initialize objects during allocation, but explicitly writes active values into new objects immediately after allocation. The garbage collector is not invoked until these writes have been performed.

5. The actual implementation represents FSBC *cells* as 32-bit binary numerals.

The proofs presented here have been extended to accommodate these optimizations.

7. Conclusion

Although the VLISP verification is quite comprehensive, and covers the great majority of the detailed implementation, there are a number of unverified aspects:

- The verification covers algorithms and data structures used, rather than the concrete code. In most cases the relationship is straightforward, and indeed particular coding approaches were often adopted so that the relationship would be transparent. However, sometimes there is an "interesting" gap between the form of the specification and that of the code.

- The VLISP implementation provides all the standard procedures stipulated in the Scheme language definition. However, because no formal specification has been provided for these user-level procedures, we have not had anything to verify these procedures against.

  To mitigate this objection, we provide all source code to the user. The majority of the standard procedures are coded in Scheme itself, and can be replaced with any variants the user considers more trustworthy.

- The Scheme language stipulates that some derived syntactic forms should be provided. However, there is no formal account of the expansion process.

  A user suspicious of these expansions can write programs directly in the primitive Scheme syntax. This is still a high level programming language by any standard.

- In some cases, such as the VLISP PreScheme Front End [13, Section 3], and the compiler proof (Section 2.5), only cases that appeared to us to be "representative" or "interesting" were selected for detailed proof.

- Proofs have not been checked using a mechanical theorem prover.

To have fully verified these aspects would have greatly increased the scale of the work.

We believe that the VLISP effort has shown that the rigorous algorithmic verification of substantial programs such as a language implementation is feasible. We have used a relatively small number of techniques which we consider now to be well-defined and broadly reusable.

We consider our decision to carry out the verification at the algorithmic level to have been one key to our success. We also consider the compact and tractable official Scheme semantics to have been another precondition. The third crucial ingredient was using an operational semantics and a state machine refinement approach to the lower levels of the verification. This enabled us to subdivide the complexities of the proof into a succession of intuitively understandable assertions. These points are developed in more detail in the companion article [7].

List of Tables

List of Figures

References

1. William Clinger. The Scheme 311 compiler: An exercise in denotational semantics. In *1984 ACM Symposium on Lisp and Functional Programming*, pages 356–364, New York, August 1984. The Association for Computing Machinery, Inc.
2. William M. Farmer. A partial functions version of Church's simple theory of types. *Journal of Symbolic Logic*, 55(3):1269–91, 1990. Also MITRE Corporation technical report M88-52, 1988; revised 1990.
3. William M. Farmer, Joshua D. Guttman, Leonard G. Monk, John D. Ramsdell, and Vipin Swarup. The faithfulness of the VLISP operational semantics. M 92B093, The MITRE Corporation, September 1992.
4. William M. Farmer, Joshua D. Guttman, and F. Javier Thayer. IMPS: an Interactive Mathematical Proof System. *Journal of Automated Reasoning*, 11(2):213–248, October 1993.
5. Joshua D. Guttman, Leonard G. Monk, William M. Farmer, John D. Ramsdell, and Vipin Swarup. The VLISP byte-code compiler. M 92B092, The MITRE Corporation, September 1992.
6. Joshua D. Guttman, Leonard G. Monk, William M. Farmer, John D. Ramsdell, and Vipin Swarup. The VLISP flattener. M 92B094, The MITRE Corporation, 1992.
7. Joshua D. Guttman, John D. Ramsdell, and Mitchell Wand. VLISP: A verified implementation of Scheme. *Lisp and Symbolic Computation*, 8(1/2):5–32, 1995.
8. C. A. R. Hoare. Notes on data structuring. In O.-J. Dahl, editor, *Structured Programming*. Academic Press, 1972.
9. IEEE Std 1178-1990. *IEEE Standard for the Scheme Programming Language*. Institute of Electrical and Electronic Engineers, Inc., New York, NY, 1991.
10. Richard A. Kelsey and Jonathan A. Rees. Scheme48 progress report. Manuscript in preparation, 1992.
11. Richard A. Kelsey and Jonathan A. Rees. A tractable Scheme implementation. *Lisp and Symbolic Computation*, 7(4):315–335, 1994.
12. Robin Milner. *Communication and Concurrency*. Prentice-Hall International, Englewood Cliffs, 1989.
13. Dino P. Oliva, John D. Ramsdell, and Mitchell Wand. The VLISP verified PreScheme compiler. *Lisp and Symbolic Computation*, 8(1/2):111–182, 1995.
14. John D. Ramsdell. The revised VLISP PreScheme front end. M 93B095, The MITRE Corporation, August 1993.
15. Jonathan A. Rees, Norman I. Adams, and James R. Meehan. *The T Manual*. Computer Science Department, Yale University, fifth edition edition, 1988.
16. Joseph E. Stoy. *Denotational Semantics: The Scott-Strachey Approach to Programming Language Theory*. MIT Press, Cambridge, MA, 1977.
17. Vipin Swarup, William M. Farmer, Joshua D. Guttman, Leonard G. Monk, and John D. Ramsdell. The VLISP byte-code interpreter. M 92B097, The MITRE Corporation, September 1992.
18. Mitchell Wand. Semantics-directed machine architecture. In *Conf. Rec. 9th ACM Symp. on Principles of Prog. Lang.*, pages 234–241, 1982.
19. Mitchell Wand and Dino P. Oliva. Proving the correctness of storage representations. In *Proceedings of the 1992 ACM Conference on Lisp and Functional Programming*, pages 151–160, New York, 1992. ACM Press.

LISP AND SYMBOLIC COMPUTATION: An International Journal, 8, 111–182 (1995)

The VLISP Verified PreScheme Compiler

DINO P. OLIVA * oliva@cse.ogi.edu
College of Computer Science
161 Cullinane Hall
Northeastern University
Boston, MA 02115

JOHN D. RAMSDELL ** ramsdell@mitre.org
The MITRE Corporation
202 Burlington Road
Bedford, MA 01730-1420

MITCHELL WAND † wand@ccs.neu.edu
College of Computer Science
161 Cullinane Hall
Northeastern University
Boston, MA 02115

Editors: Joshua D. Guttman and Mitchell Wand

Abstract. This paper describes a verified compiler for PreScheme, the implementation language for the VLISP run-time system. The compiler and proof were divided into three parts: A transformational front end that translates source text into a core language, a syntax-directed compiler that translates the core language into a combinator-based tree-manipulation language, and a linearizer that translates combinator code into code for an abstract stored-program machine with linear memory for both data and code. This factorization enabled different proof techniques to be used for the different phases of the compiler, and also allowed the generation of good code. Finally, the whole process was made possible by carefully defining the semantics of VLISP PreScheme rather than just adopting Scheme's. We believe that the architecture of the compiler and its correctness proof can easily be applied to compilers for languages other than PreScheme.

Keywords: verified, compiler

Table of Contents

* This work was supported by Rome Laboratory of the United States Air Force, contract No. F19628-89-C-0001, through the MITRE Corporation, and by NSF and DARPA under NSF grants CCR-9002253 and CCR-9014603. Author's current address: Department of Computer Science and Engineering, Oregon Graduate Institute, P.O. Box 91000, Portland, OR 97291-1000.

** The work reported here was supported by Rome Laboratory of the United States Air Force, contract No. F19628-89-C-0001. Preparation of this paper was generously supported by The MITRE Corporation.

† This work was supported by Rome Laboratory of the United States Air Force, contract No. F19628-89-C-0001, through the MITRE Corporation, and by NSF and DARPA under NSF grants CCR-9002253 and CCR-9014603.

1. Introduction

As part of the VLISP project, we have developed an architecture for the specification and implementation of verified optimizing compilers. We have used this architecture to develop a verified compiler for PreScheme.

This architecture divides the compiler into three components. In the case of PreScheme, these components are:

1. A transformational front end that translates source text into a core language called Pure PreScheme.

2. A syntax-directed compiler that translates Pure PreScheme into a combinator-based tree-manipulation language. We call this language *combinator code*.

3. An assembler that translates combinator code into code for an abstract stored-program machine with linear memory for both data and code.

We believe that this is a good architecture for the specification and implementation of verified optimizing compilers. A smaller example of this proof architecture (without the front end) is given in [31]; another example, with a more elaborate assembler, is given in [18].

The correctness of each transformation of the program is justified relative to an appropriate semantics:

- The source language and its core subset (PreScheme and Pure PreScheme in our example) share a denotational semantics.

- The language of combinators has both a denotational semantics, expressed using the same domains as the source language, and an operational semantics. The latter may be derived from the former by general theorems of the λ-calculus.

- The stored-program machine is specified using an operational semantics.

This separation of semantics allows each transformation to be proved correct using a suitable proof technique:

1. The transformational front end is shown to preserve the denotational semantics of the source language, by induction on the number of transformation steps.

2. The syntax-directed compiler is shown correct by denotational reasoning, using structural induction on the phrases of the core language. The proof establishes a relation between the denotational semantics of the core language and the denotational semantics of the combinator language. The proof is made feasible by the fact that the core and combinator semantics are expressed using the same domains.

Level	Language	Acronym	Section
Source Language	VLISP PreScheme	VLPS	2
Parsed Source Language	Macro-Free PreScheme	MFPS	2
Core Language	Pure PreScheme	PPS	2
Tree Structured Language	Combinator Code	CC	5
Linear Data Language	Linear-Data Code	LDC	6
Linear Program Language	Stored-Program Code	SPC	7
Target Language	Assembly Code	AC	9

Figure 1. Levels in the PreScheme compilation process

3. The assembler is proved correct by operational reasoning, using the operational semantics of the combinator language and the operational semantics of the stored-program machine. We define a relation, called a *storage-layout relation*, that determines when the combinator machine and the stored-program machine are in corresponding states, and we show that operation of the machines preserves this relation.

The verification of the PreScheme compiler is at the same level as that of the VLISP system itself: the algorithms are verified with respect to a formal denotational semantics of PreScheme and a formal model of an abstract target machine. The implementation of the algorithms was carried out in Scheme, and code for the abstract target machine was translated into assembly language for two real target machines (Motorola 68000 and SPARC). While neither of these implementation steps was verified, both were straightforward; for a discussion of the trustworthiness of this approach, see [8].

In the case of the PreScheme compiler, the assembler proof is performed in two steps: we first relate the combinator machine to a machine, called the *linear-data machine*, in which the data store is linear, but the program is still a tree. We then relate the linear-data machine to the *stored-program machine*, in which both the data and code are kept in linear memories.

This gives a total of five language or machine levels and four major proofs. In general, we will present level n, followed by the proof or proofs relating level n to level $n-1$. Figure 1 tabulates the various levels.

The rest of the paper is organized as follows:

1.1. Introduction

Following [2], we will give a synopsis of each section in the paper. Section n will be summarized in section $1.n$.

1.2. VLISP PreScheme

PreScheme is a dialect of Scheme intended for systems programming. PreScheme was carefully designed so that it syntactically looks like Scheme and has similar semantics. With a little care, PreScheme programs can be run and debugged as if they were ordinary Scheme programs.

However, PreScheme is particularly suitable for systems programming because every valid PreScheme program can be executed using only a C-like run-time system. A compiler for this language will reject any program that requires dynamic type checking or creation of closures at run-time. Furthermore, it is intended that PreScheme programs be runnable without the use of automatic storage reclamation.

There are a number of dialects of PreScheme that played a part in this project. VLISP PreScheme is the source language that our compiler translates. It is the least restrictive PreScheme dialect we consider. Macro-Free PreScheme programs result from VLISP PreScheme by expanding all derived syntax and performing a few simple transformations. Pure PreScheme programs are syntactically restricted, strongly typed Macro-Free PreScheme programs. The syntactic restrictions used to define Pure PreScheme imply that these programs will meet all of the run-time conditions for a valid VLISP PreScheme. Pure PreScheme programs are strongly typed, so no operator will be applied to data of the wrong type. `lambda` expressions in Pure PreScheme programs may occur only as initializers in top-level `letrec` bindings, or in the operator position of a procedure call. As a result, there is no need to represent closures at run-time. Finally, Pure PreScheme's syntax forbids non-tail-recursive procedure calls.

We present in more detail the various dialects of PreScheme used in the VLISP project and their design rationales. We also discuss the process by which the denotational semantics of PreScheme was derived.

1.3. The transformational front end and its denotational correctness

The transformational front end transforms VLISP PreScheme into Pure PreScheme. We give an overview of the transformation process and describe some of the transformations, including simplifiers, β-reduction, inlining, and lambda-lifting. We give an example to illustrate the operation of the compiler. Finally, we give an example of the correctness proof for two selected transforms.

1.4. Compiler-Oriented Semantics

As discussed in Section 2, Pure PreScheme's semantics is inherited from the semantics of Macro-Free PreScheme. However, in order to justify the compiler presented in Section 5, we reframed the semantics to distinguish some special cases syntactically and split both the environment and the continuation into a compile-time and run-time components. We call this the *compiler semantics*. The compiler reorganizes these quantities so that all the static arguments are handled before all the dynamic ones. Thus the semantics can be thought of as taking all the compile-time data and producing a code-like object π that can be applied to the run-time data, including the local data stack (*cf* the discussion in [26, p. 253]). The code-like objects are built from combinators, which will play the role of instructions in the later operational semantics.

We present some pieces of the compiler-oriented semantics. For each valuation in the semantics, we present a formal specification showing the relation that must hold between the compiler-oriented valuation and the corresponding valuation in the original semantics. These specifications are based on the induction hypotheses of [5]. The proof that the compiler oriented semantics is the same as the original then becomes a straightforward structural induction. We present some sample cases in Section 4.7.

1.5. The Combinator Code Machine and the Compiler

The combinator machine manipulates tuples of rational trees built from the combinators. A machine state is a 4-tuple $\langle q, u, z, h\rangle$, where q is the code which operates on a runtime environment, u, a stack z of stackable values, and a heap h. These rational trees are given two semantics: one denotational and one operational. The denotational semantics gives trees meanings in the same semantic domains as those used for the compiler-oriented semantics. Given the denotational semantics, the operational semantics is derived by performing β-conversion on the terms used in the compiler oriented valuations.

The Pure PreScheme compiler is similar to the compiler-oriented semantics except the compiler produces syntax rather than a denotation. Given a program, the compiler is required to produce a code tree whose denotation is the same as that given by the compiler-oriented semantics. The compiler is produced by taking the definition of the valuations in the compiler-oriented semantics, and replacing domain transformations by operations that produce trees. An adequacy theorem relates the operational semantics of the combinator machine to the denotational semantics of the original program.

We conclude by discussing some of the choices made in the design of the compiler-oriented semantics and the combinator machine.

1.6. The Linear-Data Machine

The linear-data machine uses the same machine language as the combinator machine, but instead of manipulating rational trees, its programs manipulate representations of those trees in a linear data store. It also has a heap which corresponds to the heap of the combinator machine, except that it contains untagged quantities. The state of the linear-data machine is of the form $\langle q, up, sp, s, h\rangle$, where sp

and *up* are pointers into the store representing the locations of the stack and the environment.

The representation of the stack and environment by these pointers is formalized. To aid in the intuition behind these formalisms, we first give an informal sketch of the representation. We then present the formal definitions. This is done by defining a ***storage-layout relation*** between states of the combinator-code machine and the linear-data machine. A pair of states is in this relation iff the linear-data-machine state represents the combinator-machine state. Some of the basic properties of this relation are sketched.

We define the operational semantics of the linear-data machine so that the linear-data machine simulates the behavior of the combinator machine. That is, if L_1 corresponds to C_1 and C_1 rewrites to C_2, then we want the linear-data machine to send L_1 to some state L_2 such that L_2 corresponds to C_2.

We prove that the linear-data machine satisfies the desired simulation theorem. The simulation property will need some refining, since the combinator machine keeps tag information and the linear-data machine does not. The proof relies on the global invariant that every validly compiled Pure PreScheme program runs in bounded control space.

We conclude with a theorem that shows the correctness of the compiler from the source program to linear-data machine code.

1.7. The Stored-Program Machine

The stored-program machine is very similar to the linear-data machine, except that the code is represented in cells of a linear instruction store, much like the cells of the data store. The correspondence between states of the stored-program machine and states of the linear-data machine is defined, and a simulation theorem is proved.

1.8. The Linearizer and its Correctness

The assembler takes code for the combinator or linear-data machine and produces a state of the linear instruction store which corresponds to the original according to the definition in the preceding section. We therefore call it the *linearizer*. The major technical difficulty is the treatment of branches and joins, so that code is not duplicated. The proof is by induction on the structure of the combinator code.

We conclude with a theorem that shows the correctness of the entire compiler, from the source program to the stored-program machine code.

1.9. Implementation

A compiler for PreScheme was developed in parallel with this specification. It generates code for the Motorola 68000. Representing the abstract machines with the

68000 requires a mapping similar to the ones just detailed. This section informally describes that mapping. Some performance results are presented.

1.10. Conclusions

We present some of the conclusions we have drawn from this effort. Some comparisons with other work are made. Some alternative design decisions are sketched. Directions for future work are suggested.

2. VLISP PreScheme

PreScheme is a dialect of Scheme intended for systems programming. This section describes VLISP PreScheme and various related dialects used in the VLISP project.

VLISP PreScheme was inspired by Scheme48 PreScheme [12], but differs from it in that VLISP PreScheme has no user-defined syntax, macros, or compiler directives, and in that it provides a different set of standard procedures.

Because VLISP PreScheme is intended for systems programming, programs in the language are restricted so that they make as few assumptions as possible about the facilities available at run time. In particular, the computation model underlying VLISP PreScheme has the following properties:

- VLISP PreScheme programs manipulate data objects that fit in machine words. The type of each data object is an integer, a character, a boolean, a string, a port, a pointer to an integer, or a procedure (represented as a pointer). A PreScheme data object may be a full word, without room for run-time tags. Therefore no type predicates, like those of Scheme, are possible in the language. It becomes the compiler's responsibility to ensure statically that operators are never applied to data of the wrong type.

- A valid VLISP PreScheme program can run without creating closures at run time. Thus, if p is a pointer to a procedure, the free variables of that procedure must be allocatable at compile time. However, a VLISP PreScheme program may textually contain procedures with free variables that are lambda-bound. The compiler must transform these programs so that they meet the run-time restriction.

- Implementations of VLISP PreScheme are required to be tail-recursive, which means that iterative processes can be expressed by means of procedure calls. When the last action taken by a procedure is a call, a tail-recursive implementation is required to eliminate the control information of the calling procedure so that the order of space growth of iterative processes is constant. Such a call is said to be tail-recursive. The requirement that implementations be tail-recursive is inherited from Scheme [10].

- All procedure calls in a running VLISP PreScheme program must be tail-recursive. Thus, the VLISP PreScheme compiler used in the VLISP project can only be used to specify iterative processes. This restriction was made for historical reasons, as described in Section 2.4. One of the lessons learned was how to eliminate this restriction, and new versions of the compiler allow non-tail-recursive calls [23].

A PreScheme program is said to be *legal* only if the compiler can verify statically that these properties can be guaranteed at run time. Different implementations of PreScheme may accept different sets of programs, depending on how clever the compiler is in reasoning about these properties. The strategies used by the VLISP PreScheme compiler are discussed in Section 3.

2.1. VLISP PreScheme Syntax

VLISP PreScheme was carefully designed so that it syntactically looks like Scheme and has similar semantics. With a little care, VLISP PreScheme programs can be run and debugged as if they were ordinary Scheme programs.

The syntax of the VLISP PreScheme language is identical to the syntax of the language defined in the Scheme standard [10, Chapter 7] with the following exceptions:

- Every defined procedure takes a fixed number of arguments.
- The only variables that can be modified are those introduced at top level using the syntax

  (`define` ⟨variable⟩ ⟨expression⟩),

  and whose name begins and ends with an asterisk and is at least three characters long. Variables so defined are called mutable variables. Note that a variable introduced at other than top level may have a name which begins and ends with an asterisk, but this practice is discouraged.
- If ⟨expression⟩ is a `lambda` expression, variables can also be defined using the syntax

  (`define-integrable` ⟨variable⟩ ⟨expression⟩).

  When ⟨variable⟩ occurs in the operator position of a combination, compilers must replace it with ⟨expression⟩.
- No variable may be defined more than once.
- `letrec` is not a derived expression. The initializer for each variable bound by a `letrec` expression must be a `lambda` expression.
- Constants are restricted to integers, characters, booleans, and strings.
- Finally, a different set of primitive procedures is specified. These are listed in Figure 2.

```
not, zero?, positive?, negative?, <, <=, =, >=, >, abs, +, -, *,
quotient, remainder, ashl, ashr, low-bits,
integer->char, char->integer, char=?, char<?, char<=, char>, char>=,
make-vector, vector-ref, vector-set!, vector-byte-ref,
vector-byte-set!,
addr<, addr=, addr+, addr-, addr<=, addr>, addr>=, addr->integer,
integer->addr, addr->string,
port->integer, integer->port,
read-char, peek-char, eof-object?, write-char, write-int, write,
newline,
force-output, null-port?,
open-input-file, close-input-port, open-output-file,
close-output-port, current-input-port, current-output-port,
read-image, write-image,
bytes-per-word, useful-bits-per-word,
exit, err
```

Figure 2. Primitive Operators in VLISP PreScheme

2.2. Macro-Free PreScheme

Macro-Free PreScheme programs result from VLISP PreScheme programs by expanding all derived syntax except the `case` expression, identifying which variables refer to standard procedures, and replacing single armed conditionals (`if` E E) with (`if` E E (`if #f #f`)) (while both these expressions give an unspecified result in the event that the test expression is false, the latter form allows later transformation rules to be applied more uniformly; see Section 3.1). A grammar for the resulting language is shown in Figure 3.

Not every string generated by the grammar in Figure 3 is a legal Macro-Free PreScheme program. A string is a legal program only if it is generated by the grammar and the compiler can verify that the program can be transformed to meet the runtime restrictions set forth at the beginning of this section. Macro-Free PreScheme programs must also satisfy the restriction that n-ary standard procedures must be used at one fixed arity.

VLISP PreScheme's complete formal denotational semantics is given in [24, Section 2.3]. Following the usual conventions, it assigns meanings to constructs of an abstract syntax. The abstract syntax is very similar to the syntax of Macro-Free PreScheme, so in the interest of space, it will be used as VLISP PreScheme's abstract syntax in what follows.

The semantics is presented in a form that very closely resembles Scheme's semantics [10, Appendix A]. It uses the same mathematical conventions, and many of the standard's definitions. Some of the notation from the standard is summarized in

K ∈ Con	constants
I ∈ Ide	variables
O ∈ Op	primitive operators
E ∈ Exp	expressions
B ∈ Bnd	bindings
P ∈ Pgm	programs

P ::= (`define` I)* E
B ::= (I (`lambda` (I*) E))*
E ::= K | I | (E E*) | (`lambda` (I*) E)
  | (`begin` E* E) | (`letrec` (B) E)
  | (`if` E E E) | (`if #f #f`) | (`set!` I E)
  | (O E*) | (`case` E ((K) E)* ((K) E))

Figure 3. Macro-Free PreScheme Syntax

$\langle\ldots\rangle$	Singleton sequence formation
$s \downarrow k$	kth member of the sequence s (1-based)
$\#s$	length of sequence s
$s \S t$	concatenation of sequences s and t
$s \dagger k$	drop the first k members of sequence s
$t \rightarrow a, b$	McCarthy conditional "if t then a else b"
$\rho[x/i]$	substitution "ρ with x for i"
x in D	injection of x into domain D
$x \mid$ D	projection of x to domain D

Figure 4. Notation from the IEEE Scheme Standard [10]

Figure 4. Extensions to this notation usually follow the conventions used in the programming language Standard ML [16].

The domains and valuations of the semantics are shown in Figures 5 and 6. The VLISP PreScheme formal semantics differs from Scheme's in a small number of ways:

- All variables must be defined before they are referenced or assigned and no variable may be defined more than once.

- Lambda-bound variables are immutable, so a location need not be allocated for each actual parameter of an invoked procedure. Consequently, variables may be bound to either locations or expressed values.

$\alpha \in L$		locations
$\nu \in N$		natural numbers
T	$= \{\mathit{false}, \mathit{true}\}$	booleans
H		characters
R		integers
E_v	$= L^*$	vectors
E_s		strings
E_p		ports
M	$= \{\mathit{unspecified}, \mathit{undefined}\}$	miscellaneous
$\chi \in X$		external states
$\phi \in F$	$= E^* \rightarrow K \rightarrow C$	procedure values
$\epsilon \in E$	$= T + H + R + E_v + E_s + E_p + M + F$	expressed values
$\sigma \in S$	$= L \rightarrow (E \times T)$	stores
$\delta \in D$	$= L + E$	denoted values
$\rho \in U$	$= \mathrm{Ide} \rightarrow D$	environments
$\theta \in C$	$= S \rightarrow X \rightarrow A$	command continuations
$\kappa \in K$	$= E \rightarrow C$	expression continuations
A	$= R$	answers

Figure 5. VLISP PreScheme value domains

$$\mathcal{K} : \mathrm{Con} \rightarrow E$$
$$\mathcal{L} : \mathrm{Exp} \rightarrow U \rightarrow E$$
$$\mathcal{I} : \mathrm{Bnd} \rightarrow \mathrm{Ide}^*$$
$$\mathcal{B} : \mathrm{Bnd} \rightarrow \mathrm{Ide}^* \rightarrow U \rightarrow E^* \rightarrow E^*$$
$$\mathcal{E} : \mathrm{Exp} \rightarrow U \rightarrow K \rightarrow C$$
$$\mathcal{E}^* : \mathrm{Exp}^* \rightarrow U \rightarrow (E^* \rightarrow C) \rightarrow C$$
$$\mathcal{D} : \mathrm{Pgm} \rightarrow U \rightarrow K \rightarrow C$$
$$\mathcal{P} : \mathrm{Pgm} \rightarrow X \rightarrow A$$

Figure 6. VLISP PreScheme valuations

- VLISP PreScheme procedure values do not have a location associated with them because there is no comparison operator for procedures. Vectors do not have a boolean value associated with them because all vectors are mutable.
- VLISP PreScheme `letrec` is no longer a derived expression, because the immutability of lambda-bound variables makes Scheme's definition of `letrec` inapplicable. Instead, `letrec` is defined by an explicit fixed point.
- Procedures always return exactly one value, so expression continuations map a single expressed value to a command continuation.
- The domain of answers A, unspecified in Scheme, is specified to be the flat domain of the integers. The initial continuation is also specified.
- The store is assumed to be infinite, so the storage allocator *new* always returns a location.
- The domain X of external states is added. This the domain upon which input-output operations are performed. For the PreScheme verification, this domain is unspecified. The main valuation $\mathcal{P}$ takes a program and an initial external state and produces an answer.

The following fragments of the VLISP PreScheme semantics illustrate some of these distinctions. For example, the semantics of variable reference follows. The first two lines contain the domain equations for denoted values and environments.

$$\delta \in D = E + L$$
$$\rho \in U = \text{Ide} \to D$$

$$\mathcal{E} : \text{Exp} \to U \to K \to C$$
$$\mathcal{E}[\![\text{I}]\!] = \lambda\rho\kappa.\, \mathit{hold}(\rho\,\text{I})(\lambda\epsilon.\,\epsilon = \mathit{undefined} \to \mathit{wrong}\ \text{“undefined variable”}, \kappa\epsilon)$$

$$\mathit{hold} : D \to K \to C$$
$$\mathit{hold} = \lambda\delta\kappa\sigma.\,\delta \in E \to \kappa(\delta \mid E)\sigma, \kappa(\sigma(\delta \mid L) \downarrow 1)\sigma$$

Here, as in the Scheme semantics [10, Appendix A], *undefined* $\in M$ is used to mark uninitialized variables. These semantics differ from Scheme's in that some variables are bound to expressed values instead of locations.

The semantics of a `lambda` expression provide another example.

$$\mathcal{L} : \text{Exp} \to U \to E$$
$$\mathcal{L}[\![\texttt{(lambda (I}^*\texttt{) E)}]\!] =$$
$$\lambda\rho.\,(\lambda\epsilon^*\kappa.\,\#\epsilon^* = \#\text{I}^* \to \mathcal{E}[\![\text{E}]\!](\mathit{extends}\,\rho\ \text{I}^*\ \epsilon^*)\kappa,$$
$$\mathit{wrong}\ \text{“wrong number of arguments”})$$
$$\text{in } E$$

Notice that the meaning of a `lambda` expression depends only on its environment. In contrast, the meaning of a `lambda` expression in Scheme depends on the store as well as its environment. This difference makes it easier to justify changing the time at which a PreScheme **lambda** expression is evaluated.

The semantics of a `letrec` expression are quite different from Scheme's.

$$\mathcal{B} : \text{Bnd} \to \text{Ide}^* \to U \to E^* \to E^*$$
$$\mathcal{E} : \text{Exp} \to U \to K \to C$$
$$\mathcal{B}[\![\,]\!] = \lambda \text{I}^* \rho \epsilon^* . \langle\rangle$$
$$\mathcal{B}[\![(\text{I}\ (\texttt{lambda}\ (\text{I}^*)\ \text{E}))\ \text{B}]\!] =$$
$$\quad \lambda \text{I}_0^* \rho \epsilon^* . \langle \mathcal{L}[\![(\texttt{lambda}\ (\text{I}^*)\ \text{E})]\!](\mathit{extends}\ \rho\ \text{I}_0^*\ \epsilon^*)\rangle\ \S\ \mathcal{B}[\![\text{B}]\!]\text{I}_0^* \rho \epsilon^*$$
$$\mathcal{E}[\![(\texttt{letrec}\ (\text{B})\ \text{E})]\!] = \lambda \rho \kappa . \mathcal{E}[\![\text{E}]\!](\mathit{extends}\ \rho (\mathcal{I}[\![\text{B}]\!])(\mathit{fix}(\mathcal{B}[\![\text{B}]\!](\mathcal{I}[\![\text{B}]\!])\rho)))\kappa$$

where $\mathcal{I}[\![\text{B}]\!]$ produces the sequence of identifiers bound by the `letrec` expression.

The meaning of the body of a `letrec` expression is given with an environment extended by values derived from the `letrec` bindings. As with **lambda** expressions, the values depend only on the environment and not the store. This is unlike the Scheme semantics for `letrec`, which is given in terms of assignment.

The meaning of an entire program is given by the valuation $\mathcal{P}$, which calls the valuation $\mathcal{D}$, which allocates for the global variables of the program and then invokes the expression valuation $\mathcal{E}$ on the main portion of the program.

$$\mathcal{D}[\![\text{E}]\!] = \mathcal{E}[\![\text{E}]\!]$$

$$\mathcal{D}[\![(\texttt{define}\ \text{I})\ \text{P}]\!] =$$
$$\quad \lambda \rho \kappa \sigma . \mathcal{D}[\![\text{P}]\!](\rho[(\mathit{new}\ \sigma)\ \text{in}\ D/\text{I}])\kappa(\mathit{update}(\mathit{new}\ \sigma)\ \mathit{undefined}\ \sigma)$$

$$\mathcal{P}[\![\text{P}]\!]\chi = \mathcal{D}[\![\text{P}]\!]\rho_0 \kappa_0 \sigma_0 \chi$$

$$\kappa_0 = \lambda \epsilon \sigma \chi . \epsilon \in R \to \epsilon \mid R, \mathit{wrong}\ \text{“result not an integer”}\sigma\chi$$

The environment ρ_0 maps the name of each standard procedure to its value and maps all other identifiers to *undefined*. It maps no identifier to a location. We assume that *wrong* “m” $\sigma\chi = \bot_A$.

The specification of the meaning of a procedure call is textually unchanged from the Scheme semantics. However, the semantics is somewhat different, because the domains are different. Scheme's expression continuations map a sequence of expressed values into a command continuation, but VLISP PreScheme maps a single expressed value into a command continuation.

$$\mathcal{E}[\![(\text{E}_0\ \text{E}^*)]\!] =$$
$$\quad \lambda \rho \kappa . \mathcal{E}^*(\mathit{permute}(\langle \text{E}_0 \rangle\ \S\ \text{E}^*))$$
$$\qquad \rho$$
$$\qquad (\lambda \epsilon^* . ((\lambda \epsilon^* . \mathit{applicate}(\epsilon^* \downarrow 1)(\epsilon^* \dagger 1)\kappa)$$
$$\qquad\qquad (\mathit{unpermute}\ \epsilon^*)))$$

The motivation for all these changes was efficiency for the Scheme48 version of PreScheme. However, these changes profoundly impact the ability to prove interesting properties of programs based on their semantics. In particular, these changes greatly facilitate proofs that certain program transformations preserve the meanings of programs. The utility of the changed semantics will be demonstrated later in the paper.

2.3. Pure PreScheme

Pure PreScheme programs are syntactically restricted, strongly typed Macro-Free PreScheme programs. As in Standard ML [16], types are inferred, not declared, but unlike Standard ML, there are no polymorphic variables. All expressions are monomorphic except (`if #f #f`) and (`set!` I E). The static semantics is given as a conventional set of inference rules, except that when an expression is unconstrained by the rules, the expression is assigned the integer type [24, Section 3.3].

The syntax of Pure PreScheme programs is given in Figure 7. The syntactic restrictions used to define Pure PreScheme imply that these programs will meet all of the run-time conditions of a VLISP PreScheme program presented at the beginning of this section. Pure PreScheme programs are strongly typed, so no operator will be applied to data of the wrong type. **`lambda`** expressions in Pure PreScheme programs may occur only as initializers in top-level `letrec` bindings, or in the operator position of a procedure call. As a result, there is no need to represent closures at run-time. Finally, Pure PreScheme's syntax forbids non-tail-recursive procedure calls.

There is a further syntactic restriction. The first selection criteria of a `case` clause must be zero and the selection criteria for other clauses must be the successor of the previous clause's selection criterion. This restriction is imposed to allow an `case` expression to be compiled into a computed goto.

Pure PreScheme's semantics are inherited from Macro-Free PreScheme's semantics, but they assume particular values for *permute* and *unpermute*, that is, the arguments of a call are always evaluated left-to-right, and then the operator is evaluated.

2.4. Challenges in the Design of VLISP PreScheme

The design process for VLISP PreScheme was considerably more complex than the preceding presentation might suggest. At the beginning of the VLISP project, we knew that the architecture of VLISP would be modeled after Scheme48, but we did not know how to build a verified compiler for a language like PreScheme. We also knew that the VLISP byte-code interpreter would mostly be an iterative process.

We began by concentrating on the run-time conditions for VLISP PreScheme programs presented at the beginning of this section. Pure PreScheme was the first language defined, and its syntax and semantics directly reflected the run-time con-

K ∈ Con	constants
I ∈ Ide	variables
O ∈ Op	primitive operators
S ∈ Smpl	simple expressions
T ∈ Tail	tail recursive expressions
E ∈ Exp	top level expressions
B ∈ Bnd	bindings
P ∈ Pgm	programs

P ::= (`define` I)* E
E ::= (`letrec` (B) T)
B ::= (I (`lambda` (I*) T))*
T ::= S | (S S*) | (`if` S T T) | (`case` S ((K) T)*)
  | (`begin` S* T) | ((`lambda` (I*) T) S*)
S ::= K | I | (O S*) | (`if` S S S) | (`if` `#f` `#f`) | (`set!` I S)
  | (`begin` S* S) | ((`lambda` (I*) S) S*) | (`case` S ((K) S)*)

Figure 7. Pure PreScheme Syntax

ditions. When it was defined, Pure PreScheme's syntax and semantics were given independently; only later did we work out the simple embedding of that semantics in the more general semantics of VLISP PreScheme discussed here.

Unfortunately, the VLISP byte-code interpreter is not conveniently described using only tail-recursive calls. While the byte-code interpreter is a finite state machine, it would have been more natural to allow non-tail-recursive calls to the interpreter's garbage collector. The implementation of a purely iterative byte-code interpreter is described in [7, Section 1.2.2]. In retrospect, we suffered from attempting to produce a language too finely tuned to our specific task. When we found our analysis of the task was wrong, the language was not general enough to conveniently handle the task when properly specified.

3. The Transformational Front End

The Front End translates VLISP PreScheme into Pure PreScheme. The translation occurs in three phases.

Parse: Expands usages of derived syntax by rules consistent with those presented in the Scheme standard. In addition, the program's bound variables are changed so that no variable occurs both bound and free, and no variable is bound more than once. This implies that a variable bound in the program is changed if it is also bound to a standard procedure. Other syntactic checks are made. The result is a Macro-Free PreScheme program.

Apply transformation rules: Translates a Macro-free PreScheme program into the syntax of Pure PreScheme using meaning-refining transformations. More will be said about this phase later.

Type check: Ensures that a syntactically restricted Macro-Free PreScheme program is strongly typed, and is therefore a Pure PreScheme program. This phase implements Algorithm W. That algorithm's correctness was demonstrated by Robin Milner [15]. The unifier is based on a published program by Laurence Paulson [21, p. 381].

A compiler for for VLISP PreScheme cannot accept all syntactically correct programs, because many Macro-Free PreScheme programs cannot be translated into Pure PreScheme. Furthermore, the set of Macro-Free programs that can be translated by a particular compiler depends on the transformation rules used by that compiler.

While there is no precise characterization of what constitutes a VLISP PreScheme program, knowledgeable programmers know one when they see one. Their intuition is based on an understanding of the run-time conditions and the knowledge that existing compilers perform β-conversion, procedure inlining, and closure hoisting.

For example, the following VLISP PreScheme program cannot be translated into Pure PreScheme. The procedure `loop` must be unwound if there are to be only tail-recursive procedure calls, but the compiler cannot predict how many times it should be unwound because `*x*` is a mutable variable.

```
(define *x* 2)
(define-integrable (loop x)
  (if (positive? x) (loop (- x 1)) x))
(some-hairy-command-which-modifies-*x*!)
(+ (loop *x*) 3)
```

In contrast, the following loop will be unwound at compile-time.

```
(define bytes-per-word 4)
(define-integrable (floor-log2 x a)
  (if (<= x 1)
      a
      (floor-log2 (quotient x 2) (+ 1 a))))
(define log-bytes-per-word
  (floor-log2 bytes-per-word 0))
log-bytes-per-word
```

The most complex and error-prone phase of the VLISP PreScheme Front End translates Macro-free PreScheme programs into a syntactically restricted form. The program is transformed by applying a set of rules. Each rule can be shown to be *meaning-refining*, in a sense to be defined below.

The selection and application of rules is performed by an intricate set of procedures. However, since each rule is meaning-refining, the output of the transformation process will be a program that is a refinement of the original, regardless of the choice of transformation rules. Therefore, the verification effort focused solely on the transformation rules. The consequences of this strategy are discussed in Section 3.3.

3.1. Transformation Rules

Each rule is a conditional rewrite rule. It has a pattern, a predicate, and a replacement. An expression matches a pattern if there is an assignment of pattern variables which makes the two expressions equal. The rewrite is performed if the matching expression satisfies the predicate.

To avoid name conflicts, the matching system works only on expressions that are α-converted. An expression is *α-converted* if no variable occurs both bound and free, and no variable is bound more than once. The output of the parsing phase is already α-converted, and the matching system α-converts the output of each transformation step.

A rule with pattern E_0 and replacement E_1 is written $\mathrm{E}_0 \Longrightarrow \mathrm{E}_1$, and its predicate is given in the text. If no predicate is given, the predicate is assumed to be true of any α-converted expression.

Several rules require certain subexpressions to be side-effect-free. More precisely:

Definition. E is side-effect-free iff $(\forall\rho,\sigma)(\exists\epsilon)(\forall\kappa,\chi)$

$$\mathcal{E}[\![\mathrm{E}]\!]\rho\kappa\sigma\chi = (\epsilon = \mathit{undefined} \rightarrow \bot_A, \kappa\epsilon\sigma\chi) \tag{1}$$

This definition says that the evaluation of E can read from the environment ρ and the store σ, and may then either return a value to its continuation, with the store and external state unchanged, or yield an erroneous result. Here we use the miscellaneous value *undefined* $\in M$ (used in the Scheme semantics [10, Appendix A] to mark uninitialized variables) to distinguish the two cases. Without loss of generality, we can always choose $\epsilon \neq \bot_E$, since when $\epsilon = \bot_E$ the right-hand side of Equation 1 equals $\bot_A$, so the same result could be obtained by choosing $\epsilon = \mathit{undefined}$.

It is, of course, undecidable to determine if an expression is side-effect-free, so instead we introduce the notion of an *evaluative* expression. Evaluative expressions are defined so as to allow them to be recognized by a simple recursive function on syntax, and so that every evaluative expression is side-effect-free. We then use this syntactic approximation in the transformation rules.

Definition. The *evaluative* expressions are defined inductively by the following rules:

- A primitive O is evaluative only if its invocation returns a value without modifying the store and without reading or modifying the external state. We assume this information is known in advance for the finite number of primitives in the language.
- K is evaluative.
- I is evaluative.
- If O is evaluative, and $E_1 \ldots E_n$ are evaluative, then so is (O $E_1 \ldots E_n$).
- (`lambda` (I*) E) is evaluative.
- If $E_0, \ldots, E_n$ are evaluative, then so is (`begin` $E_0 \ldots E_n$).
- If E is evaluative, then so is (`letrec` (B) E).
- If E_0, E_1, and E_2 are evaluative, then so is (`if` E_0 E_1 E_2).
- If $E_0, \ldots, E_n$ are evaluative, then so is (`case` E_0 ((K) E_1)...).

If an expression is evaluative, it returns a value without modifying the store, as will be shown in Theorem 1. A evaluative expression can be eliminated when its value is ignored.

THEOREM 1 *If* E *is evaluative, then* E *is side-effect-free.*

Proof: This is proved by structural induction on evaluative expressions. The cases of E being I and (`if` E_0 E_1 E_2) are shown.

Case E = I: Fix ρ and σ. Let $\epsilon = \rho\mathrm{I} \in E \to \rho\mathrm{I} \mid E, \sigma(\rho\mathrm{I} \mid L) \downarrow 1$. Notice ϵ is independent of κ and χ. Expanding definitions gives the desired result that for all κ and χ

$$\mathcal{E}[\![\mathrm{I}]\!]\rho\kappa\sigma\chi = (\epsilon = \mathit{undefined} \to \bot_A, \kappa\epsilon\sigma\chi).$$

Case E = (`if` E_0 E_1 E_2): Fix ρ and σ. By the induction hypothesis, there is at least one ϵ_0 such that for all κ, χ

$$\mathcal{E}[\![\mathrm{E}_0]\!]\rho\kappa\sigma\chi = (\epsilon_0 = \mathit{undefined} \to \bot_A, \kappa\epsilon_0\sigma\chi).$$

By the note following the definition of side-effect-free, we can assume without loss of generality that $\epsilon_0 \neq \bot_E$. If $\epsilon_0 = \mathit{undefined}$ the result is immediate. Otherwise, for any κ and χ,

$$\begin{aligned}
&\mathcal{E}[\![(\texttt{if}\ \mathrm{E}_0\ \mathrm{E}_1\ \mathrm{E}_2)]\!]\rho\kappa\sigma\chi \\
&= \mathcal{E}[\![\mathrm{E}_0]\!]\rho(\lambda\epsilon.\, \mathit{truish}\,\epsilon \to \mathcal{E}[\![\mathrm{E}_1]\!]\rho\kappa, \mathcal{E}[\![\mathrm{E}_2]\!]\rho\kappa)\sigma\chi \\
&= \mathit{truish}\,\epsilon_0 \to \mathcal{E}[\![\mathrm{E}_1]\!]\rho\kappa\sigma\chi, \mathcal{E}[\![\mathrm{E}_2]\!]\rho\kappa\sigma\chi.
\end{aligned}$$

Therefore, when $\epsilon_0 \neq \mathit{false}$ (and therefore $\mathit{truish}\,\epsilon_0$ is true),

$$\mathcal{E}[\![(\texttt{if}\ \mathrm{E}_0\ \mathrm{E}_1\ \mathrm{E}_2)]\!]\rho\kappa\sigma\chi = \mathcal{E}[\![\mathrm{E}_1]\!]\rho\kappa\sigma\chi,$$

otherwise

$$\mathcal{E}[\![(\texttt{if}\ \mathrm{E}_0\ \mathrm{E}_1\ \mathrm{E}_2)]\!]\rho\kappa\sigma\chi = \mathcal{E}[\![\mathrm{E}_2]\!]\rho\kappa\sigma\chi.$$

Use of the induction hypothesis verifies both alternatives. ■

There are several other recursively defined predicates on expression syntax which are used by a variety of rules. There is a predicate which determines if a variable is free in an expression. Another predicate is true of expressions which are evaluative and have values which do not depend on modifiable values. Yet another one recognizes expressions that do not modify the store until their last action.

The predicates have been carefully chosen so as to work with the rule application mechanism. For example, the definition of evaluative expressions could have included the following clause.

- If $\mathrm{E}_0, \ldots, \mathrm{E}_n$ are evaluative, then $((\texttt{lambda}\ (\mathrm{I}_1 \ldots \mathrm{I}_n)\ \mathrm{E}_0)\ \mathrm{E}_1 \ldots \mathrm{E}_n)$ is evaluative.

This clause generates expressions that are side-effect-free. It was eliminated because its addition caused looping of the rule application mechanism.

The Front End implements a variety of rules [24, Section 5.1.2]. There are roughly five categories of rules. One category contains rules specific to primitive operators. These rules help implement constant folding. For example, the rules associated with the plus operator follow.

$(+\ \mathrm{K}_0\ \mathrm{K}_1) \Longrightarrow \mathrm{K}_0 + \mathrm{K}_1$	constant folding
$(+\ 0\ \mathrm{E}) \Longrightarrow \mathrm{E}$	idempotency
$(+\ \mathrm{E}\ \mathrm{K}) \Longrightarrow (+\ \mathrm{K}\ \mathrm{E})$	commutativity
$(+\ \mathrm{E}_0\ (+\ \mathrm{E}_1\ \mathrm{E}_2)) \Longrightarrow (+\ (+\ \mathrm{E}_0\ \mathrm{E}_1)\ \mathrm{E}_2)$	associativity

The next category of rules focus on conditional expressions. As with the previous category of rules, the form of the rules are quite conventional, as the following example shows.

Definition. The `if`-in-an-`if`'s-Consequence Rule.

$$(\texttt{if}\ \mathrm{E}_0\ (\texttt{if}\ \mathrm{E}_0\ \mathrm{E}_1\ \mathrm{E}_2)\ \mathrm{E}_3) \Longrightarrow (\texttt{if}\ \mathrm{E}_0\ \mathrm{E}_1\ \mathrm{E}_3)$$
$$(\texttt{if}\ \mathrm{E}_0\ \mathrm{E}_1\ (\texttt{if}\ \mathrm{E}_0\ \mathrm{E}_2\ \mathrm{E}_3)) \Longrightarrow (\texttt{if}\ \mathrm{E}_0\ \mathrm{E}_1\ \mathrm{E}_3)$$

when E_0 is evaluative.

For this rule to be sound, we must guarantee that E_0 is side-effect-free, so we use instead the approximation that E_0 be evaluative.

The remaining categories of rules implement β-conversion, closure hoisting, and defined constant substitution. Many of the rules in these categories look unusual. The forms of these rules was intended to facilitate correctness proofs. For example, two distinct rules produce the effect of β-conversion. Closures are hoisted by the use of several other rules, including the rule below.

```
(define number 77)                    ; This program
(define (dec x) (- x 1))              ; produces zero
(define (even x)                      ; if NUMBER is even
  (if (zero? x)                       ; and non-negative,
      0                               ; otherwise it
      (odd (dec x))))                 ; produces one.
(define (odd x)
  (if (zero? x)
      1
      (even (dec x))))
(if (negative? number)
    1
    (even number))
```

Figure 8. Example VLISP PreScheme Program

```
(define number)
(define dec)
(define even)
(define odd)
(begin
  (set! number 77)
  (set! dec (lambda (x) (- x 1)))
  (set! even (lambda (y) (if (= 0 y) 0 (odd (dec y)))))
  (set! odd (lambda (z) (if (= 0 z) 1 (even (dec z)))))
  (if (> 0 number) 1 (even number)))
```

Figure 9. Expand into Macro-Free PreScheme

Definition. The `letrec` Expression Merging Rule.

$$(\texttt{letrec}\ (B_0)\ (\texttt{letrec}\ (B_1)\ E)) \Longrightarrow (\texttt{letrec}\ (B_0\ B_1)\ E)$$

The rules result in program transformations similar to those produced by other compilers [11, 13]. Consider the even-odd program given in Figure 8. It specifies a simple iterative process. Figures 9–14 show how this program might be translated into Pure PreScheme using transformations implemented in the Front End. Notice that unlike [11, 13], this compiler does not convert the program into continuation-passing style [1, 25].

```
(define number) (define dec) (define even) (define odd)
(begin
  (set! number 77)
  (set! dec (letrec ((dec-0 (lambda (x) (- x 1)))) dec-0)))
  (set! even (letrec ((even-0 (lambda (y)
                                (if (= 0 y)
                                    0
                                    (odd (dec y))))))
                  even-0)))
  (set! odd (letrec ((odd-0 (lambda (z)
                              (if (= 0 z)
                                  1
                                  (even (dec z))))))
                 odd-0)))
  (if (> 0 number) 1 (even number)))
```

Figure 10. Name Anonymous Lambda Expressions

```
(define number) (define dec) (define even) (define odd)
(letrec
    ((dec-0 (lambda (x) (- x 1)))
     (even-0 (lambda (y) (if (= 0 y) 0 (odd (dec y)))))
     (odd-0 (lambda (z) (if (= 0 z) 1 (even (dec z))))))
  (begin
    (set! number 77)
    (set! dec dec-0)
    (set! even even-0)
    (set! odd odd-0)
    (if (> 0 number) 1 (even number))))
```

Figure 11. Closure Hoisting

```
(define number) (define dec) (define even) (define odd)
(letrec
    ((dec-0 (lambda (x) (- x 1)))
     (even-0 (lambda (y) (if (= 0 y) 0 (odd-0 (dec-0 y)))))
     (odd-0 (lambda (z) (if (= 0 z) 1 (even-0 (dec-0 z))))))
  (begin
    (set! number 77) (set! dec dec-0)
    (set! even even-0) (set! odd odd-0)
    (if (> 0 77)                          ; Which simplifies
        1                                 ; to (even-0 77).
        (even-0 77))))
```

Figure 12. Constant Folding

```
(define number) (define dec) (define even) (define odd)
(letrec
    ((dec-0 (lambda (x) (- x 1)))
     (even-0 (lambda (y) (if (= 0 y) 0 (odd-0 (- y 1)))))
     (odd-0 (lambda (z) (if (= 0 z) 1 (even-0 (- z 1))))))
  (begin
    (set! number 77) (set! dec dec-0)
    (set! even even-0) (set! odd odd-0)
    (even-0 77)))
```

Figure 13. Inline Non-Tail-Recursive Procedure Calls

```
(define number) (define dec) (define even) (define odd)
(letrec
    ((even-0 (lambda (y) (if (= 0 y) 0 (odd-0 (- y 1)))))
     (odd-0 (lambda (z) (if (= 0 z) 1 (even-0 (- z 1))))))
  (begin
    (set! number (if #f #f)) (set! dec (if #f #f))
    (set! even (if #f #f)) (set! odd (if #f #f))
    (even-0 77)))
```

Figure 14. Eliminate Unused Lambda Expressions and Initializers

3.2. Justification of the Rules

The application of a rule is justified if it transforms a Macro-free PreScheme program into another, and both programs have the same meaning as given by the formal semantics. Some of the rules have another interesting property—they can transform a program which has bottom denotation into a program which produces a non-bottom answer. For example, the program

```
(define two (+ 1 one))
(define one 1)
two
```

is transformed into a program which produces the answer 2!

This odd behavior is tolerated so as to allow constant propagation without performing a dependency analysis. In the above example, `1` is substituted for the occurrence of the immutable variable `one` even though *undefined* should have been substituted.

Definition. A rule is *meaning-refining* iff whenever its application transforms a program P_0 to a program P_1, then $\mathcal{P}[\![P_0]\!] \sqsubseteq \mathcal{P}[\![P_1]\!]$.

A rule is meaning-refining if its application does not affect non-erroneous computational results: if a meaning-refining rule transforms program P_0 to a program P_1, and $\mathcal{P}[\![P_0]\!]\chi = n$, then $\mathcal{P}[\![P_1]\!]\chi = n$ as well. Since errors denote $\bot_A$, a meaning-refining rule may transform a looping or erroneous program to a terminating one.

To show that a rule transforming E_0 to E_1 is meaning-refining, it suffices to show that $\mathcal{E}[\![E_0]\!] \sqsubseteq \mathcal{E}[\![E_1]\!]$, for if $\mathcal{E}[\![E_0]\!] \sqsubseteq \mathcal{E}[\![E_1]\!]$ and P_1 is a program which results from P_0 by the replacement of E_0 by E_1, then compositionality implies that $\mathcal{P}[\![P_0]\!] \sqsubseteq \mathcal{P}[\![P_1]\!]$.

The proof of each rule usually requires the consideration of many details. Many rules are proved using structural induction on the syntax of Macro-Free PreScheme. Some rules have predicates which oblige certain expressions not modify the store, others require certain expressions not modify the store or reference mutable data. Some of the proofs in [24] are incomplete as only the cases that appeared to us to be "interesting" were selected for detailed consideration.

As a result, there is no proof which is representative of all of the others. However, the proofs of the `if`-in-an-`if`'s-Consequence Rule and the `letrec` Expression Merging Rule give some flavor of the other proofs.

3.2.1. The `if`-in-an-`if`'s-Consequence Rule

This rule has a predicate which requires one of its expressions to be evaluative. Evaluative expressions are side-effect-free.

THEOREM 2 *If* E_0 *is evaluative,*

$$\mathcal{E}[\![(\texttt{if}\ E_0\ (\texttt{if}\ E_0\ E_1\ E_2)\ E_3)]\!] = \mathcal{E}[\![(\texttt{if}\ E_0\ E_1\ E_3)]\!].$$

Hence the `if`*-in-an-*`if`*'s-Consequence Rule is meaning-refining.*

Proof: By Theorem 1, for any ρ and σ there exists an ϵ_0 such that for all κ and χ,

$$\mathcal{E}[\![\mathrm{E}_0]\!]\rho\kappa\sigma\chi = (\epsilon_0 = \mathit{undefined} \rightarrow \bot_A, \kappa\epsilon_0\sigma\chi).$$

If $\epsilon_0 = \mathit{undefined}$, the proof is immediate, so assume $\epsilon_0 \neq \mathit{undefined}$.

$$\begin{aligned}
&\mathcal{E}[\![(\texttt{if}\ \mathrm{E}_0\ (\texttt{if}\ \mathrm{E}_0\ \mathrm{E}_1\ \mathrm{E}_2)\ \mathrm{E}_3)]\!]\rho\kappa\sigma\chi\\
&\quad = \mathcal{E}[\![\mathrm{E}_0]\!]\rho(\lambda\epsilon.\, \mathit{truish}\,\epsilon \rightarrow \mathcal{E}[\![(\texttt{if}\ \mathrm{E}_0\ \mathrm{E}_1\ \mathrm{E}_2)]\!]\rho\kappa, \mathcal{E}[\![\mathrm{E}_3]\!]\rho\kappa)\sigma\chi\\
&\quad = \mathit{truish}\,\epsilon_0 \rightarrow \mathcal{E}[\![(\texttt{if}\ \mathrm{E}_0\ \mathrm{E}_1\ \mathrm{E}_2)]\!]\rho\kappa\sigma\chi, \mathcal{E}[\![\mathrm{E}_3]\!]\rho\kappa\sigma\chi\\
&\quad = \mathit{truish}\,\epsilon_0 \rightarrow \mathcal{E}[\![\mathrm{E}_0]\!]\rho(\lambda\epsilon.\, \mathit{truish}\,\epsilon \rightarrow \mathcal{E}[\![\mathrm{E}_1]\!]\rho\kappa, \mathcal{E}[\![\mathrm{E}_2]\!]\rho\kappa)\sigma\chi, \mathcal{E}[\![\mathrm{E}_3]\!]\rho\kappa\sigma\chi\\
&\quad = \mathit{truish}\,\epsilon_0 \rightarrow \mathit{truish}\,\epsilon_0 \rightarrow \mathcal{E}[\![\mathrm{E}_1]\!]\rho\kappa\sigma\chi, \mathcal{E}[\![\mathrm{E}_2]\!]\rho\kappa\sigma\chi, \mathcal{E}[\![\mathrm{E}_3]\!]\rho\kappa\sigma\chi\\
&\quad = \mathit{truish}\,\epsilon_0 \rightarrow \mathcal{E}[\![\mathrm{E}_1]\!]\rho\kappa\sigma\chi, \mathcal{E}[\![\mathrm{E}_3]\!]\rho\kappa\sigma\chi\\
&\quad = \mathcal{E}[\![\mathrm{E}_0]\!]\rho(\lambda\epsilon.\, \mathit{truish}\,\epsilon \rightarrow \mathcal{E}[\![\mathrm{E}_1]\!]\rho\kappa, \mathcal{E}[\![\mathrm{E}_3]\!]\rho\kappa)\sigma\chi\\
&\quad = \mathcal{E}[\![(\texttt{if}\ \mathrm{E}_0\ \mathrm{E}_1\ \mathrm{E}_3)]\!]\rho\kappa\sigma\chi
\end{aligned}$$

The proof of the other form of the rule is similar. ■

3.2.2. The `letrec` *Expression Merging Rule*

The correctness proof of this rule is interesting because it demonstrates the use of fixed points in a denotational semantics to prove something that would be difficult using an operational semantics.

The proof makes use of the following lemmas which are presented without proofs. The *extends* auxiliary function is similar to Scheme's except that it associates identifiers with expressed values instead of locations. Recall from [10, Appendix A] that *dropfirst s k* drops the first k elements of the sequence s (a mnemonic for $s \dagger k$), and *takefirst s k* produces a sequence consisting of the first k elements of the sequence s.

LEMMA 1 *If* $\mathrm{I}_0^* \S \mathrm{I}_1^*$ *is a sequence of distinct identifiers, then*

$$\mathit{extends}\,(\mathit{extends}\,\rho\,\mathrm{I}_0^*\,\epsilon_0^*)\,\mathrm{I}_1^*\,\epsilon_1^* = \mathit{extends}\,\rho\,(\mathrm{I}_0^* \S \mathrm{I}_1^*)\,(\epsilon_0^* \S \epsilon_1^*).$$

LEMMA 2

$$\begin{aligned}
&\mathcal{B}[\![\mathrm{B}_0\mathrm{B}_1]\!](\mathcal{I}[\![\mathrm{B}_0\mathrm{B}_1]\!])\rho\\
&\quad = \lambda\epsilon^*.\, \mathcal{B}[\![\mathrm{B}_0]\!](\mathcal{I}[\![\mathrm{B}_0]\!])\\
&\qquad\qquad (\mathit{extends}\ \rho\,(\mathcal{I}[\![\mathrm{B}_1]\!])\ (\mathit{dropfirst}\,\epsilon^*\ \#\mathrm{B}_0))\\
&\qquad\qquad (\mathit{takefirst}\,\epsilon^*\ \#\mathrm{B}_0)\\
&\qquad\ \S\ \mathcal{B}[\![\mathrm{B}_1]\!](\mathcal{I}[\![\mathrm{B}_1]\!])\\
&\qquad\qquad (\mathit{extends}\,\rho\,(\mathcal{I}[\![\mathrm{B}_0]\!])\ (\mathit{takefirst}\,\epsilon^*\ \#\mathrm{B}_0))\\
&\qquad\qquad (\mathit{dropfirst}\,\epsilon^*\ \#\mathrm{B}_0)
\end{aligned}$$

The following theorem shows that the `letrec` expression merging rule is meaning-refining:

THEOREM 3 *If* $\mathcal{I}[\![\mathrm{B}_0\mathrm{B}_1]\!]$ *is a sequence of distinct identifiers, then*

$$\mathcal{E}[\![\texttt{(letrec (}\mathrm{B}_0\texttt{) (letrec (}\mathrm{B}_1\texttt{) E))}]\!] = \mathcal{E}[\![\texttt{(letrec (}\mathrm{B}_0\ \mathrm{B}_1\texttt{) E)}]\!].$$

Proof:

$$\begin{aligned}\text{Let } f_0 &= \mathcal{B}[\![\mathrm{B}_0]\!](\mathcal{I}[\![\mathrm{B}_0]\!])\rho,\\ \rho' &= \mathit{extends}\,\rho\,(\mathcal{I}[\![\mathrm{B}_0]\!])(\mathit{fix}\ f_0),\\ f_1 &= \mathcal{B}[\![\mathrm{B}_1]\!](\mathcal{I}[\![\mathrm{B}_1]\!])\rho'.\end{aligned}$$

Then we have

$$\begin{aligned}&\mathcal{E}[\![\texttt{(letrec (}\mathrm{B}_0\texttt{) (letrec (}\mathrm{B}_1\texttt{) E))}]\!]\rho\kappa\sigma\chi\\ &= \mathcal{E}[\![\texttt{(letrec (}\mathrm{B}_1\texttt{) E)}]\!]\rho'\kappa\sigma\chi\\ &= \mathcal{E}[\![\mathrm{E}]\!](\mathit{extends}\,\rho'\,(\mathcal{I}[\![\mathrm{B}_1]\!])(\mathit{fix}\ f_1))\kappa\sigma\chi\end{aligned}$$

Because expressions are α-converted,

$$\begin{aligned}&\mathit{extends}\,\rho'\,(\mathcal{I}[\![\mathrm{B}_1]\!])\,(\mathit{fix}\ f_1)\\ &\quad= \mathit{extends}\,\rho\,(\mathcal{I}[\![\mathrm{B}_0\mathrm{B}_1]\!])\,(\mathit{fix}\ f_0\ \S\ \mathit{fix}\ f_1).\end{aligned}$$

Let $f_{01} = \mathcal{B}[\![\mathrm{B}_0\mathrm{B}_1]\!](\mathcal{I}[\![\mathrm{B}_0\mathrm{B}_1]\!])\rho$.

$$\begin{aligned}&\mathcal{E}[\![\texttt{(letrec (}\mathrm{B}_0\ \mathrm{B}_1\texttt{) E)}]\!]\rho\kappa\sigma\chi\\ &\quad= \mathcal{E}[\![\mathrm{E}]\!](\mathit{extends}\,\rho\,(\mathcal{I}[\![\mathrm{B}_0\mathrm{B}_1]\!])\,(\mathit{fix}\ f_{01}))\kappa\sigma\chi\end{aligned}$$

The proof is completed by showing $\mathit{fix}\ f_{01} = \mathit{fix}\ f_0\ \S\ \mathit{fix}\ f_1$.

$$\begin{aligned}f_{01} = \lambda\epsilon^*.\ &\mathcal{B}[\![\mathrm{B}_0]\!](\mathcal{I}[\![\mathrm{B}_0]\!])\\ &\qquad(\mathit{extends}\,\rho\,(\mathcal{I}[\![\mathrm{B}_1]\!])\,(\mathit{dropfirst}\,\epsilon^*\#\mathrm{B}_0))\\ &\qquad(\mathit{takefirst}\,\epsilon^*\#\mathrm{B}_0)\\ &\S\ \mathcal{B}[\![\mathrm{B}_1]\!](\mathcal{I}[\![\mathrm{B}_1]\!])\\ &\qquad(\mathit{extends}\,\rho\,(\mathcal{I}[\![\mathrm{B}_0]\!])\,(\mathit{takefirst}\,\epsilon^*\#\mathrm{B}_0))\\ &\qquad(\mathit{dropfirst}\,\epsilon^*\#\mathrm{B}_0)\\ = \lambda\epsilon^*.\ &\mathcal{B}[\![\mathrm{B}_0]\!](\mathcal{I}[\![\mathrm{B}_0]\!])\rho\,(\mathit{takefirst}\,\epsilon^*\#\mathrm{B}_0)\\ &\S\ \mathcal{B}[\![\mathrm{B}_1]\!](\mathcal{I}[\![\mathrm{B}_1]\!])\\ &\qquad(\mathit{extends}\,\rho\,(\mathcal{I}[\![\mathrm{B}_0]\!])\,(\mathit{takefirst}\,\epsilon^*\#\mathrm{B}_0))\\ &\qquad(\mathit{dropfirst}\,\epsilon^*\#\mathrm{B}_0)\\ = \lambda\epsilon^*.\ &f_0(\mathit{takefirst}\,\epsilon^*\#\mathrm{B}_0)\\ &\S\ \mathcal{B}[\![\mathrm{B}_1]\!](\mathcal{I}[\![\mathrm{B}_1]\!])\\ &\qquad(\mathit{extends}\,\rho\,(\mathcal{I}[\![\mathrm{B}_0]\!])\,(\mathit{takefirst}\,\epsilon^*\#\mathrm{B}_0))\\ &\qquad(\mathit{dropfirst}\,\epsilon^*\#\mathrm{B}_0)\end{aligned}$$

because no binding in B_0 references a variable bound by B_1.

Let $g = \lambda\epsilon^*.\, f_0(\mathit{takefirst}\,\epsilon^*\#\mathrm{B}_0)\ \S\ \mathit{dropfirst}\,\epsilon^*\#\mathrm{B}_0$. Superscripts will denote function iteration: $f^0 = \lambda\epsilon^*.\epsilon^*$ and $f^{n+1} = f \circ f^n$. Observe that $f_{01}^n(\mathit{fix}\ g) = \mathit{fix}\ f_0\ \S\ f_1^n\bot$, therefore, $\bigsqcup\{f_{01}^n(\mathit{fix}\ g)\} = \mathit{fix}\ f_0\ \S\ \mathit{fix}\ f_1$.

$\mathit{fix}\ f_0 \S \mathit{fix}\ f_1$ is a fixed point of f_{01} because

$$\begin{aligned} & f_{01}(\mathit{fix}\ f_0 \S \mathit{fix}\ f_1) \\ & = f_{01}(\bigsqcup\{f_{01}^n(\mathit{fix}\ g)\}) \\ & = \bigsqcup\{f_{01}^{n+1}(\mathit{fix}\ g)\} && \text{by continuity} \\ & = \bigsqcup\{f_{01}^n(\mathit{fix}\ g)\} && \text{as } \mathit{fix}\ g \sqsubseteq f_{01}(\mathit{fix}\ g) \\ & = \mathit{fix}\ f_0 \S \mathit{fix}\ f_1. \end{aligned}$$

$\mathit{fix}\ f_0 \S \mathit{fix}\ f_1$ is the least fixed point of f_{01} because, by construction, $g^m\bot \sqsubseteq f_{01}^m\bot$ so $f_{01}^n(g^m\bot) \sqsubseteq f_{01}^{m+n}\bot$.

$$\begin{aligned} & f_{01}^n(\mathit{fix}\ g) = f_{01}^n(\bigsqcup\{g^m\bot\}) = \bigsqcup\{f_{01}^n(g^m\bot)\} \\ & \quad \sqsubseteq \bigsqcup\{f_{01}^n(f_{01}^m\bot)\} = f_{01}^n(\mathit{fix}\ f_{01}) = \mathit{fix}\ f_{01} \end{aligned}$$

Therefore $f_{01}^n(\mathit{fix}\ g) \sqsubseteq \mathit{fix}\ f_{01}$ and $\mathit{fix}\ f_{01} = \mathit{fix}\ f_0 \S \mathit{fix}\ f_1$. ∎

3.3. Selection and Proof of Rules

The most significant contribution of the work on the Front End is the identification of a collection of transformation rules that can both be verified relative to the formal semantics of the source language, and can also form the basis of a practical optimizing compiler.

It is difficult to quantify the quality of the rule set implemented in the Front End. The Front End implements many of the rules used in successful compilers, and so its performance should be comparable. We studied the result of translating the VLISP Byte-Code Interpreter into Pure PreScheme and could identify no other plausible general transformation that would improve the code. The general nature of each implemented rule suggests the rule set should be useful for a wide range of VLISP PreScheme programs.

There were two distinct prototypes of the Front End before the final version was implemented. Early guesses of the form the transformation rules were quite naïve, because we tried to use rules designed for unverified compilers. The first prototype explored various rule sets. It also became apparent that the mechanism used in the prototype to control rule application would not scale so as to allow the compilation of a program as large as the VLISP Byte-Code Interpreter. The second prototype had the control mechanism nearly right and its rule set seemed to generate reasonable code. Attempts to prove the correctness of its rules failed miserably. The exercise led to changes in both the rules and VLISP PreScheme's semantics. For example, we had to split the β-conversion rule into two rules. The prototypes gave us extremely valuable information and made the identification of the final, finely tuned rule set possible. Our motto is prototype but verify!

There are several unverified aspects of the Front End. The algorithm used to translate VLISP PreScheme into Macro-Free PreScheme was not studied rigorously. The lack of rigor is of little concern because the process is clearly specified in the Scheme Report section on derived expression types [10, Section 7.4].

The most unsatisfying part of the Front End is the fact that the algorithms describing the control procedures are unverified. All parts of the Front End were written in a simple and direct style. We studiously avoided tricky or obscure coding practices, partially so that someone reading the code which applies transformation rules will easily conclude that the control procedures only cause changes to the program which are consistent with the set of rules, but there is no formal verification of this fact. Further work is needed to design a formalism that when given a rule set produces an efficient and verified rule application mechanism.

4. Compiler-Oriented Semantics

As discussed in Section 2, Pure PreScheme's semantics is inherited from the semantics of Macro-Free PreScheme. However, in order to justify the compiler presented in Section 5, we reframed the semantics to distinguish some special cases syntactically and split both the environment and the continuation into a compile-time and run-time components. We call this the *compiler semantics*.

The architecture of this semantics is motivated by a binding-time analysis of the semantics:

- The program is always compile-time data (that is, it is available at compile time).
- The environment is split into a symbol table γ (available at compile time), and a run-time environment or display μ (available at run-time).
- The continuation is also split into static (compile-time) and dynamic (run-time) components.
- The store σ and external state χ are always run-time data.

In addition, the compiler semantics introduces a data stack for the values of subexpressions. This stack is "partially static" in that its size is statically determinable, but its contents are dynamic.

The compiler semantics reorganizes these quantities so that all the static arguments are handled before all the dynamic ones. Thus the semantics can be thought of as taking all the compile-time data and producing a code-like object π that can be applied to the run-time data, including the local data stack (*cf* the discussion in [26, p. 253]).

In addition, the semantics distinguishes between simple expressions and tail-recursive expressions, following the grammar of Figure 7. An easy proof via structural induction shows that valuations of tail-recursive expressions always use the initial continuation κ_0, a fact exploited in the new semantics.

The compiler-oriented semantics also distinguishes commands (expressions executed only for effect) from expressions executed for their value. An easy proof via structural induction shows that valuations of commands always use a continuation which ignores its value. This separation allows the compiler to know that the value of a simple expression can be ignored. In principle, we could have preserved the semantic principle of "one non-terminal, one valuation" by creating a separate syntactic category for commands, but the programming principle of orthogonality ("a phrase should be usable anywhere it is meaningful") won out, since in Scheme in any (simple) expression can be evaluated for effect only.

As noted above, the new semantics relies on the usual division of environments into a compile-time and a run-time component. We introduce a new domain D_c of compile-time denotations (lexical addresses), and represent an environment ρ : Ide $\rightarrow D$ by a symbol table γ : Ide $\rightarrow D_c$ and a runtime environment $\mu : D_c \rightarrow D$ such that $\rho = (\mu \circ \gamma)$. We need to ensure that the run-time and compile-time extension functions behave consistently. The behavior of these functions must satisfy the following for any μ and γ:

$$\mathit{extends}\,(\mu \circ \gamma)\, \mathrm{I}^* \epsilon^* = (\mathit{extends}_{rl}\ \mu\, \epsilon^*) \circ (\mathit{extends}_{cl}\ \gamma\, \mathrm{I}^*)$$

with similar conditions for global variables.[1] Because the scoping structure of Pure PreScheme programs is very simple, our semantics uses integers for lexical addresses.

The domain of code-like objects π is

$$Q = U_r \rightarrow E^* \rightarrow S \rightarrow X \rightarrow A$$

where U_r is the domain of run-time environments (displays), E is the domain of expressed values, S is the domain of stores, X is the domain of external states, and A is the domain of answers. In general, the elements of Q will be built out of certain combinators, which we call *instructions*. The justification for this terminology will become evident in Section 5.

The compiler will be defined compositionally: that is, it will consist of a valuation for each non-terminal in the language, and these valuations will be defined by structural induction.

Our goal is to prove that the compiler oriented semantics is the same as the original, i.e., $\mathcal{CP}[\![\mathrm{P}]\!] = \mathcal{P}[\![\mathrm{P}]\!]$, by induction on the grammatical structure of P. This is feasible because both $\mathcal{P}$ and $\mathcal{CP}$ are defined compositionally, that is, by structural induction.

To do this, however, we will need to specify not only how the compiler behaves on entire programs, but how it behaves on phrases of each syntactic category in the language. For each non-terminal of the language, we need to write a formal specification showing the relation that must hold between the compiler-oriented valuation and the corresponding valuation in the original semantics. In each case, the relation specifies how the compiled code for phrases of that non-terminal behaves when executed. For example, consider the case of simple expressions. The compiler valuation for simple expressions will be specified by:

[1] For historical reasons, this semantics assumes that the identifiers have been partitioned into local and global identifiers. Global identifiers can only be used for defined variables, and local identifiers can only be used for `letrec` and `lambda` bound variables.

type: $\mathcal{CSE} : \text{Smpl} \to U_c \to Q \to Q$
specification: $(\mathcal{CSE}[\![S]\!]\gamma\pi)\mu\zeta = \mathcal{E}[\![S]\!](\mu \circ \gamma)(\lambda\epsilon.\, \pi\mu(\epsilon :: \zeta))$

Here $\mathcal{CSE}$ takes all the static arguments before all the dynamic arguments, as discussed above.

This specification says that the answer obtained by running a simple expression compiled using symbol table γ with code to follow π in runtime environment μ with runtime stack ζ should be the same as the semantics for that expression using composition of μ and γ for an environment with a continuation executing π in with the same runtime environment but with the result pushed onto the runtime stack.

We will write a similar specification for each non-terminal (or equivalently, for each valuation), and then give a definition for each valuation. The structural induction proof will establish that each valuation satisfies its specification. Thus the specifications like the one above also play the role of induction hypotheses for the proof. We will therefore refer to them interchangeably as specifications or induction hypotheses. We will present some sample cases of the proof in Section 4.7. The complete semantics and proof can be found in [19].

We next present some pieces used to construct the compiler oriented semantics, $\mathcal{CP}[\![P]\!]$. For each valuation we give the following data:

1. an informal specification of the valuation
2. the domain of the valuation
3. the induction hypothesis (formal specification) for the valuation
4. the rules for each production, and last
5. The semantics of typical instructions introduced in those rules

4.1. Simple Expressions

Compile Simple Expressions. Generates code that evaluates the expression and pushes the value onto the runtime stack.[2]

type: $\mathcal{CSE} : \text{Smpl} \to U_c \to Q \to Q$
specification: $(\mathcal{CSE}[\![S]\!]\gamma\pi)\mu\zeta = \mathcal{E}[\![S]\!](\mu \circ \gamma)(\lambda\epsilon.\, \pi\mu(\epsilon :: \zeta))$

This specification is explained above.

definition:
$\mathcal{CSE}[\![I]\!] = \lambda\gamma\pi.\, \mathit{fetch}_l\ (\gamma\, I)\ \pi$
$\mathcal{CSE}[\![(\texttt{if}\ S_0\ S_1\ S_2)]\!] = \lambda\gamma\pi.\, \mathcal{CSE}[\![S_0]\!]\gamma(\mathit{brf}(\mathcal{CSE}[\![S_1]\!]\gamma(\mathit{label}\ \pi))$

[2] The runtime stack in this semantics contains expressed values. The actual compiler allows environments as well [20]. The use of ζ instead of ϵ^* reminds us of the fact that the presentation has been simplified.

$$(\mathcal{CSE}[\![S_2]\!]\gamma(goto\ \pi)))$$
$$\mathcal{CSE}[\![(\texttt{set!}\ G\ S)]\!] = \lambda\gamma\pi.\,\mathcal{CSE}[\![S]\!]\gamma(update\text{-}store\ (\gamma\ G)\ \pi)$$
$$\mathcal{CSE}[\![(O\ S^*)]\!] = \lambda\gamma\pi.\,\mathcal{CSE}^*[\![S^*]\!]\gamma(prim\text{-}apply\ \#S^*\ \mathcal{O}[\![O]\!]\ \pi)$$

These clauses introduce six new instructions.

$$fetch_l : D_c \to Q \to Q$$
$$fetch_l = \lambda\iota\pi.\,\lambda\mu\zeta.(\mu\,\iota) \in E \to \pi\mu(((\mu\,\iota) \mid E) :: \zeta), (wrong\ \text{“Local variable given storage.”})$$

$$brf\colon Q \to Q \to Q$$
$$brf = \lambda\pi_0\pi_1\lambda\mu\zeta.\,truish((\zeta \downarrow 1)) \to (\pi_0\mu(\zeta \dagger 1)), (\pi_1\mu(\zeta \dagger 1))$$

$$label\colon Q \to Q$$
$$label = \lambda\pi\mu\zeta.\pi\mu\zeta$$

$$goto : Q \to Q$$
$$goto = \lambda\pi\mu\zeta.\pi\mu\zeta$$

The *label* and *goto* instructions are used as directives to the linearizer (Section 8).

$$update\text{-}store : D_c \to Q \to Q$$
$$update\text{-}store = \lambda\iota\pi.\,\lambda\mu\zeta.(\mu\,\iota) \in L \to (assign\ ((\mu\,\iota) \mid L)\ (\zeta \downarrow 1)\ (\pi\mu\zeta)), (wrong\ \text{“Can't assign to a local variable”})$$

$$prim\text{-}apply : N \to F \to Q \to Q$$
$$prim\text{-}apply = \lambda\nu\upsilon\pi.\,\lambda\mu\zeta.(apply\text{-}primitive\ \upsilon\ (takefirst\ \nu\ \zeta)\ (\lambda\epsilon.\,\pi\mu(\epsilon :: (dropfirst\ \nu\ \zeta))))$$

4.2. Simple Expression Sequences

Compile Simple Expression Sequences. Generates code that evaluates the sequence of simple expressions and pushes the sequence of values onto the runtime stack.

type: $\mathcal{CSE}^* : \mathrm{Smpl}^* \to U_c \to Q \to Q$
specification: $(\mathcal{CSE}^*[\![S^*]\!]\gamma\pi)\mu\zeta = \mathcal{E}^*[\![S^*]\!](\mu \circ \gamma)(\lambda\epsilon^*.\,\pi\mu(\epsilon^*\ \S\ \zeta))$

The induction hypothesis states that running simple expression sequences compiled using symbol table γ with code to follow π in runtime environment μ with runtime stack ζ is the same as the semantics using composition of μ and γ for an environment with a continuation executing π in with the same runtime environment but with the resulting values pushed onto the runtime stack.

$$\mathcal{CSE}^*[\![\,]\!] = \lambda\gamma\pi.\,\pi$$
$$\mathcal{CSE}^*[\![S\ S^*]\!] = \lambda\gamma\pi.\,\mathcal{CSE}[\![S]\!]\gamma(\mathcal{CSE}^*[\![S^*]\!]\gamma\pi)$$

4.3. Simple Commands

Compile Simple Commands. Generates code that evaluates the expression and but does not push the value onto the runtime stack.

type: $\mathcal{CSC} : \text{Smpl} \rightarrow U_c \rightarrow Q \rightarrow Q$
specification: $(\mathcal{CSC}[\![\text{S}]\!]\gamma\pi)\mu\zeta = \mathcal{E}[\![\text{S}]\!](\mu \circ \gamma)(\lambda\epsilon.\,\pi\mu\zeta)$

The induction hypothesis states that running simple commands compiled using symbol table γ with code to follow π in runtime environment μ with runtime stack ζ is the same as the semantics using composition of μ and γ for an environment with a continuation executing π with the same runtime environment and stack (i.e. the value is ignored).

definition:
$\mathcal{CSC}[\![\text{I}]\!] = \lambda\gamma\pi.\,\pi$
$\mathcal{CSC}[\![(\texttt{if}\ \text{S}_0\ \text{S}_1\ \text{S}_2)]\!] = \lambda\gamma\pi.\,\mathcal{CSE}[\![\text{S}_0]\!]\gamma(\mathit{brf}(\mathcal{CSC}[\![\text{S}_1]\!]\gamma\pi)\ (\mathcal{CSC}[\![\text{S}_2]\!]\gamma\pi))$
$\mathcal{CSC}[\![(\texttt{set!}\ \text{G}\ \text{S})]\!] = \lambda\gamma\pi.\,\mathcal{CSE}[\![\text{S}]\!]\gamma(\mathit{update\text{-}store}_i\ (\gamma\ \text{G})\ \pi)$
$\mathcal{CSC}[\![(\text{O}\ \text{S}^*)]\!] = \lambda\gamma\pi.\,\mathcal{CSE}^*[\![\text{S}^*]\!]\gamma(\mathit{prim\text{-}apply}_i\ \#S^*\ \mathcal{O}[\![\text{O}]\!]\ \pi)$

This valuation introduces two new instructions, *update-store*$_i$ and *prim-apply*$_i$, which are like their expression counterparts but do not push a value onto the runtime stack.

4.4. Tail-Recursive Expressions

Compile Tail-recursive Expressions. Generates code that evaluates the tail-recursive expression and pushes the value onto the runtime stack. As the expressions are tail-recursive, no static continuation is necessary for compilation.

type: $\mathcal{CT} : \text{Tail} \rightarrow U_c \rightarrow Q$
specification: $(\mathcal{CT}[\![\text{T}]\!]\gamma)\mu\langle\rangle = \mathcal{E}[\![\text{T}]\!](\mu \circ \gamma)\kappa_0$

The induction hypothesis states that running tail recursive expressions compiled using symbol table γ in runtime environment μ with an empty runtime stack is the same as the semantics using composition of μ and γ for an environment.

$\mathcal{CT}[\![\text{S}]\!] = \lambda\gamma.\,\mathcal{CSE}[\![\text{S}]\!]\gamma(\mathit{halt})$
$\mathcal{CT}[\![(\texttt{if}\ \text{S}\ \text{T}_0\ \text{T}_1)]\!] = \lambda\gamma.\,\mathcal{CSE}[\![\text{S}]\!]\gamma(\mathit{brf}(\mathcal{CT}[\![\text{T}_0]\!]\gamma)\ (\mathcal{CT}[\![\text{T}_1]\!]\gamma))$
$\mathcal{CT}[\![(\texttt{begin}\ \text{S}^*\ \text{T})]\!] = \lambda\gamma.\,\mathcal{CSC}^*[\![\text{S}^*]\!]\gamma(\mathcal{CT}[\![\text{T}]\!]\gamma)$
$\mathcal{CT}[\![((\texttt{lambda}\ (\text{I}^*)\ \text{T})\ \text{S}^*)]\!] = \lambda\gamma.\mathcal{CSE}^*[\![\text{S}^*]\!]\gamma$
$\qquad(\mathit{add\text{-}to\text{-}env}(\mathcal{CT}[\![\text{T}]\!](\mathit{extends}_{cl}\ \gamma\ \text{I}^*)))$
$\mathcal{CT}[\![(\text{S}\ \text{S}^*)]\!] = \lambda\gamma.\,\mathcal{CSE}^*[\![\text{S}^*]\!]\gamma(\mathcal{CSE}[\![\text{S}]\!]\gamma(\mathit{tail\text{-}call}))$

These clauses introduce three more new instructions, *halt*, *add-to-env*, and *tail-call*:

$halt : Q$
$halt = \lambda\mu\zeta.\,\kappa_0(\zeta \downarrow 1)$

$add\text{-}to\text{-}env : Q \rightarrow Q$
$add\text{-}to\text{-}env = \lambda\pi.\,\lambda\mu\zeta.\,\pi(extends_{rl}\,\mu\,\zeta)\langle\rangle$

$tail\text{-}call : Q$
$tail\text{-}call = \lambda\mu\zeta.\,(tail\text{-}apply\,(\zeta \downarrow 1)\,(\zeta \dagger 1))$

where *tail-apply* is defined by

$tail\text{-}apply : E \rightarrow E^* \rightarrow C$
$tail\text{-}apply = \lambda\epsilon\epsilon^*.\,\epsilon \in F \rightarrow (\epsilon \mid F)\epsilon^*\kappa_0,\ (wrong\ \text{“Non-function to apply”})$

4.5. Recursive Procedures

Compile Recursive Declarations. Takes a set of local procedure declarations and generates code that extends the run-time environment by making the indicated mutually-recursive declarations.

type: $\mathcal{CE} : \text{Exp} \rightarrow U_c \rightarrow Q$
specification:
$(\mathcal{CE}[\![(\texttt{letrec}\ (\text{B})\ \text{T})]\!]\gamma)\mu\langle\rangle = \mathcal{E}[\![(\texttt{letrec}\ (\text{B})\ \text{T})]\!](\mu \circ \gamma)\kappa_0$
definition:
$\mathcal{CE}[\![(\texttt{letrec}\ (\text{B})\ \text{T})]\!]\gamma = closerecs(\mathcal{CB}[\![\text{B}]\!](\mathcal{I}[\![\text{B}]\!])\gamma)(\mathcal{CT}[\![\text{T}]\!](extends_{cl}\,\gamma\,(\mathcal{I}[\![\text{B}]\!])))$

The induction hypothesis says that executing the code generated by the compiler is equivalent to executing the code for T in an appropriate recursively-extended environment.

The auxiliary valuation $\mathcal{CB}$ produces a sequence of code segments which will turn into the bodies of the procedures.

type: $\mathcal{CB} : \text{Bnd} \rightarrow \text{LocIde}^* \rightarrow U_c \rightarrow Q^*$
specification:
$closerecs(\mathcal{CB}[\![\text{B}]\!](\mathcal{I}[\![\text{B}]\!])\gamma)\pi\mu = \pi(extends_{rl}\,\mu(fix(\mathcal{B}[\![\text{B}]\!](\mathcal{I}[\![\text{B}]\!])(\mu \circ \gamma))))$
definition:
$\mathcal{CB}[\![\ ]\!] = \lambda\text{I}^*\gamma.\,\langle\rangle$
$\mathcal{CB}[\![(\text{I}\ (\texttt{lambda}(\text{I}^*)\ \text{T}))\ \text{B}]\!] =$
$\lambda\text{I}_0^*\gamma.\,\mathcal{CT}[\![\text{T}]\!](extends_{cl}(extends_{cl}\,\gamma\,\text{I}_0^*)\text{I}^*) :: (\mathcal{CB}[\![\text{B}]\!]\text{I}_0^*\gamma)$

This valuation introduces a single new instruction *closerecs*, defined by:

$closerecs\,\pi^*\pi = \lambda\mu\zeta.\,\pi(fix(\lambda\mu'.\,extends_{rl}\,\mu\,(map(close_r\,\mu')\pi^*)))\zeta$

where

$close_r = \lambda\mu\pi.\,(\lambda\epsilon^*.\,\pi(extends_{rl}\,\mu\,\epsilon^*)\langle\rangle)\ \text{in}\ E$

4.6. Programs

Takes an entire program and compiles it.

type: $\mathcal{CP} : \text{Pgm} \rightarrow Q$
specification: $\mathcal{CP}[\![\text{P}]\!] = \mathcal{P}[\![\text{P}]\!]$
definition:
$\mathcal{CP}[\![\text{P}]\!] = \mathcal{CD}[\![\text{P}]\!]\gamma_0$

where γ_0 has the property that $\rho_0 = (\mu_0 \circ \gamma_0)$, and $\mathcal{CD}$ is an auxiliary valuation that relates to the valuation $\mathcal{D}$:

type: $\mathcal{CD} : \text{Pgm} \rightarrow U_c \rightarrow Q$
specification: $(\mathcal{CD}[\![\text{P}]\!]\gamma)\mu\langle\rangle = \mathcal{D}[\![\text{P}]\!](\mu \circ \gamma)\kappa_0$
definition:
$\mathcal{CD}[\![\text{E}]\!]\gamma = \mathcal{CE}[\![\text{E}]\!]\gamma$
$\mathcal{CD}[\![(\texttt{define}\ \text{I})\ \text{P}]\!]\gamma = \textit{add-to-env}_g(\mathcal{CD}[\![\text{P}]\!](\textit{extends}_{cg}\,\gamma\text{I}))$

where $\textit{add-to-env}_g$ is an instruction similar to *add-to-env*, except that it uses $\textit{extends}_{rg}$ instead of $\textit{extends}_{rl}$.

4.7. Correctness of the Compiler-Oriented Semantics

The main statement of correctness of the compiler is:

THEOREM 4 (CORRECTNESS OF THE COMPILER ORIENTED SEMANTICS) *For any program* P*:*

1. $\mathcal{P}[\![\text{P}]\!] = \mathcal{CP}[\![\text{P}]\!]$
2. $(\mathcal{CD}[\![\text{P}]\!]\gamma)\mu\langle\rangle = \mathcal{D}[\![\text{P}]\!](\mu \circ \gamma)\kappa_0$

The first part of the theorem is the main result, but the second part is the one that is actually used in Theorem 6.

The proof is a tedious but straightforward structural induction, verifying each of the 13 simultaneous induction hypotheses, one for each function in the compiler. These are two clauses actually used in other proofs. There is one induction step for each clause in the definitions. Most of the induction steps are easy calculations: the only exceptions are the ones for recursive declarations. Here we include a few sample cases to illustrate the calculations. We show a few simple cases and the cases for recursive declarations in more detail.

We begin with two cases for simple expressions. The induction hypothesis to be verified is

specification:
$(\mathcal{CSE}[\![\text{S}]\!]\gamma\pi)\mu\zeta = \mathcal{E}[\![\text{S}]\!](\mu \circ \gamma)(\lambda\epsilon\,.\,\pi\mu(\epsilon :: \zeta))$

The following three cases are typical.

$(\mathcal{CSE}[\![\mathrm{I}]\!]\gamma\pi)\mu\zeta$
$=$ [by definition of $\mathcal{CSE}$]
$(\mathit{fetch}_l\,(\gamma\,\mathrm{I})\,\pi)\mu\zeta$
$=$ [by definition of fetch_l]
$((\mu\circ\gamma)\mathrm{I})\in E\rightarrow\pi\mu((((\mu\circ\gamma)\mathrm{I})\mid E)::\zeta),$
$\quad(\mathit{wrong}$ "Local variable given storage.")
$=$ [by definition of $\mathcal{E}$]
$\mathcal{E}[\![\mathrm{I}]\!](\mu\circ\gamma)(\lambda\epsilon.\,\pi\mu(\epsilon::\zeta))$

$(\mathcal{CSE}[\![(\texttt{if}\ \mathrm{S}_0\ \mathrm{S}_1\ \mathrm{S}_2)]\!]\gamma\pi)\mu\zeta$
$=$ [by definition of $\mathcal{CSE}$]
$(\mathcal{CSE}[\![\mathrm{S}_0]\!]\gamma(\mathit{brf}(\mathcal{CSE}[\![\mathrm{S}_1]\!]\gamma(\mathit{label}\,\pi))\ (\mathcal{CSE}[\![\mathrm{S}_2]\!]\gamma(\mathit{goto}\ \pi))))\mu\zeta$
$=$ [by induction hypothesis at S_0]
$\mathcal{E}[\![\mathrm{S}_0]\!](\mu\circ\gamma)(\lambda\epsilon.\,(\mathit{brf}(\mathcal{CSE}[\![\mathrm{S}_1]\!]\gamma(\mathit{label}\ \pi))\ (\mathcal{CSE}[\![\mathrm{S}_2]\!]\gamma(\mathit{goto}\ \pi)))\mu(\epsilon::\zeta))$
$=$ [by definitions of brf, label, goto]
$\mathcal{E}[\![\mathrm{S}_0]\!](\mu\circ\gamma)(\lambda\epsilon.\,(\mathit{truish}(\epsilon)\rightarrow((\mathcal{CSE}[\![\mathrm{S}_1]\!]\gamma\pi)\mu\zeta),$
$\quad((\mathcal{CSE}[\![\mathrm{S}_2]\!]\gamma\pi)\mu\zeta)))$
$=$ [by induction hypothesis at S_1, S_2]
$\mathcal{E}[\![\mathrm{S}_0]\!](\mu\circ\gamma)(\lambda\epsilon.\,(\mathit{truish}(\epsilon)\rightarrow\mathcal{E}[\![\mathrm{S}_1]\!](\mu\circ\gamma)(\lambda\epsilon.\,\pi\mu(\epsilon::\gamma))$
$\quad\mathcal{E}[\![\mathrm{S}_2]\!](\mu\circ\gamma)(\lambda\epsilon.\,\pi\mu(\epsilon::\zeta))))$
$=$ [by definition of $\mathcal{E}$]
$\mathcal{E}[\![(\texttt{if}\ \mathrm{S}_0\ \mathrm{S}_1\ \mathrm{S}_2)]\!](\mu\circ\gamma)(\lambda\epsilon.\,\pi\mu(\epsilon::\zeta))$

$(\mathcal{CSE}[\![(\texttt{set!}\ \mathrm{G}\ \mathrm{S})]\!]\gamma\pi)\mu\zeta$
$=$ [by definition of $\mathcal{CSE}$]
$(\mathcal{CSE}[\![\mathrm{S}]\!]\gamma(\mathit{update\text{-}store}\,(\gamma\,\mathrm{G})\,\pi))\mu\zeta$
$=$ [by induction hypothesis at S]
$\mathcal{E}[\![\mathrm{S}]\!](\mu\circ\gamma)(\lambda\epsilon.\,(\mathit{update\text{-}store}\,(\gamma\,\mathrm{G})\,\pi)\mu(\epsilon::\zeta))$
$=$ [by definition of $\mathit{update\text{-}store}$]
$\mathcal{E}[\![\mathrm{S}]\!](\mu\circ\gamma)(\lambda\epsilon.\,((\mu\circ\gamma)\mathrm{G})\in L\rightarrow(\mathit{assign}\,(((\mu\circ\gamma)\mathrm{G})\mid L)\,\epsilon\,(\pi\mu(\epsilon::\zeta))),$
$\quad(\mathit{wrong}$ "Can't assign to a local variable"))
$=$ [by definition of $\mathcal{E}$]
$\mathcal{E}[\![(\texttt{set!}\ \mathrm{G}\ \mathrm{S})]\!](\mu\circ\gamma)(\lambda\epsilon.\,\pi\mu(\epsilon::\zeta))$

Several valuations recur on sequences of syntactic elements; $\mathcal{CSE}^*$ is typical. The induction hypothesis is

specification:
$(\mathcal{CSE}^*[\![\mathrm{S}^*]\!]\gamma\pi)\mu\zeta=\mathcal{E}^*[\![\mathrm{S}^*]\!](\mu\circ\gamma)(\lambda\epsilon^*.\,\pi\mu(\epsilon^*\,\S\,\zeta))$

There are two productions (clauses), which are proved as follows:

$(\mathcal{CSE}^*[\![\ ]\!]\gamma\pi)\mu\zeta$

$=$ [by definition of $\mathcal{CSE}^*$]
$\pi\mu\zeta$
$=$ [by definition of $\mathcal{E}^*$]
$\mathcal{E}^*[\![\ ]\!](\mu \circ \gamma)(\lambda\epsilon^*.\, \pi\mu(\epsilon^* \S \zeta))$

$(\mathcal{CSE}^*[\![\mathrm{S}\ \mathrm{S}^*]\!]\gamma\pi)\mu\zeta$
$=$ [by definition of $\mathcal{CSE}^*$]
$(\mathcal{CSE}[\![\mathrm{S}]\!]\gamma(\mathcal{CSE}^*[\![\mathrm{S}^*]\!]\gamma\pi))\mu\zeta$
$=$ [by induction hypothesis at S]
$\mathcal{E}[\![\mathrm{S}]\!](\mu \circ \gamma)(\lambda\epsilon.\, (\mathcal{CSE}^*[\![\mathrm{S}^*]\!]\gamma\pi)\mu(\epsilon :: \zeta))$
$=$ [by induction hypothesis at S^*]
$\mathcal{E}[\![\mathrm{S}]\!](\mu \circ \gamma)(\lambda\epsilon.\, \mathcal{E}^*[\![\mathrm{S}^*]\!](\mu \circ \gamma)(\lambda\epsilon^*.\, \pi\mu(\epsilon^* \S (\epsilon :: \zeta))))$
$=$ [by definition of $\mathcal{E}^*$]
$\mathcal{E}^*[\![\mathrm{S}\ \mathrm{S}^*]\!](\mu \circ \gamma)(\lambda\epsilon^*.\, \pi\mu(\epsilon^* \S \zeta))$

The only difficult proof is the one for recursive procedure declarations. The induction hypothesis is

specification:
$closerecs(\mathcal{CB}[\![\mathrm{B}]\!](\mathcal{I}[\![\mathrm{B}]\!])\gamma)\pi\mu = \pi(extends_{rl}\, \mu(fix(\mathcal{B}[\![\mathrm{B}]\!](\mathcal{I}[\![\mathrm{B}]\!])(\mu \circ \gamma))))$

This calculation is complicated by the necessity to reason both about sequences of values and about fixed points. To simplify this calculation, we write $\langle e \ldots \rangle$ for a sequence of values whose typical element is given by e, and "X… " for a sequence of syntactic elements whose typical element is given by X.

To verify the induction hypothesis, let

$$\begin{aligned} \mathrm{B} &= (\mathrm{I}\ (\texttt{lambda}\ (\mathrm{I}^*)\ \mathrm{T}))\ldots \\ \mathrm{I}_0^* &= \mathcal{I}[\![\mathrm{B}]\!] \\ \gamma' &= extends_{cl}\, \gamma \mathrm{I}_0^* \end{aligned}$$

Then, calculating from the left-hand side of the induction hypothesis, we get:

$closerecs(\mathcal{CB}[\![\mathrm{B}]\!]\mathrm{I}_0^*\gamma)\pi\mu$
$=$ [by definition of $closerecs$]
$\pi(fix(\lambda\mu'.\, extends_{rl}\, \mu(map\ (close_{\ r}\ \mu')(\mathcal{CB}[\![\mathrm{B}]\!]\mathrm{I}_0^*\gamma))))$
$=$ [by definition of $\mathcal{CB}$]
$\pi(fix(\lambda\mu'.\, extends_{rl}\, \mu(map\ (close_{\ r}\ \mu')\langle\mathcal{CT}[\![\mathrm{T}]\!](extends_{cl}\, \gamma'\mathrm{I}^*)\ldots\rangle)))$
$=$ [by definition of map and $close_{\ r}$]
$\pi(fix(\lambda\mu'.\, extends_{rl}\, \mu\langle(\lambda\epsilon^*.\, \mathcal{CT}[\![\mathrm{T}]\!](extends_{cl}\, \gamma'\mathrm{I}^*) \circ (extends_{rl}\, \mu'\epsilon^*)\langle\rangle)\ \mathrm{in}\ E$
$\ldots\rangle))$
$=$ [by induction hypothesis at T]
$\pi(fix(\lambda\mu'.\, extends_{rl}\, \mu\langle(\lambda\epsilon^*.\, \mathcal{E}[\![\mathrm{T}]\!]((extends_{cl}\, \gamma'\mathrm{I}^*) \circ (extends_{rl}\, \mu'\epsilon^*))\kappa_0)\ \mathrm{in}\ E$
$\ldots\rangle))$
$=$ [by consistency of $extends_{rl}$, $extends_{cl}$]
$\pi(fix(\lambda\mu'.\, extends_{rl}\, \mu\langle(\lambda\epsilon^*.\, \mathcal{E}[\![\mathrm{T}]\!](extends(\mu' \circ \gamma')\mathrm{I}^*\epsilon^*)\kappa_0)\ \mathrm{in}\ E\ldots\rangle))$
$=$ [by definition of $\mathcal{L}$]
$\pi(fix(\lambda\mu'.\, extends_{rl}\, \mu\langle\mathcal{L}[\![(\texttt{lambda}\ (\mathrm{I}^*)\ \mathrm{T})]\!](\mu' \circ \gamma')\ldots\rangle))$

Working from the right-hand side, we calculate:

$\pi(\mathit{extends}_{rl}\ \mu(\mathit{fix}(\mathcal{B}[\![\mathrm{B}]\!]\mathrm{I}_0^*(\mu \circ \gamma))))$
$=$ [by definition of $\mathcal{B}$]
$\pi(\mathit{extends}_{rl}\ \mu(\mathit{fix}(\lambda\epsilon^*.\ \langle\mathcal{L}[\![\texttt{(lambda}\ (\mathrm{I}^*)\ \mathrm{T})]\!](\mathit{extends}(\mu \circ \gamma)\mathrm{I}_0^*\epsilon^*)\ldots\rangle)))$

Let $f = \lambda\mu'.\ \mathit{extends}_{rl}\ \mu\langle\mathcal{L}[\![\texttt{(lambda}\ (\mathrm{I}^*)\ \mathrm{T})]\!](\mu' \circ \gamma')\ldots\rangle$
and $g = \lambda\epsilon^*.\ \langle\mathcal{L}[\![\texttt{(lambda}\ (\mathrm{I}^*)\ \mathrm{T})]\!](\mathit{extends}\,(\mu \circ \gamma)\mathrm{I}_0^*\epsilon^*)\ldots\rangle$

The theorem is proved once we show that:

$$\mathit{fix}\, f = \mathit{extends}_{rl}\ \mu\,(\mathit{fix}\, g)$$

The right-hand side is a fixed point of f because:

$$\begin{aligned} f(\mathit{extends}_{rl}\ \mu\,\epsilon^*) &= \mathit{extends}_{rl}\ \mu\,(g\epsilon^*) && \text{[by substitution]} \\ f(\mathit{extends}_{rl}\ \mu\,(\mathit{fix}\, g)) &= \mathit{extends}_{rl}\ \mu\,(g(\mathit{fix}\, g)) && \text{[by use of previous line]} \\ &= \mathit{extends}_{rl}\ \mu\,(\mathit{fix}\, g) \end{aligned}$$

The right-hand side is a least fixed point of f because:

$$\mathit{extends}_{rl}\ \mu\,(g^n \bot) \sqsubseteq f^{n+1} \bot$$

The proof is by induction on n.

$$\begin{aligned} \mathit{extends}_{rl}\ \mu\,(g^0 \bot) &= \mathit{extends}_{rl}\ \mu\, \bot \\ &\sqsubseteq \mathit{extends}_{rl}\ \mu\,\langle\mathcal{L}[\![\texttt{(lambda}\ (\mathrm{I}^*)\ \mathrm{T})]\!](\bot \circ \gamma')\ldots\rangle \\ &= f^1 \bot \end{aligned}$$

$$\begin{aligned} \mathit{extends}_{rl}\ \mu\,(g^{n+1} \bot) &= \mathit{extends}_{rl}\ \mu\,(g(g^n \bot)) \\ &= f(\mathit{extends}_{rl}\ \mu\,(g^n \bot)) \\ &\sqsubseteq f(f^{n+1} \bot) && \text{[by induction hypothesis]} \\ &= f^{n+2} \bot \end{aligned}$$

5. The Combinator Machine and the Compiler

5.1. The Combinator Machine

The combinator machine manipulates tuples of rational trees. Rational (or regular) trees [6] are finite or infinite trees that have only finitely many distinct subtrees. Such a tree can always be represented as a finite graph that unwinds to a possibly-infinite tree.

A machine state is a 4-tuple $\langle q, u, z, h\rangle$, where q is the code which operates on a runtime environment, u, a stack of stackable values, z, and a heap h. A portion of the grammar for permissible states $\langle q, u, z, h\rangle$ is shown in Figure 15. The combinator machine has a total of 20 instructions, of which 15 are shown.[3] The permissible states of the machine are those configurations $\langle q, u, z, h\rangle$ where q, u, z, and h are elements of the greatest fixed point defined by the operators of the grammar. The only infinite trees that arise during execution, however, are those generated for recursive environments, and these trees are rational.

The stack z consists of a list of stackable values v. These values are procedures (closed in the representation u_0 of a global environment, to be described later), environments, vectors, and other values, which we call *immediate* values. Immediate values are values that we conceive as fitting in a machine word: integers, booleans, characters, strings, L-values, and ports. Strings are treated with the immediates because they are immutable; mutable strings would have been treated like vectors. L-values a (addresses, or pointers into the store) are tagged integers.

The heap h represents both the store σ and the external state χ in the semantics. Since these components are only rarely manipulated in the subsequent proofs, it is convenient to represent them together. The store is represented as a pair consisting of a map from heap pointers (as above) to immediate values, and an integer representing a free-location counter. The external state χ is represented by an unspecified third element x. We use the notation $h.1$, $h.2$, and $h.3$ for the three components.

Non-bottom elements n of the answer domain A are represented as $\langle \mathbf{ok}, n\rangle$. $\langle \mathbf{error}\rangle$ denotes the bottom element $\perp_A$ of A.

The operational semantics of each machine instruction is shown in Figure 16. The machine halts normally by executing a *halt* instruction, returning the value $\langle \mathbf{ok}, n\rangle$ for some integer n. The last rule in Figure 16 specifies that if the machine state does not match any of the preceding left-hand sides, then the machine goes into an error state and halts, returning the value $\langle \mathbf{error}\rangle$. `fix` builds an infinite rational tree with a loop in it. For example, if $t = \mathtt{fix}(\lambda u.\ \mathit{extends}_{rg}\, ua)$, then t is a tree such that $t = \mathit{extends}_{rg}\, ta$. It is easy to see that there is exactly one infinite tree that has this property, namely the one generated by the finite graph in which the left subtree of the $\mathit{extends}_{rg}$ loops back to the top of the tree [6]. The auxiliary `lookup` is an operation on syntax trees that simulates environment lookup. `truish` is a test on rational trees, simulating the operator *truish* of [10, Appendix A]. `apply-prim` handles the application of primitive procedures p.

Each set of terms manipulated has an analogous domain in the compiler oriented semantics for Pure PreScheme. The relation between syntactic and denotational variables is shown in Figure 17. Each set also has a natural valuation motivated by the form of the equations of the compiler oriented semantics. Some sample clauses of these valuations are:

$\mathcal{U}[\![\mathit{emptydisplay}]\!] = \mu_0$ the initial runtime environment

$$\mathcal{Q}[\![(\mathit{brf}\ q_0\ q_1)]\!] = \lambda\mu\zeta.\ \mathit{truish}((\zeta \downarrow 1)) \rightarrow \mathcal{Q}[\![q_0]\!]\mu(\zeta \dagger 1),\ \mathcal{Q}[\![q_1]\!]\mu(\zeta \dagger 1)$$

[3]The five omitted instructions are: *constant*, fetch_g, $\mathit{restore\text{-}env}_i$, a single-argument version of *add-to-env*, and a multi-way branch. None of these instructions cause any new problems.

$$
\begin{array}{rcll}
q & ::= & (\mathit{halt}) \mid (\mathit{goto}\ q) \mid (\mathit{label}\ q) & \text{code} \\
& \mid & (\mathit{fetch}_l\ i\, q) \mid (\mathit{brf}\ q_1\, q_2) & \\
& \mid & (\mathit{save\text{-}env}\ q) \mid (\mathit{restore\text{-}env}\ q) & \\
& \mid & (\mathit{update\text{-}store}\ i\, q) \mid (\mathit{prim\text{-}apply}\, n\, p\, q) & \\
& \mid & (\mathit{update\text{-}store}_i\ i\, q) \mid (\mathit{prim\text{-}apply}_i\ n\, p\, q) & \\
& \mid & (\mathit{add\text{-}to\text{-}env}\ n\, q) \mid (\mathit{add\text{-}to\text{-}env}_g\ q) & \\
& \mid & (\mathit{closerecs}(q_1 \ldots q_n)\, q) \mid (\mathit{tail\text{-}call}) & \\
\\
u & ::= & \mathit{emptydisplay} & \text{run-time} \\
& & & \text{environments} \\
& \mid & (\mathit{extends}_{rl}\, u\, (v_1 \ldots v_n)) & \\
& \mid & (\mathit{extends}_{rg}\ ua) & \\
\\
z & ::= & v^* & \text{stacks} \\
\\
v & ::= & i \mid \langle \mathbf{proc}, \langle q, u \rangle\rangle \mid \langle \mathbf{env}, u \rangle & \text{stackable values} \\
& \mid & \langle \mathbf{vector}, a_1, \ldots, a_n \rangle & \\
\\
i & ::= & \langle \mathbf{int}, n \rangle \mid \langle \mathbf{bool}, b \rangle & \text{immediate values} \\
& \mid & \langle \mathbf{char}, c \rangle \mid \langle \mathbf{string}, s \rangle \mid a \mid \langle \mathbf{port}, p \rangle & \\
\\
a & ::= & \langle \mathbf{hptr}, n \rangle & \text{L-values} \\
\\
h & ::= & \langle \phi, n, x \rangle & \text{heaps} \\
\\
\phi & \in & a \rightarrow v & \\
\\
\mathit{ans} & ::= & \langle \mathbf{ok}, n \rangle \mid \langle \mathbf{error} \rangle & \text{answers}
\end{array}
$$

Figure 15. Grammar for states of the combinator machine

$$
\begin{array}{ll}
\langle (\mathit{halt}), u, (\langle \mathbf{int}, n\rangle) :: z), h\rangle & \Longrightarrow \langle \mathbf{ok}, n\rangle \\
\langle (\mathit{goto}\ q), u, z, h\rangle & \Longrightarrow \langle q, u, z, h\rangle \\
\langle (\mathit{label}\ q), u, z, h\rangle & \Longrightarrow \langle q, u, z, h\rangle \\
\langle (\mathit{fetch}_l\ i\, q), u, z, h\rangle & \Longrightarrow \langle q, u, ((\mathtt{lookup}\ u\, i) :: z), h\rangle \\
\langle (\mathit{brf}\ q_0\, q_1), u, (v :: z), h\rangle & \Longrightarrow \langle (\mathtt{truish}(v) \rightarrow q_0, q_1), u, z, h\rangle \\
\langle (\mathit{save\text{-}env}\ q), u, z, h\rangle & \Longrightarrow \langle q, u, (\langle \mathbf{env}, u\rangle :: z), h\rangle \\
\langle (\mathit{restore\text{-}env}\ q), u, z, h\rangle & \Longrightarrow \langle q, u', (v :: z'), h\rangle \\
\quad \text{where } z = (v :: \langle \mathbf{env}, u'\rangle :: z') & \\
\langle (\mathit{update\text{-}store}\ i\, q), u, (v :: z), h\rangle & \Longrightarrow \langle q, u, (v :: z), (\mathtt{update}\,(\mathtt{lookup}\ u\, i)\, v\, h)\rangle \\
\langle (\mathit{prim\text{-}apply}\ n\, p\, q), u, z, h\rangle & \Longrightarrow \langle q, u, (w_1 :: z'), h_1\rangle \\
\quad \text{where } z = (v_1 :: \ldots :: v_n :: z') & \\
\quad \text{and } (w_1, h_1) = (\mathtt{apply\text{-}prim}\ p(v_1 \ldots v_n) h) & \\
\langle (\mathit{add\text{-}to\text{-}env}\ n\, q), u, z, h\rangle & \Longrightarrow \langle q, (\mathit{extends}_{rl}\ u\,(v_1 \ldots v_n)), z', h\rangle \\
\quad \text{where } z = (v_1 :: \ldots :: v_n :: z') & \\
\langle (\mathit{add\text{-}to\text{-}env}_g\ q), u, (v :: z), h\rangle & \Longrightarrow \\
\quad \langle q, (\mathit{extends}_{rg}\ u\,(\mathtt{new}\ h)), z, (\mathtt{update}\,(\mathtt{new}\ h)\, v\, h)\rangle & \\
\langle (\mathit{closerecs}\,(q_1 \ldots q_n)\, q), u, z, h\rangle & \Longrightarrow \\
\quad \langle q, (\mathtt{fix}\,(\lambda u'.\,(\mathit{extends}_{rl}\ u\,(\langle \mathbf{proc}, \langle q_1, u'\rangle\rangle \ldots \langle \mathbf{proc}, \langle q_n, u'\rangle\rangle)))), z, h\rangle & \\
\langle (\mathit{tail\text{-}call}), u, z_1, h\rangle & \Longrightarrow \langle q, (\mathit{extends}_{rl}\ u_1\,(v_1 \ldots v_n)), \langle\rangle, h\rangle \\
\quad \text{where } z_1 = (\langle \mathbf{proc}, \langle q, u_1\rangle\rangle :: v_1 :: \ldots :: v_n :: \langle\rangle) & \\
\text{otherwise} & \Longrightarrow \langle \mathbf{error}\rangle
\end{array}
$$

Auxiliaries:

$$
\mathtt{lookup}\,(\mathit{extends}_{rl}\ u(v_0 \ldots v_{n-1}))\,(i) = \begin{cases} v_i & 0 \leq i < n \\ \mathtt{lookup}\ u(i-n) & n \leq i \end{cases}
$$

$$\mathtt{lookup}\,(\mathit{extends}_{rg}\ u\, a)\,(0) = a$$

$$\mathtt{lookup}\,(\mathit{extends}_{rg}\ u\, a)\,(i+1) = \mathtt{lookup}\ u\, i$$

$\mathtt{lookup}\ \mathit{emptydisplay}\ i$ is an error

Figure 16. Operational Semantics of the Combinator Machine

Syntactic	Denotational	Description
v	ϵ	expressed value
q	π	code sequence
u	μ	runtime environment
z	ζ	stack
h	σ, χ	store and external state
i	ι	global variable reference
a	α	location
g	γ	symbol table

Figure 17. Analogous syntactic and denotational variables

$$\mathcal{V}[\![\langle \mathbf{proc}, \langle q, u \rangle \rangle]\!] = \lambda \epsilon^* . \, \mathcal{Q}[\![q]\!](\mathit{extends}_{rl}(\mathcal{U}[\![u]\!])\epsilon^*) \text{ in } E$$

$$\mathcal{A}[\![\langle \mathbf{ok}, n \rangle]\!] = n$$
$$\mathcal{A}[\![\langle \mathbf{error} \rangle]\!] = \bot_A$$

The semantics for machine states is given by

$$\mathcal{M}[\![\langle q, u, z, h \rangle]\!] = (\mathcal{Q}[\![q]\!])(\mathcal{U}[\![u]\!])(\mathcal{Z}[\![z]\!])(\mathcal{S}[\![h.1, h.2]\!])(\mathcal{X}[\![h.3]\!])$$

We have given these valuations as if they were for finite trees. To accommodate infinite trees, we actually define a sequence of approximate valuations; for example, we write

$$\mathcal{V}_0 \, [\![v]\!] = \bot$$
$$\mathcal{V}_{n+1} \, [\![\langle \mathbf{proc}, \langle q, u \rangle \rangle]\!] = \lambda \epsilon^* . \, \mathcal{Q}_n \, [\![q]\!](\mathit{extends}_{rl}(\mathcal{U}_n \, [\![u]\!])\epsilon^*) \text{ in } E$$

Given the valuations, the transitions of the machine were derived by performing β-conversion on the terms used in the compiler oriented valuations. The *brf* rule is derived by simple calculations:

$$\mathcal{M}[\![\langle (\mathit{brf} \, q_0 \, q_1), u, (v :: z), h \rangle]\!]$$
$$= \quad [\text{by definition of } \mathcal{M}]$$
$$\mathcal{Q}[\![(\mathit{brf} \, q_0 \, q_1)]\!](\mathcal{U}[\![u]\!])(\mathcal{Z}[\![(v :: z)]\!])(\mathcal{H}[\![h]\!])$$
$$= \quad [\text{by definition of } \mathcal{Z}]$$
$$\mathcal{Q}[\![(\mathit{brf} \, q_0 \, q_1)]\!](\mathcal{U}[\![u]\!])(\mathcal{V}[\![v]\!] :: \mathcal{Z}[\![z]\!])(\mathcal{H}[\![h]\!])$$
$$= \quad [\text{by definition of } \mathcal{Q} \text{ and } \mathit{brf}]$$
$$\mathit{truish}(\mathcal{V}[\![v]\!]) \rightarrow \mathcal{Q}[\![q_0]\!](\mathcal{U}[\![u]\!])(\mathcal{Z}[\![z]\!])(\mathcal{H}[\![h]\!]), \mathcal{Q}[\![q_1]\!](\mathcal{U}[\![u]\!])(\mathcal{Z}[\![z]\!])(\mathcal{H}[\![h]\!])$$
$$= \quad [\text{by definition of } \mathtt{truish}]$$
$$\mathtt{truish}(v) \rightarrow \mathcal{Q}[\![q_0]\!](\mathcal{U}[\![u]\!])(\mathcal{Z}[\![z]\!])(\mathcal{H}[\![h]\!]), \mathcal{Q}[\![q_1]\!](\mathcal{U}[\![u]\!])(\mathcal{Z}[\![z]\!])(\mathcal{H}[\![h]\!])$$
$$= (\mathtt{truish}(v) \rightarrow \mathcal{Q}[\![q_0]\!], \mathcal{Q}[\![q_0]\!]) \, (\mathcal{U}[\![u]\!]) \, (\mathcal{Z}[\![z]\!]) \, (\mathcal{H}[\![h]\!])$$

$= \mathcal{Q}[\![\texttt{truish}(v) \rightarrow q_0,\, q_1]\!](\mathcal{U}[\![u]\!])(\mathcal{Z}[\![z]\!])(\mathcal{H}[\![h]\!])$
$= \mathcal{M}[\![\langle(\texttt{truish}(v) \rightarrow q_0,\, q_1), u, z, h\rangle]\!]$

Observe that the reduction semantics of the instructions in the compiler oriented semantics determine the transitions of the combinator machine. One could regard each instruction as a combinator, so that each transition corresponds to the reduction of one combinator. This interpretation of the machine gives it its name.

The soundness of the machine can be stated as follows:

THEOREM 5 (SOUNDNESS OF THE COMBINATOR MACHINE)
If $\langle q, u, z, h\rangle \Longrightarrow \langle q', u', z', h'\rangle$*, then* $\mathcal{M}[\![\langle q, u, z, h\rangle]\!] = \mathcal{M}[\![\langle q', u', z', h'\rangle]\!]$.
If $\langle q, u, z, h\rangle \Longrightarrow ans$*, then* $\mathcal{M}[\![\langle q, u, z, h\rangle]\!] = \mathcal{A}[\![ans]\!]$

Proof: By calculation for each transition in Figure 16. In the case of a *closerecs*, we unwind the fixed-point one time to see that u' is a legal runtime environment. The valuation $\mathcal{Q}$ is carefully written to check the length of the stack and the tags of the operands so that the error transition is sound. ■

5.2. The Combinator-Code Compiler

The Pure PreScheme compiler cp is similar to the compiler oriented semantics except the compiler produces syntax rather than a denotation. For each program p, we want to produce a piece of combinator code q such that $\mathcal{CP}[\![p]\!] = \mathcal{Q}[\![q]\!]$. This can be done easily by replacing each clause in the definition of $\mathcal{CP}$ by an analogous constructor for q. For example, the analog of $\mathcal{CSE}$ is `cse`. For the case of a primitive application we have

$$\mathcal{CSE}[\![(\mathrm{O}\ \mathrm{S}^*)]\!] = \lambda\gamma\pi.\, \mathcal{CSE}^*[\![\mathrm{S}^*]\!]\gamma(\textit{prim-apply}\ \#\mathrm{S}^*\ \mathcal{O}[\![\mathrm{O}]\!]\ \pi)$$

in the compiler-oriented semantics, so we define

$$\texttt{cse}\,[\![(\mathrm{O}\ \mathrm{S}^*)]\!]gq = \texttt{cse}^*[\![\mathrm{S}^*]\!]g(\textit{prim-apply}\ \#\mathrm{S}^*\ \mathrm{O}\, q)$$

where in the latter, $(\textit{prim-apply}\ \#\mathrm{S}^*\ \mathrm{O}\, q)$ represents the construction of a combinator, a piece of syntax rather than a denotation.

In practice, Scheme program text defined `cse`. For example, we could write

```
(define cse
  (lambda (exp symtab q)
    (record-case exp
      (primapply (op s*)
        (cse* s* symtab
          (prim-apply (length s*) (meaning-of-primop op) q)))
      ...)))
```

This Scheme code could be used to simulate $\mathcal{CSE}$ by defining, following Section 4,

```
(define prim-apply
  (lambda (n primop q)
    (lambda (mu zeta)
      (apply-primitive primop (take-first n zeta)
        (lambda (epsilon)
          (q mu (cons epsilon (drop-first n zeta))))))))
```

or it could be used as part of the definition of `cse` by defining

```
(define prim-apply
  (lambda (n primop q)
    (list 'prim-apply n primop q)))
```

which emits a representation of a *prim-apply* instruction. With these conventions, it is easy to show that $\mathcal{CP} = (\mathcal{Q} \circ \mathtt{cp})$.

The syntactic structure of Pure PreScheme programs allows us to characterize the structure of a compiled program $\mathtt{cp}\,[\![\mathrm{P}]\!]$. Every compiled program consists of a prelude that allocates globals with a sequence of $\textit{add-to-env}_g$ instructions, followed by a *closerecs* instruction that creates all the procedures. This prelude is followed by the code for the body of the program. The effect of the prelude is to create an environment u_0 in which all the global procedures are closed.

We can now give a summary of how we run a program. Given a program P, we compile it to get $\mathtt{cp}\,[\![\mathrm{P}]\!]$. Given an initial external state χ, we run the compiled program by starting the machine in a state $\langle \mathtt{cp}\,[\![\mathrm{P}]\!], \textit{emptydisplay}, \langle\rangle, h_0(\chi)\rangle$, where h_0 is a function that creates a suitably initialized heap h where $h.3$ denotes χ.

Our results so far can be summarized as follows:

THEOREM 6 *For any program* P, *external state* χ *and answer ans, if*

$$\langle \mathtt{cp}\,[\![\mathrm{P}]\!], \textit{emptydisplay}, \langle\rangle, h_0(\chi)\rangle \overset{*}{\Longrightarrow} \textit{ans}$$

then $\mathcal{A}[\![\textit{ans}]\!] = \mathcal{P}[\![\mathrm{P}]\!]\chi$

Proof: Here *ans* ranges over syntactic answers, as in Figure 15. Let $h = h_0(\chi)$. By the conditions on h_0, we know that $\mathcal{X}[\![h.3]\!] = \chi$. So

$$\begin{aligned}
&\mathcal{M}[\![\langle \mathtt{cp}\,[\![\mathrm{P}]\!], \textit{emptydisplay}, \langle\rangle, h_0(\chi)\rangle]\!] \\
&= (\mathcal{Q}[\![\mathtt{cp}\,[\![\mathrm{P}]\!]]\!])(\mathcal{U}[\![\textit{emptydisplay}]\!])(\mathcal{Z}[\![\langle\rangle]\!])(\mathcal{S}[\![h.1, h.2]\!])(\mathcal{X}[\![h.3]\!]) \\
&\qquad\qquad\qquad\qquad \text{definition of } \mathcal{M} \\
&= \mathcal{CP}[\![\mathrm{P}]\!]\mu_0\langle\rangle\sigma_0\chi \qquad \text{definition of } \mathcal{U}, \text{ etc., } h_0 \\
&= \mathcal{CD}[\![\mathrm{P}]\!]\gamma_0\mu_0\langle\rangle\sigma_0\chi \qquad \text{definition of } \mathcal{CP} \\
&= \mathcal{D}[\![\mathrm{P}]\!](\mu_0 \circ \gamma_0)\kappa_0\sigma_0\chi \qquad \text{Theorem 4} \\
&= \mathcal{D}[\![\mathrm{P}]\!]\rho_0\kappa_0\sigma_0\chi \qquad \text{definition of } \mu_0, \gamma_0 \\
&= \mathcal{P}[\![\mathrm{P}]\!]\chi \qquad \text{definition of } \mathcal{P}
\end{aligned}$$

But, by the soundness of the combinator machine (Theorem 5), we know that

$$\langle \texttt{cp}\,[\![\mathrm{P}]\!], \mathit{emptydisplay}, \langle\rangle, h_0(\chi)\rangle \stackrel{*}{\Longrightarrow} \mathit{ans}$$

implies that

$$\mathcal{M}[\![\langle \texttt{cp}\,[\![\mathrm{P}]\!], \mathit{emptydisplay}, \langle\rangle, h_0(\chi)\rangle]\!] = \mathcal{A}[\![\mathit{ans}]\!]$$

So $\mathcal{P}[\![\mathrm{P}]\!]\chi = \mathcal{A}[\![\mathit{ans}]\!]$. ■

So, if the machine halts, either with a number or with an error, the machine's answer denotes the denotational answer. Of course this would be true even if the machine's transition relation were empty. For the machine to be satisfactory, we need to know that whenever the denotational semantics specifies a non-bottom answer, then the machine finds it. This is the converse of Theorem 6.

To obtain this converse, we use some results from the λ-calculus. We first observe that the translation $\mathcal{CP}$ also factors through the λ-calculus. In the example above, we can generate λ-terms, rather than (Scheme simulations of) denotations or combinator code terms, by writing something like

```
(define prim-apply
  (lambda (n primop q)
    char'`(lambda (mu zeta)
       (,apply-primitive ,primop (,take-first ,n zeta)
         (lambda (epsilon)
           (,q mu (,cons epsilon (,drop-first ,n zeta))))))))
```

where `apply-primitive`, `take-first`, etc., are bound to suitable λ-terms.

Similarly, we can transform the valuations $\mathcal{M}$, $\mathcal{Q}$, etc, to factor through the λ-calculus. Since the grammar for machine states includes infinite trees, we need to replace the grammar of Figure 15 with a more refined grammar that generates only the rational trees using *closerecs*. These rational trees are then translated using Turing's fixed-point combinator Θ [2, Definition 6.1.4]. Let us call this translation $\mathcal{M}_\lambda$. This translation has the property that no term $\mathcal{M}_\lambda[\![\langle q,u,z,h\rangle]\!]$ is in head normal form, since $\mathcal{Q}[\![q]\!]$ is always an abstraction. Similarly, let $\mathcal{A}_\lambda$ denote the translation from answers *ans* to λ-terms; $\mathcal{A}_\lambda[\![\langle\mathbf{error}\rangle]\!]$ will be a term with no head normal form, such as ΘI.

We can sharpen the soundness theorem (Theorem 5), to factor through this translation and to characterize the λ-calculus reduction sequence corresponding to each machine step:

THEOREM 7
If $\langle q,u,z,h\rangle \Longrightarrow \langle q',u',z',h'\rangle$, *then* $\mathcal{M}_\lambda[\![\langle q,u,z,h\rangle]\!]$ *β-reduces to* $\mathcal{M}_\lambda[\![\langle q',u',z',h'\rangle]\!]$ *via a reduction whose first step is a head reduction. Furthermore, if* $\langle q,u,z,h\rangle \Longrightarrow$ *ans, then* $\mathcal{M}[\![\langle q,u,z,h\rangle]\!]$ *β-reduces to* $\mathcal{A}_\lambda[\![ans]\!]$ *by a reduction whose whose first step is a head reduction.*

Proof: By calculation for each transition, as above. ■

Now we invoke a lemma from the λ-calculus:

THEOREM 8 *Let M be any λ-term. If M has an infinite reduction sequence in which head reductions occur infinitely often, then M has no head normal form.*

Proof: The proof of [2, Theorem 13.2.6] is easily modified to show that if M has an infinite reduction sequence in which head reductions occur infinitely often, then M has an infinite head reduction, and hence has no head normal form. ■

We can now put the pieces together:

THEOREM 9 (ADEQUACY) *For any program* P, *external state χ and answer ans* $\mathcal{P}[\![\mathrm{P}]\!]\chi = \mathcal{A}[\![ans]\!]$ *if and only if* $\langle \mathtt{cp}\,[\![\mathrm{P}]\!], \mathit{emptydisplay}, \langle\rangle, h_0(\chi)\rangle \stackrel{*}{\Longrightarrow} ans$

Proof: The "if" is Theorem 6. To establish the other direction, consider the inverse: If the machine runs infinitely, then by Theorem 7 there is an infinite reduction sequence starting at $\mathcal{M}_\lambda[\![\langle \mathtt{cp}\,[\![\mathrm{P}]\!], \mathit{emptydisplay}, \langle\rangle, h_0(\chi)\rangle]\!]$ which contains infinitely many head reductions. Hence this term has no head normal form. Now, any continuous model is sensible [2, Proposition 19.3.3], which means that any term with no head normal form denotes $\bot$. Since all the usual models are continuous, we conclude that if the machine runs infinitely, it must have denoted $\bot_A$. ■

An important property of the combinator machine is that the size of the terms (except for the heap) is statically bounded. To express this, we define $dom(u) = \{i \mid \mathtt{lookup}\ u\, i \text{ is not an error}\}$. Then we have:

THEOREM 10 (BOUNDED SPACE) *If* P *is a valid Pure PreScheme program, then there exist integers N_0 and N such that for any state $\langle q, u, z, h\rangle$ in the computation sequence of* $\langle \mathtt{cp}\,[\![\mathrm{P}]\!], \mathit{emptydisplay}, \langle\rangle, h_0\rangle$, $|dom(u)| \leq N$. *Furthermore, after the execution of the single closerecs instruction in* $\mathtt{cp}\,[\![\mathrm{P}]\!]$,

$$N_0 \leq |dom(u)| \leq N$$

Proof: (Sketch) A Pure PreScheme program must consist of a set of global simple declarations followed by a set of local procedure declarations followed by a tail-recursive expression. Let N_0 be total number of global simple declarations and local procedure declarations, and let N be N_0 plus the deepest lexical depth in the program. Since all procedures are closed in the global environment, which has N_0 elements, it must be that $N_0 \leq |dom(u)|$; the usual argument about static scoping establishes $|dom(u)| \leq N$. A completely formal proof would have to consider the details of the syntax of Pure PreScheme and the compiler. ■

5.3. Design Choices in the Compiler

The translation from Pure PreScheme to combinator code was patterned after [5]. In this section, we discuss some of the innovations and design choices that we made in the process of developing our translator.

An important change from [5] is the explicit separation of the syntax and semantics of the combinator code. This separation was already present in [27], but was dropped in [28, 29] in favor of punning between λ-terms and their denotations. At the time, the pun was useful in deriving the compiler-oriented semantics, but many people found it confusing. Furthermore, a clear separation between syntax trees and domain elements allowed us to understand when continuity arguments were permissible, and when they were not. This was even more important once rational trees became part of the structure.

We slightly modified the architecture of the machine. Clinger used a value register ϵ and a value stack ϵ^* where we use the value stack ζ. Clinger's value register serves to cache the top element of the stack. As a result, his induction hypotheses are asymmetrical because they need to keep track of when the cache is active: in Clinger's induction hypotheses A and B, ϵ occurs free on the left but not on the right, and in his induction hypothesis C, it appears free, but one has a precondition that says its value is ignored [5, page 360]. He also needs to generate *push* instructions to copy the value register onto the top of the stack. By replacing these with a single value stack, our induction hypotheses became more symmetrical and easier to work with; we did not need any pesky side conditions such as the one for Clinger's hypothesis C. We could rely on a later register allocation phase, such as that in [18], to deal with caching strategies.

Another change was in the separation of the different compiler modes. Clinger's compiler used two different compiling valuations, t (for general expressions) and e (for expressions in tail position). The choice of which valuation to use was embedded in the code of the compiler [5, Figure 5]. We chose instead to separate tail-recursive expressions from simple expressions in the syntax. This made it clearer which valuation should be used at any point in the compiler.

Another distinction in the compiler was between simple expressions evaluated for value or for effect. It is advantageous for the compiler to distinguish between these cases so that it need not worry about handling the value of an expression evaluated for effect. There were a number of different ways of organizing the compiler to treat this distinction. We could have made a separate syntactic category for commands. This would be the obvious approach for an ordinary procedural language. However, in our language, the set of commands would have been exactly the same as the set of simple expressions, so introducing a new syntactic category would have been redundant. We could have had commands leave their values on the top of the stack, and introduced an instruction that would drop the top value of the stack when it was to be ignored. This would have led to unacceptably inefficient code. In the end, we simply used a separate compiler valuation for expressions in command position, and we introduced a few extra instructions, such as *update-store*$_i$, to perform primitive operations without pushing a value on the stack. This is also consistent with modern ideas about machine architecture, which condone and even encourage new instructions to handle common special cases.

A more subtle change was in the role of the specifications. In [5], induction hypotheses were introduced only as part of the internals of the proof. Indeed, Clinger writes, "... the algorithm was designed and a compiler built before any thought was given to a formal correctness proof." [5, page 356]. Instead, in keeping with the ideas of [30], we viewed the induction hypotheses as *specifications* for the compiler: they described what the code generated by the compiler was supposed to do. This idea, along with our simplified machine design, allowed us to write down the specifications for the different valuations in a relatively systematic way. Given the specifications and a few general ideas about the form of the code, it was easy to write the clauses for the various productions. Thus the design of the specifications preceded the writing of the compiler. Most (though not all) of the proofs were easy, as was shown in Section 4.7. We believe that the induction hypotheses were a major work product, and should be considered a major work product of future compiler verification projects.

6. The Linear-Data Machine

The linear-data machine differs from the combinator machine in that it uses a linearly-addressed data memory to represent the environment and stack of the combinator machine. It uses two pointers into this memory, sp and up, to represent the stack and the environment. It also has a heap which corresponds to the heap of the combinator machine. Thus the state of the linear-data machine is of the form $\langle q, up, sp, m, h\rangle$, where sp and up are integers, and m is a map from integers to tree-structured values.

In this section we will formalize the way in which the sp and up pointers represent the stack and the environment. To aid in the intuition behind these formalisms, we will first give an informal sketch of the representation. We will then present the formal definitions.

The representation utilizes the fact that any PreScheme program uses only a bounded, statically-determinable amount of space in the data memory. By analyzing the program, we may define two constants for that program. The first, N, is the total amount of environment space required by the program. The second, N_0, is the amount of space initially required by the environment for globals and procedure declarations. These constants are easily calculated (see Theorem 10) and are used for setting the initial parameters of the linear-data machine.

6.1. Informal Presentation

We can take advantage of this by using locations 0 through N of the linear data memory for the environment u, and the locations above N for the local stack z.

We can describe the representation pictorially as follows:

1. Stackable values (integers, booleans, characters, strings, ports, vectors, procedures, environments). In keeping with the assumptions of the runtime model discussed in Section 2, runtime tags are not used. This restricts our correctness result but only for those programs that result in an error. All quantities are represented by a single machine word (i.e. one location in m). Strings and procedures are represented by pointers into a static space; since all procedures in a PreScheme program share the same environment, there is no need for a separate environment pointer in a procedure object. Vectors are represented by contiguous blocks of storage, and are represented on the stack by a pointer to their first location. Environments need to be stacked, but they are not expressible; when stacked they are represented as pointers to the environment representation. Since all other data is either immediate or a pointer to static space, these environment pointers are the only real "pointers" in the system (that is, they are the only references that can potentially dangle).

2. Runtime environment u. As all values are represented by a single word in memory, this suggests that u be represented by locations 0 through up in m:

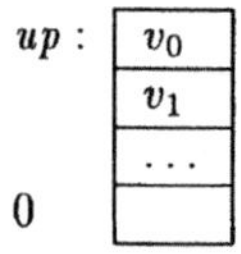

where $v_0 = \texttt{lookup}\, u\, 0$, $v_1 = \texttt{lookup}\, u\, 1$, etc. By Theorem 10, $0 \leq up \leq N$.

3. The local stack z. Since all values are represented by a single word in m and up ranges between 0 and N, a local stack $z = (v_1 :: v_2 :: \ldots :: v_n :: \langle\rangle)$ can be represented using m as a stack growing upward from position $N + 1$:

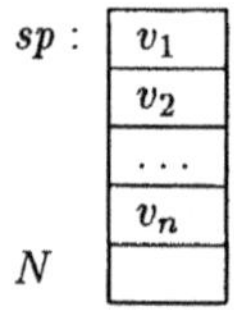

In the initial startup of the machine, up is started at -1 and the stack pointer sp starts at N, so that both the environment and stack are empty. The prelude to the program allocates globals with a sequence of $add\text{-}to\text{-}env_g$ instructions. These instructions allocate a sequence of heap pointers at the low end of the data memory. We use heap pointers because we are trying to model the semantics as closely as possible. See [18] for details on how to model this using a mutable stack instead.

The $add\text{-}to\text{-}env_g$ instructions are followed by a *closerecs* instruction. The effect of these instructions is to create an environment u_0 in which all the global procedures are closed. At this point *up* has value N_0. This is the ground configuration which is used as a reference for all tail calls.

After the globals and procedures have been allocated, *up* will have value N_0 and will not drop below this value for the remainder of program execution. This configuration is the configuration restored at tail call:

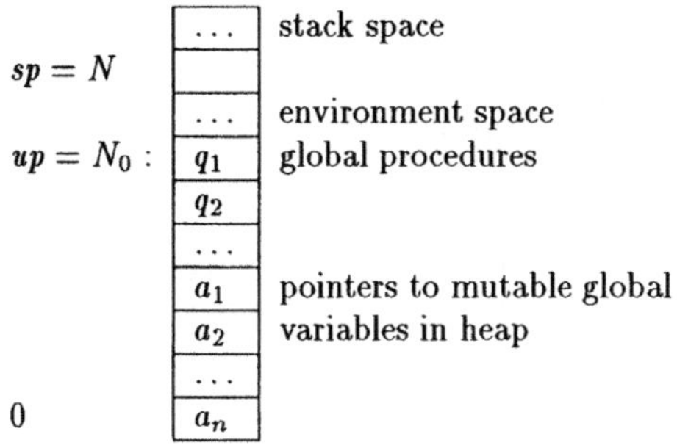

6.2. Formal Presentation

To formalize this representation, we will introduce the notion of *storage layout relation* [9] which is defined in [7, Section 4.2]. A storage layout relation is a predicate asserting that some concrete values (that is, values in the linear-data machine) represent some abstract term (that is, a term in the language of the combinator machine). A typical example is the relation for environments, which is a judgement of the form $(m, b) \models_U p \simeq u$. This predicate asserts that pointer p into memory m represents run-time environment u. (Here the parameter b marks the upper boundary of environment space). Such a relation is typically defined by a least fixed-point induction on a powerset $P(X \times Y)$ for suitable sets X and Y.

We will have one storage layout relation for each kind of data manipulated by the combinator and linear-data machines. These are: immediate data, stackable values, stacks, environments, heaps, and programs. These will be defined as the least fixed point of a simultaneous induction. There is no difficulty in defining these relations on infinite trees; certain infinite trees will be in the relation because one of the base cases in the induction (the one for recursive environments) will require it. The definition of the relations is a relatively straightforward transcription of the data in the diagrams above; the primary difficulty is in guarding against off-by-one errors.

As suggested by the diagrams above, the exact correspondences will depend on the values of N, N_0, and u_0, which in turn depend on the particular program being compiled. N and N_0 are obtained from Theorem 10 and u_0 is obtained from the semantics of the program. Since these quantities are constant throughout, they are treated as silent parameters.

6.2.1. *Relating Immediate Data*

If i and i' are immediate data, then $i \simeq_{imm} i'$ (read "i represents i'") iff i is the untagged version of i'. This is a degenerate storage-layout relation, since it does not involve the data memory.

6.2.2. *Relating Stackable Values*

$$
\begin{array}{ll}
\multicolumn{2}{l}{(m,b) \models_V c \simeq v \iff} \\
\text{either} & c \simeq_{imm} v \\
\text{or} & v = \langle \mathbf{vector}, a_1, \ldots, a_n \rangle \\
 & \text{and } (\forall i : 1 \le i \le n)(a_i = \langle \mathbf{hptr}, c + i - 1 \rangle)) \\
\text{or} & v = \langle \mathbf{proc}, \langle q, u_0 \rangle \rangle \text{ and } c = q \\
\text{or} & v = \langle \mathbf{env}, u \rangle \\
 & \text{and } (m,b) \models_U c \simeq u \\
 & \text{and } c \le b \\
\text{or} &
\end{array}
$$

We use c to range over concrete values (the values in the linear-data machine), and v to range over rational trees as in Section 5.

A stackable value that is immediate is represented by its untagged version. A vector is represented by a pointer to its first element. This requires the implementation to represent vectors by contiguous locations, a requirement not visible at higher levels of the semantics.

Procedures are represented only by their code components, since all procedures in a PreScheme program are closed in the environment u_0 at the end of the prelude. In general, u_0 may be an infinite rational tree, so any solution to this equation, including its least fixed point, will have infinite trees in the relation.

An environment is represented by an environment pointer. The parameter b marks the upper boundary of environment space; the condition on environments ensures that no environment pointer is ever dangling. This parameter will almost always be the environment pointer up.

6.2.3. *Relating Pointers and Stacks*

$$
\begin{array}{ll}
\multicolumn{2}{l}{(m,b) \models_Z \langle p, p' \rangle \simeq z \iff} \\
\text{either} & z = \langle\rangle \text{ and } p = p' \\
\text{or} & z = (v :: z') \text{ and } p > p' \text{ and } (m,b) \models_V m(p) \simeq v \\
 & \text{and } (m,b) \models_Z \langle p-1, p' \rangle \simeq z'
\end{array}
$$

Here the stack elements are in locations $p' + 1$ through p, so $p = p'$ marks an empty stack. In the proof, p' will always be N.

6.2.4. Relating Pointers and Environments

$$
\begin{array}{ll}
\multicolumn{2}{l}{(m,b) \models_U p \simeq u \iff} \\
\text{either} & u = \mathit{emptydisplay} \text{ and } p = -1 \\
\text{or} & u = (\mathit{extends}_{rl}\, u'\, (v_1 \ldots v_n)) \text{ and } p \leq b \\
& \text{and } (m,b) \models_V m(p) \simeq v_n \ldots (m,b) \models_V m(p-(n-1)) \simeq v_1 \\
& \text{and } (m,b) \models_U (p-n) \simeq u' \\
\text{or} & u = (\mathit{extends}_{rg}\, u' a) \text{ and } p \leq b \\
& \text{and } m(p) \simeq a \\
& \text{and } (m,b) \models_U (p-1) \simeq u'
\end{array}
$$

6.2.5. Relating Programs

Programs in the linear-data and combinator machines differ only in the format of the literals embedded in them. Thus we define

$$
\begin{array}{ll}
\multicolumn{2}{l}{q_l \simeq q_c \iff} \\
\text{either} & q_c = (\mathit{constant}\; i\, q_c') \text{ and } q_l = (\mathit{constant}\; i'\, q_l') \\
& \text{and } i \simeq_{imm} i' \text{ and } q_l' \simeq q_c' \\
& q_c = (\mathit{fetch}_l\; i\, q_c') \text{ and } q_l = (\mathit{fetch}_l\; i\, q_l') \\
& \text{and } q_l' \simeq q_c' \\
\text{or} & q_c = (\mathit{fetch}_g\; i\, q_c') \text{ and } q_l = (\mathit{fetch}_g\; i\, q_l') \\
& \text{and } q_l' \simeq q_c' \\
\text{or} & q_c = (\mathit{goto}\, q_c') \text{ and } q_l = (\mathit{goto}\, q_l') \\
& \text{and } q_l' \simeq q_c' \\
\text{or} & q_c = (\mathit{halt}) \text{ and } q_l = (\mathit{halt}) \\
& \text{etc.}
\end{array}
$$

where *constant* is an instruction that pushes a literal on the stack. As this is the only place where this instruction causes problems, this is the only place we have included it in our extracts.

6.2.6. Relating Heaps

The linear-data heap is like the combinator-machine heap except that its L-values are *untagged* integers, and its first component contains immediate values in their linear-data representation. Hence the first component maps untagged integers to immediate values in their linear-data representation, the second component is an integer-valued free-storage counter, and the third component is the same as that for the combinator machine. Heaps correspond if their free-storage counters and third components agree, and if the allocated portions of their first components correspond:

$$\begin{aligned} &h_l \simeq h_c \iff \\ &\quad h_c.2 = h_l.2 \\ &\quad \text{and } (\forall i : 0 \le i \le h_l.2)(h_l.1(i) \simeq h_c.1(\langle \mathbf{hptr}, i \rangle)) \\ &\quad \text{and } h_c.3 = h_l.3 \end{aligned}$$

6.3. Relating the Combinator and Linear-Data Machines

We can now define the correspondence between combinator and linear-data machine states.

The effect of the prelude is to establish the invariants

$$N_0 \le up \le N \le sp$$

and

$$(m, N_0) \models_U N_0 \simeq u_0$$

The first invariant expresses the disjointness of the environment and stack spaces, and the second establishes the correct representation of the globals.

Definition. We say a linear-data machine state $\langle q, up, sp, m, h \rangle$ *corresponds* to a combinator-machine state $\langle q', u, z, h' \rangle$, written

$$\langle q, up, sp, m, h \rangle \simeq \langle q', u, z, h' \rangle$$

if and only if the following conditions are satisfied:

1. $q \simeq q'$,
2. $(m, up) \models_U up \simeq u$,
3. $(m, up) \models_Z (sp, N) \simeq z$,
4. $h \simeq h'$
5. $N_0 \le up \le N \le sp$, and
6. $(m, u_0) \models_U N_0 \simeq u_0$

6.4. Basic Properties of the Representation

Before proceeding, we state several lemmas that express the basic properties of these relations. These are used constantly in the proof.

LEMMA 3 (IMMEDIATE VALUES) *If* $c \simeq_{imm} v$, *then for all* m *and* b, $(m, b) \models_V c \simeq v$.

Definition. We say $m =_{[p,p']} m'$ if $p \le p'$ and $(\forall x : p \le x \le p')(m(x) = m'(x))$.

LEMMA 4 (FREE-STORAGE LEMMA) *1. If* $(m, b) \models_V c \simeq v$ *and* $m =_{[0,b]} m'$ *then* $(m', b) \models_V c \simeq v$.

2. If $(m, b) \models_Z \langle p, p' \rangle \simeq z$ *and* $m =_{[0,b]} m'$ *and* $m =_{[p'+1,p]} m'$ *then* $(m', b) \models_Z \langle p, p' \rangle \simeq z$.

3. If $(m, b) \models_U p \simeq u$ *and* $m =_{[0,p]} m'$ *then* $(m', b) \models_U p \simeq u$.

Proof: By induction on the definitions of $\models_V, \models_Z$, and $\models_U$. ∎

LEMMA 5 *If* $(m, b) \models_V c \simeq v$ *and* $b \leq b'$ *then* $(m, b') \models_V c \simeq v$.

Proof: The parameter b is only used in the case $(m, b) \models_V c \simeq \langle \mathbf{env}, u \rangle$. In that case, $c \leq b \leq b'$, so $(m, b') \models_V c \simeq \langle \mathbf{env}, u \rangle$. The rest of the proof follows by tedious induction. ∎

LEMMA 6 *If* $(m, b) \models_U p \simeq u$ *then* $(m, b) \models_V m(p - n) \simeq \texttt{lookup}\ u\ n$.

Proof: By induction on n. ∎

6.5. Definition of the Linear-Data Machine

We define the operational semantics of the linear-data machine by considering the representation of each possible combinator-machine state, so that the linear-data machine simulates the behavior of the combinator machine. That is, if $L_1 \simeq C_1$ and $C_1 \Longrightarrow C_2$, then we want the linear-data machine to send L_1 to some state L_2 such that $L_2 \simeq C_2$.

In general, we will only be able to perform this simulation when C_1 is a state arising from reducing a properly compiled Pure PreScheme program. There are a number of things that might go wrong:

- The linear-data machine does not have tags to distinguish different data types. The combinator machine uses these tags to distinguish an error state. Since the linear-data machine cannot mimic this behavior, we will require the linear-data machine to behave correctly only if C_2 is not an error state. If C_2 is an error state, the behavior of the linear-data machine is unspecified. For type-checked PreScheme programs, such as the Scheme 48 Virtual Machine, this restriction is moot, because the typing rules guarantee that the program will never reach an error state.

- Similarly, if C_1 is a combinator-machine state with some arbitrary program q, executing it may cause other errors, such as underflowing the stack or overflowing the environment. However, this will not happen if C_1 is a state that is reached when the combinator machine is started with a correctly compiled Pure PreScheme program. The simulation theorem will have to take this into account.

$$
\begin{array}{ll}
\langle (\mathit{halt}), \mathit{up}, \mathit{sp}, m, h\rangle & \Longrightarrow \langle \mathbf{ok}, m(\mathit{sp})\rangle \\
\langle (\mathit{goto}\ q), \mathit{up}, \mathit{sp}, m, h\rangle & \Longrightarrow \langle q, \mathit{up}, \mathit{sp}, m, h\rangle \\
\langle (\mathit{label}\ q), \mathit{up}, \mathit{sp}, m, h\rangle & \Longrightarrow \langle q, \mathit{up}, \mathit{sp}, m, h\rangle \\
\langle (\mathit{fetch}_l\ i\, q), \mathit{up}, \mathit{sp}, m, h\rangle & \Longrightarrow \langle q, \mathit{up}, \mathit{sp}+1, m', h\rangle \\
\quad \text{where } m' = m[(\mathtt{lookup}\ i\ \mathit{up}\ m)/\mathit{sp}+1] & \\
\langle (\mathit{brf}\ q_1 q_2), \mathit{up}, \mathit{sp}, m, h\rangle & \Longrightarrow \langle (\mathtt{truish}(m(\mathit{sp})) \rightarrow q_1, q_2), \mathit{up}, \mathit{sp}-1, m, h\rangle \\
\langle (\mathit{save\text{-}env}\ q), \mathit{up}, \mathit{sp}, m, h\rangle & \Longrightarrow \langle q, \mathit{up}, \mathit{sp}+1, m[\mathit{up}/\mathit{sp}+1], h\rangle \\
\langle (\mathit{restore\text{-}env}\ q), \mathit{up}, \mathit{sp}, m, h\rangle & \Longrightarrow \langle q, m(\mathit{sp}-1), \mathit{sp}-1, m_1, h\rangle \\
\quad \text{where } m_1 = m[m(\mathit{sp})/\mathit{sp}-1] & \\
\langle (\mathit{update\text{-}store}\ i\, q), \mathit{up}, \mathit{sp}, m, h\rangle & \Longrightarrow \langle q, \mathit{up}, \mathit{sp}, m, h_1\rangle \\
\quad \text{where } h_1 = (\mathtt{update}\ m(\mathit{up}-i)\ m(\mathit{sp})\ h) & \\
\langle (\mathit{prim\text{-}apply}\ n\, p\, q), \mathit{up}, \mathit{sp}, m, h\rangle & \Longrightarrow \langle q, \mathit{up}, \mathit{sp}-(n-1), m_1, h_1\rangle \\
\quad \text{where } (w_1, h_1) = (\mathtt{apply\text{-}prim'}\ p\, (\mathtt{collect}\ m\ \mathit{sp}\ n)\, h) & \\
\quad \text{and } m_1 = m[w_1/\,\mathit{sp}-(n-1)] & \\
\langle (\mathit{add\text{-}to\text{-}env}\ n\, q), \mathit{up}, \mathit{sp}, m, h\rangle & \Longrightarrow \langle q, (\mathit{up}+n), (\mathit{sp}-n), m_1, h\rangle \\
\quad \text{where } m_1 = (\mathtt{copy}\ m\, n\, (\mathit{up}+1)\ \mathit{sp}) & \\
\langle (\mathit{add\text{-}to\text{-}env}_g\ q), \mathit{up}, \mathit{sp}, m, h\rangle & \Longrightarrow \\
\quad \langle q, \mathit{up}+1, \mathit{sp}-1, (m[(\mathtt{new}\ h)/(\mathit{up}+1)]), (\mathtt{update}(\mathtt{new}\ h)\, m(\mathit{sp})\, h)\rangle & \\
\langle (\mathit{closerecs}\, (q_1 \ldots q_n)\, q), \mathit{up}, \mathit{sp}, m, h\rangle & \\
 & \Longrightarrow \langle q, \mathit{up}+n, \mathit{sp}, m_1, h\rangle \\
\quad \text{where } m_1 = (\mathtt{spread}\ m(\mathit{up}+n)\, (q_1 \ldots q_n)) & \\
\langle (\mathit{tail\text{-}call}), \mathit{up}, \mathit{sp}, m, h\rangle & \Longrightarrow \langle m(\mathit{sp}), (N_0+n), (N-1), m_1, h\rangle \\
\quad \text{where } n = \mathit{sp}-N-1 & \\
\quad \text{and } m_1 = (\mathtt{copy}\ m\, n\, (N_0+1)\, (\mathit{sp}-1)) & \\
\text{otherwise} & \Longrightarrow \langle \mathbf{error}\rangle
\end{array}
$$

Figure 18. Operational Semantics of the Linear-Data Machine

The operational semantics of the linear-data machine is shown in Figure 18. The various auxiliaries used by the machine are shown in Figure 19. `apply-prim′` is unspecified, but it must satisfy the constraint that when `apply-prim` and `apply-prim′` are applied to congruent arguments, they return congruent immediate values and congruent heaps.

6.6. Correctness of the Linear-Data Machine

The correctness of the linear-data machine is shown in two parts. First, we show that $\simeq$ is a simulation between the combinator and linear-data machines. Then we show that execution of the compiled code for any Pure PreScheme program eventually causes this relation to be established.

$$(\texttt{new}\ h) = h.2 + 1$$

$$(\texttt{update}\ l\, v\, h) = \langle h.1[v/l], l > h.2 \rightarrow l, h.2, h.3\rangle$$

$$(\texttt{lookup}\ i\ up\ m) = m(up - i)$$

$$(\texttt{copy}\ m\, n\, d\, s) = (n = 0) \rightarrow m, (\texttt{copy}\ m[m(s)/d]\,(n-1)\,(d+1)\,(s-1))$$

$$(\texttt{spread}\ m\, n\, \langle\rangle) = m$$
$$(\texttt{spread}\ m\, n\, v :: \langle v_0 \ldots v_n\rangle) = (\texttt{spread}\ m[v/n]\,(n-1)\,\langle v_0 \ldots v_n\rangle)$$

$$(\texttt{collect}\ m\, i\, 0) = \langle\rangle$$
$$(\texttt{collect}\ m\, i\, n) = m(i) :: (\texttt{collect}\ m\,(i-1)\,(n-1))$$

Figure 19. Auxiliaries for the Linear-Data Machine

THEOREM 11 *Let N, N_0, and u_0 be chosen as in Theorem 10, and $L_1 \simeq C_1$. Then*

1. *if $C_1 \Longrightarrow C_2$, then there exists L_2 such that $L_1 \Longrightarrow L_2$ and $L_2 \simeq C_2$.*

2. *if $L_1 \Longrightarrow L_2$, then either there exists C_2 such that $C_1 \Longrightarrow C_2$ and $L_2 \simeq C_2$, or $C_1 \Longrightarrow \langle\mathbf{error}\rangle$.*

Proof: We read the proposition so that L_2 and C_2 are allowed to include answers. The proof is by a tedious analysis of each instruction, using the definitions of the storage layout relations and Lemma 4. In the second part of the theorem, we need the alternative $C_1 \Longrightarrow \langle\mathbf{error}\rangle$ because if the current instruction is a *halt* or *tail-call*, the combinator machine may terminate with an error while the linear-data machine proceeds, because its data has no tags that it can check. ∎

We believe that the second half of this theorem, and consequently Theorem 12, can be strengthened. We discuss this possibility at the end of this section.

Thus, since both machines are deterministic, once the machines become synchronized they must proceed in lockstep:

COROLLARY 1 *Let N, N_0, and u_0 be chosen as in Theorem 10, and $L_1 \simeq C_1$. Then if $C_1 \stackrel{*}{\Longrightarrow} \langle\mathbf{ok}, n\rangle$ then $L_1 \stackrel{*}{\Longrightarrow} \langle\mathbf{ok}, n\rangle$.*

The converse of this corollary is false because the linear-data machine may continue to operate after the combinator machine terminates with an error, as noted above.

The hard part is showing that the machines become synchronized. To this end, let conc be the operation that converts a combinator machine program to a linear-data machine program by removing the tags on the operands of all the *constant* instructions, so for all combinator-machine programs q, $\mathbf{conc}(q) \simeq q$. Let m_0 denote the empty memory, and let h_0^L denote a function analogous to h_0 for the linear-data machine. Now we can state the simulation theorem:

THEOREM 12 (CORRECTNESS OF THE LINEAR-DATA MACHINE) *For any Pure Pre-Scheme program* P, *there exists an integer N such that for all integers n and external states χ, if $\mathcal{P}[\![\mathrm{P}]\!]\chi = \mathcal{A}[\![\langle \mathbf{ok}, n\rangle]\!]$ then*

$$\langle \mathbf{conc}(\mathbf{cp}\,[\![\mathrm{P}]\!]), -1, N, m_0, h_0^L(\chi)\rangle \stackrel{*}{\Longrightarrow} \langle \mathbf{ok}, n\rangle$$

Proof: For any χ and n we know by the adequacy of the combinator machine (Theorem 9 that $\mathcal{P}[\![\mathrm{P}]\!]\chi = \mathcal{A}[\![\langle \mathbf{ok}, n\rangle]\!]$ iff

$$\langle \mathbf{cp}\,[\![\mathrm{P}]\!], \mathit{emptydisplay}, \langle\rangle, h_0(\chi)\rangle \stackrel{*}{\Longrightarrow} \langle \mathbf{ok}, n\rangle \tag{2}$$

So it will suffice to show that if (2) holds then

$$\langle \mathbf{conc}(\mathbf{cp}\,[\![\mathrm{P}]\!]), -1, N, m_0, h_0^L(\chi)\rangle \stackrel{*}{\Longrightarrow} \langle \mathbf{ok}, n\rangle \tag{3}$$

holds as well.

Choose N_0, N, and u_0 as in Theorem 10. By the preceding corollary, it will suffice to show that after sufficiently many states, the two machines reach states that are related by $\simeq$.

We observe that the programs for both the linear-data and combinator machines begin with a sequence of *add-to-env$_g$* instructions, followed by a *closerecs* instruction. Let k_0 be the number of steps to execute these instructions.

The machines start in states

$$\langle q, -1, N, m_0, h_0^L(\chi)\rangle$$

for the linear-data machine and

$$\langle q', \mathit{emptydisplay}, \langle\rangle, h_0(\chi)\rangle$$

for the combinator machine. Comparing these states with the definition of $\simeq$ for states, we see that all of the conditions for correspondence hold, except for $N_0 \leq up$ and $(m, N) \models_U N_0 \simeq u_0$ Let $\simeq_0$ denote this weakened relation. Since there are no procedures represented during the preamble, this relation does not depend on u_0. Let L_k and C_k denote the states of the linear-data and combinator machines after k steps.

We then show the following:

For all $k < k_0$, $L_k \simeq_0 C_k$.
$L_{k_0} \simeq C_{k_0}$.

The programs q and q' begin with a sequence of *add-to-env$_g$* instructions. A straightforward calculation, using the definitions of the storage layout relations and Lemma 4, shows that these instructions preserve $\simeq_0$. This establishes the first proposition.

Next, we turn to the *closerecs* instruction that ends the prelude. Assume we have

$$\begin{aligned}&\langle(\mathit{closerecs}\,(q_1 \ldots q_n)\,q), up, sp, m, h\rangle \\ &\quad \simeq_0 \langle(\mathit{closerecs}\,(q'_1 \ldots q'_n)\,q'), u, z, h'\rangle\end{aligned}$$

We must show that

$$\langle q, up{+}n, sp, m', h\rangle \simeq \langle q', u_0, z, h'\rangle$$

where

$$\begin{aligned}m' &= (\mathtt{spread}\ m(up{+}n)\,(q_1 \ldots q_n)) \\ u_0 &= (\mathtt{fix}(\lambda u'.\,(\mathit{extends}_{rl}\ u\,(\langle \mathbf{proc}, \langle q'_1, u'\rangle\rangle \ldots \langle \mathbf{proc}, \langle q'_n, u'\rangle\rangle))))\end{aligned}$$

Here we need to establish $\simeq$, not $\simeq_0$.

At the end of this instruction, we have $up = N_0$, by the definition of N_0.

By the definition of m', for $1 \le i \le n$ we have $m'(up{+}n - i + 1) = q_i$, so by the definition of $\models_V$ we have $(m', up) \models_V m'(up{+}n - i + 1) \simeq \langle \mathbf{proc}, \langle q'_i, u_0\rangle\rangle$, and $(m', up) \models_U up \simeq u$, so by the definition of $\models_U$ we have $(m', up) \models_U up{+}n \simeq u_1$, where

$$u_1 = (\mathit{extends}_{rl}\ u\,(\langle \mathbf{proc}, \langle q'_1, u_0\rangle\rangle \ldots \langle \mathbf{proc}, \langle q'_n, u_0\rangle\rangle))$$

But u_1 is just one unwinding of u_0, so $u_1 = u_0$.

All the other conditions are established trivially. This establishes $L_{k_0} \simeq C_{k_0}$. By Corollary 1, we are done. ■

6.7. Development of Storage-Layout Relations

Storage-layout relations, as we have described them, allow us to structure a proof by induction on computation steps. Many early compiler-correctness proofs used congruences between domains as a way of structuring such proofs, e.g. [26]. Such proofs were complicated because the relations were formulated between elements of domains, and inverse-limit constructions acted as a surrogate for operational reasoning.

Instead, relying on the development of natural semantics [22], our predicates relate pairs of trees, thus avoiding most of these complications. Our definitions are patterned on those of Hannan [9]. In [31], we introduced these ideas, showing how the relations of [9] could be generalized and the proofs simplified.

Theorem 12 would be considerably stronger if it were an iff, like Theorem 9. The converse of Theorem 12 would be true if a valid PreScheme program, which must be syntactically well-typed (see Section 3), never produced $\langle$**error**$\rangle$. Unfortunately, there is nothing to prevent primitive operations, and especially operations on the external state, from producing errors. We believe that we could obtain the converse if operations on the external state were restricted in this way. There are a number of ways in which this might be achieved, but such a proof was not attempted.

7. The Stored-Program Machine

The stored-program machine is identical to the linear-data machine, except that the code is represented in cells of a linear program memory M, much like the cells of the data memory.

The formal definition of the stored-program machine appears in Figure 20. The machine uses a fetch-execute cycle. It has two kinds of states: fetch states and execute states. In a fetch state, denoted $F(ip, up, sp, m, h)$, the machine retrieves the contents of the location pointed to by ip and goes into the execute state $E(ip, M(ip), up, sp, m, h)$. In the execute state, the machine decodes the current instruction and behaves accordingly, going into a fetch state. This organization allows a finite presentation of the machine's behavior using conventional operational-semantics notation. The program memory is treated as a global since it remains constant throughout execution.

We use storage-layout relations to specify the correspondence between the two machines. The machine's goal is to preserve correspondence with the behavior of the linear-data machine.

We first show how linear-data machine code is represented in the linear program memory. For example the representation of bytecode $(\mathit{fetch}_l \; i \, q_0)$ at location p in M is:

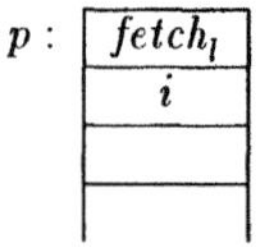

where $p + 2$ represents q_0. This notion is formalized by the storage-layout relation $\models_P$:

$$
\begin{array}{lll}
\multicolumn{3}{l}{M \models_P p \simeq q \iff} \\
& \text{either} & M(p) = \mathit{halt} \text{ and } q = (\mathit{halt}) \\
& \text{or} & M(p) = \mathit{goto} \text{ and } q = (\mathit{goto}\; q_0) \\
& & \text{and } M \models_P M(p+1) \simeq q_0 \\
& \text{or} & q = (\mathit{label}\; q_0) \\
& & \text{and } M \models_P p \simeq q_0 \\
& \text{or} & M(p) = \mathit{fetch}_l \text{ and } q = (\mathit{fetch}_l \; i \, q_0) \\
& & \text{and } M(p+1) = i \text{ and } M \models_P p + 2 \simeq q_0 \\
& \text{or} & M(p) = \mathit{brf} \text{ and } q = (\mathit{brf}\; q_0 \, q_1) \\
& & \text{and } M \models_P p + 2 \simeq q_0 \text{ and } M \models_P M(p+1) \simeq q_1 \\
& \text{etc.} &
\end{array}
$$

Fetch state :

$F(ip, up, sp, m, h) \Longrightarrow E(ip, M(ip), up, sp, m, h)$

Execute state :

$E(ip, halt, up, sp, m, h) \Longrightarrow \langle \mathbf{ok}, m(sp)\rangle$

$E(ip, goto, up, sp, m, h) \Longrightarrow F(M(ip+1), up, sp, m, h)$

$E(ip, fetch_l, up, sp, m, h) \Longrightarrow F(ip+2, up, sp+1, m_1, h)$
  where $m_1 = m[(\texttt{lookup}\ M(ip+1)\ up\ m)/(sp+1)]$

$E(ip, brf, up, sp, m, h) \Longrightarrow F(ip_1, up, sp-1, m, h)$
  where $ip_1 = (\texttt{truish}(m(sp)) \rightarrow (ip+2), M(ip+1))$

$E(ip, save\text{-}env, up, sp, m, h) \Longrightarrow F(ip+1, up, sp+1, m[up/sp+1], h)$

$E(ip, restore\text{-}env, up, sp, m, h) \Longrightarrow F(ip+1, m(sp-1), sp-1, m_1, h)$
  where $m_1 = m[m(sp)/sp-1]$

$E(ip, update\text{-}store, up, sp, m, h) \Longrightarrow F(ip+2, up, sp, m, h_1)$
  where $h_1 = (\texttt{update}\ m(up-M(ip+1))\ m(sp)\ h)$

$E(ip, prim\text{-}apply, up, sp, m, h) \Longrightarrow F(ip+3, up, sp_1, m_1, h_1)$
  where $sp_1 = sp-(M(ip+1)-1)$
  and $(w_1, h_1) = (\texttt{apply-prim}\ M(ip+2)\,(\texttt{collect}\ m\ sp\ M(ip+1))\,h)$
  and $m_1 = m[w_1/\,sp-(M(ip+1)-1)]$

$E(ip, update\text{-}store_i, up, sp, m, h) \Longrightarrow F(ip+2, up, sp-1, m, h_1)$
  where $h_1 = (\texttt{update}\ m(up-M(ip+1))\ m(sp)\ h)$

$E(ip, prim\text{-}apply_i, up, sp, m, h) \Longrightarrow F(ip+3, up, sp-M(ip+1), m, h_1)$
  where $(w_1, h_1) = (\texttt{apply-prim}\ M(ip+2)\,(\texttt{collect}\ m\ sp\ M(ip+1))\,h)$

$E(ip, add\text{-}to\text{-}env, up, sp, m, h) \Longrightarrow F(ip+2, up_1, sp_1, s_1, h)$
  where $up_1 = (up+M(ip+1))$
  and $sp_1 = (sp-M(ip+1))$
  and $m_1 = (\texttt{copy}\ m\,M(ip+1)\,(up+1)\ sp)$

$E(ip, add\text{-}to\text{-}env_g, up, sp, m, h) \Longrightarrow F(ip+1, up+1, sp-1, m_1, h_1)$
  where $m_1 = (m[(\texttt{new}\ h)/(up+1)])$
  and $h_1 = (\texttt{update}\,(\texttt{new}\ h)\,m(sp)\,h)$

$E(ip, closerecs, up, sp, m, h) \Longrightarrow F(M(ip+1), up+M(ip+2), sp, m_1, h)$

where $m_1 = (\texttt{spread}\ m(up+M(ip+2))\,(ip+3\ldots ip+M(ip+2)+2))$

$E(ip, tail\text{-}call, up, sp, m, h) \Longrightarrow F(m(sp), N_0+n, (N-1), m_1, h)$
  where $n = sp-N-1$
  and $m_1 = (\texttt{copy}\ m\,M(ip+1)\,(N_0+1)\,(sp-1))$

otherwise $\Longrightarrow$ **error**

Figure 20. The fetch/execute cycle of the stored-program machine.

This change propagates through the other classes of data that are represented in the machine. Values correspond if they are alike except for the representation of programs. Data memories correspond up to pointer p if they correspond location by location for all smaller locations. Heaps correspond if they both have the same number of used cells, the values of corresponding cells are related, and the third components (the external states) are equal. All these can be written easily using the language of storage-layout relations in the style of Section 6.

Given these relations, we can define the correspondence between states of the linear-data machine and fetch states of the stored-program machine. For correspondence, the stored-program machine's instruction pointer must correspond to the linear-data machine's program. Furthermore the dedicated registers must have the same values in both machines and data in the data memories and heaps must correspond.

Definition. We say that under linear program memory M, stored-program machine state $F(ip, up, sp, m, h)$ corresponds to a linear-data machine state $\langle q, up', sp', m', h'\rangle$ (written $M \models F(ip, up, sp, m, h) \simeq \langle q, up', sp', m', h'\rangle$) if and only if:

1. $M \models_P ip \simeq q$
2. $up = up'$
3. $sp = sp'$
4. $M \models_{[0,sp]} m \simeq m'$
5. $M \models_H h \simeq h'$

In the fourth item, the notation $M \models_{[0,sp]} m \simeq m'$ means that m and m' agree pointwise for values between 0 and sp.

The simulation theorem says that machines in corresponding states remain in corresponding states as they execute, except that the stored-program machine takes exactly two steps (one fetch and one execute) for each step of the linear-data machine.

THEOREM 13 *Let L_1 and L_2 be states of the linear-data machine and P_1 and P_2 be fetch states of the stored-program machine. If $M \models P_1 \simeq L_1$, then*

1. *If $L_1 \Longrightarrow L_2$, then there exists an execute state P_1' and a fetch state P_2 of the stored-program machine such that $P_1 \Longrightarrow P_1' \Longrightarrow P_2$ such that $M \models P_2 \simeq L_2$.*
2. *If $P_1 \Longrightarrow P_1' \Longrightarrow P_2$, then there exists a state L_2 of the linear-data machine such that $L_1 \Longrightarrow L_2$ and $M \models P_2 \simeq L_2$.*

Proof: By analysis of each instruction. ∎

As before, since both machines are deterministic, this ensures that once the machines are started in corresponding states, they are guaranteed to return identical answers.

8. The Linearizer and its Correctness

In Theorem 13, we showed that if L and P were corresponding states of the linear-data machine and the stored-program machine, then L and P would always compute in corresponding states. In particular, if L halted with an integer n, then so would P. Theorem 12 specified how to get from a Pure PreScheme program P to a suitable linear-data machine state by using **cp** and **conc**, but Theorem 13 gives no corresponding specification for how to get to a stored-program machine state.

In this section, we describe an algorithm that takes the combinator code for a program q and an initial code address p, and produces a linear instruction store M such that $M \models_P p \simeq q$, that is, M contains a program, starting at p, that corresponds to q.

We call this algorithm the *linearizer*. This would be a straightforward tree traversal, except that splits and joins must be accounted for. Splits occur at conditionals. For example, consider the combinator code emitted for a simple conditional expression. The syntax-directed compiler gives:

$$\begin{aligned}\texttt{cse}\,[\![(\texttt{if}\ \mathrm{S}_0\ \mathrm{S}_1\ \mathrm{S}_2)]\!] g q = \texttt{cse}\,[\![\mathrm{S}_0]\!] g(\mathit{brf}(&\texttt{cse}\,[\![\mathrm{S}_1]\!] g(\mathit{label}\ q))\\ &(\texttt{cse}\,[\![\mathrm{S}_2]\!] g(\mathit{goto}\ q)))\end{aligned}$$

The linearizer must avoid making two copies of q. It does this by relying on the syntax-directed compiler to mark the join point with *label* and *goto* instructions. More precisely, the linearizer assumes that the left path into a join is marked by a *label* and the right path is marked by a *goto*. This requirement is formalized by the predicate *legal*(q) in Figure 21, which also defines the join point *join*(q) of a combinator program q. It is easy to confirm that code generated by the compiler satisfies these restrictions:

THEOREM 14 *For any program* P, conc(cp $[\![$P$]\!]$) *is legal.*

Proof: Routine induction. ■

The linearizer is a set of three valuations on combinator-code programs. We present it in a style similar to that employed for the compiler. For each valuation, we present an informal description of its intended purpose, its formal specification, and some excerpts from its definition. As in Section 4, formulating the specification was the most difficult part of the process; once that was done, writing the linearizer and its proof was relatively straightforward. We therefore give the specifications in some detail, and the algorithm and proof in less detail.

We begin with some preliminary definitions needed for the specification.

Definition. For code stores M and M', $M =_p^{p'} M'$ if and only if $(\forall i : p \leq i < p')\ M(i) = M'(i)$.

Definition. The instructions *tail-call* and *halt* are called *leaves* and *leaf* (q) is true if and only if q is a leaf.

q	$join(q)$	$legal(q)$
$(halt)$	$(halt)$	$true$
$(goto\ q_0)$	$(goto\ q_0)$	$legal(q_0)$
$(label\ q_0)$	$(label\ q_0)$	$legal(q_0)$
$(fetch_l\ i\ q_0)$	$join(q_0)$	$legal(q_0)$
$(brf\ q_0\ q_1)$	$join(join(q_0))$	$join(q_0) = (label\ q')$ and $join(q_1) = (goto\ q')$ and $legal(q')$
$(save\text{-}env\ q_0)$	$join(q_0)$	$legal(q_0)$
$(restore\text{-}env\ q_0)$	$join(q_0)$	$legal(q_0)$
$(update\text{-}store\ i\ q_0)$	$join(q_0)$	$legal(q_0)$
$(prim\text{-}apply\ n\ p\ q_0)$	$join(q_0)$	$legal(q_0)$
$(update\text{-}store_i\ i\ q_0)$	$join(q_0)$	$legal(q_0)$
$(prim\text{-}apply_i\ n\ p\ q_0)$	$join(q_0)$	$legal(q_0)$
$(add\text{-}to\text{-}env\ nu\ q_0)$	$join(q_0)$	$legal(q_0)$
$(add\text{-}to\text{-}env_g\ q_0)$	$join(q_0)$	$legal(q_0)$
$(closerecs\,(q_1 \ldots q_n)\,q_0)$	$join(q_0)$	$(\forall i : 0 \leq i \leq n)$ $legal(q_i)$ and $leaf\,(join(q_i))$
$(tail\text{-}call\ n)$	$(tail\text{-}call\ n)$	$true$

Figure 21. Specification of legal combinator code.

We are now ready to describe the linearizer.

$\mathcal{L}$ is the initial linearization function. It takes as input a combinator-code program q representing an entire program or procedure, a code store M, and a pointer p to the next free position in M. It returns two values $\langle M', p'\rangle$, where M' is a code store just like M except that $M' \models_P p \simeq q$, and p' is the next free position in M'.

This informal specification must be refined to clarify the meaning of phrases like "just like" and "next free position." This must be done in a way that will support the eventual induction proof. After considerable experimentation, we arrived at the following formal specification of $\mathcal{L}$:

If q is legal and the join point of q is a leaf then $\mathcal{L}[\![q]\!]Mp = \langle M', p'\rangle$ such that

1. $M =_0^p M'$
2. $p' \geq p$
3. $(\forall\, M'')$ if $M'' =_p^{p'} M'$, then $M'' \models_P p \simeq q$

The first condition guarantees that the linearizer does not change the locations in M below p, corresponding to the informal statement that p is the first free location in M and M' is "just like" M. The third condition guarantees that the linearization of q lies between locations p and $p' - 1$.

$\mathcal{L}$ is defined by:

$$\mathcal{L}[\![(halt)]\!]Mp = \langle M[halt/p], p+1\rangle$$

$$\mathcal{L}[\![(tail\text{-}call\ n)]\!]Mp = \langle M[tail\text{-}call/p, n/p+1], p+2\rangle$$

otherwise

$$\begin{aligned}\mathcal{L}[\![q]\!]Mp = \texttt{let}\ &\langle M', p', q'\rangle = \mathcal{L}'[\![q]\!]M(p+2)\\ \texttt{in}\ &\mathcal{L}[\![q']\!]M'p'\end{aligned}$$

The idiom $M[tail\text{-}call/p, n/p+1]$ corresponds to the emission of code: Here location p is loaded with *tail-call* and location $p+1$ is loaded with the number n.

$\mathcal{L}'$ does the major work. It takes as input a combinator-code program q, a code store M, and a code pointer p (the next free position in M). It returns three values $\langle M', p', q'\rangle$, where M' is a modified code store, p' is a pointer into the code store, and q' is a combinator-code program.

The formal specification for $\mathcal{L}'$ is: If q is legal then $\mathcal{L}'[\![q]\!]Mp = \langle M', p', q'\rangle$ such that

1. $M =_0^p M'$
2. $p' \geq p$
3. $q' = join(q)$
4. $(\forall\, M'')$ if $M'' =_p^{p'} M'$ and $M'' \models_P p' \simeq q'$, then $M'' \models_P p \simeq q$.

The first and second conditions are similar to those for $\mathcal{L}$. The third condition states that $\mathcal{L}'$ computes $join(q)$. The fourth condition says that if M'' has a linearization of q' beginning at p', and is identical with M' for positions between p and p', then M'' has a linearization of q starting at p. So p' is a position in the code store at which the linearizer expects an image of q' to be placed.

When both sides of the conditional are linearized, the linearizer chooses which copy of q' to linearize (they are guaranteed to be the same because q is legal), and it inserts a goto at the place in the code store where the other branch wanted to put q. This is illustrated in the clause for linearizing a *brf*:

$$
\begin{aligned}
&\mathcal{L}'[\![(brf\; q_0\, q_1)]\!]Mp \\
&= \texttt{let*}\ \langle M', p', (goto\ q')\rangle = \mathcal{L}'[\![q_0]\!]M(p+2) \\
&\qquad\quad \langle M'', p'', (label\ q')\rangle = \mathcal{L}'[\![q_1]\!]M'(p'+2) \\
&\quad \texttt{in}\ \mathcal{L}'[\![q']\!]M''[brf/p, (p'+2)/(p+1), goto/p', p''/(p'+1)]p''
\end{aligned}
$$

Here q' represents the common code after q_0 and q_1 rejoin each other. Though q' is bound twice in this definition, the two bindings are guaranteed to coincide because of the assumption that $(brf\; q_0\, q_1)$ is legal. If $\mathcal{L}'[\![(brf\; q_0\, q_1)]\!]Mp = \langle M''', p''', q''\rangle$, then M''' will look like

p :	*brf*	
	$p'+2$	
	...	linearization of q_0
p' :	*goto*	
	p''	
	...	linearization of q_1
p'' :	...	linearization of q'
p''' :		starting address for q''

We give some additional excerpts from the definition of $\mathcal{L}'$ to suggest the other cases.

$$\mathcal{L}'[\![(halt)]\!]Mp = \langle M, p, (halt)\rangle$$

$$\mathcal{L}'[\![(goto\ q_0)]\!]Mp = \langle M, p, (goto\ q_0)\rangle$$

$$\mathcal{L}'[\![(label\ q_0)]\!]Mp = \langle M, p, (label\ q_0)\rangle$$

$$\mathcal{L}'[\![(fetch_l\ i\, q_0)]\!]Mp = \mathcal{L}'[\![q_0]\!]M[fetch_l/p, i/p+1](p+2)$$

$$
\begin{aligned}
&\mathcal{L}'[\![(closerecs\,(q_1 \ldots q_n)\, q_0)]\!]Mp = \\
&\quad \texttt{let}\ \langle M', (p_1 \ldots p_n), p'\rangle = \mathcal{L}^*[\![(q_1 \ldots q_n)]\!]M(p+n+3) \\
&\qquad \texttt{in}\ \mathcal{L}'[\![q_0]\!]r'[closerecs/p, p'/p+1, n/p+2, \\
&\qquad\qquad\qquad p_1/p+3, \ldots, p_n/(p+n+2)]p'
\end{aligned}
$$

$$\mathcal{L}'[\![(tail\text{-}call\ n)]\!]Mp = \langle M, p, (tail\text{-}call\ n)\rangle$$

The last valuation, $\mathcal{L}^*$, is used for linearizing a sequence of combinator-code programs. It takes as input a list of combinator-code programs $(q_1 \ldots q_n)$, a code store M, and a code pointer p (the next free position in M) and returns three values $\langle M', (p_1 \ldots p_n), p' \rangle$. M' is a code store just like M except that $(\forall i : 1 \leq i \leq n)\ M' \models_P p_i \simeq q_i$. Again, p' is the next free position in M'. $\mathcal{L}^*$ is used to linearize the procedure definitions in a *closerecs*.

The formal specification of $\mathcal{L}^*$ is: if $(\forall i : 1 \leq i \leq n)$ q_i is legal and the join point of q_i is a leaf then $\mathcal{L}^*[\![(q_1 \ldots q_n)]\!]Mp = \langle M', (p_1 \ldots p_n), p' \rangle$ such that

1. $M =_0^p M'$

2. $p' \geq p$

3. $(\forall\ M : M =_p^{p'} M'), (\forall i : 1 \leq i \leq n)\ M \models_P p_i \simeq q_i$

$\mathcal{L}^*$ is defined by:

$$\mathcal{L}^*[\![()]\!]Mp = \langle M, (), p \rangle$$

$$\begin{aligned}\mathcal{L}^*[\![q :: (q_1 \ldots q_n)]\!]Mp = \texttt{let*}\ & \langle M', p' \rangle = \mathcal{L}[\![q]\!]Mp \\ & \langle M'', (p_1 \ldots p_n), p'' \rangle = \mathcal{L}^*[\![(q_1 \ldots q_n)]\!]M'p' \\ \texttt{in}\ & \langle M'', p :: (p_1 \ldots p_n), p'' \rangle\end{aligned}$$

The correctness of the linearizer is given as follows:

THEOREM 15 *$\mathcal{L}$, $\mathcal{L}'$ and $\mathcal{L}^*$ satisfy their specifications.*

Proof: By induction on the definitions of $\mathcal{L}$, $\mathcal{L}'$ and $\mathcal{L}^*$. ■

We can now give a summary of how we run a program. Given a program P, we compile it to get **cp** [\![P]\!]. We then remove tags from the literal data in the program, getting conc(**cp** [\![P]\!]). We then run the linearizer $\mathcal{L}$ on this linear-data machine code, to assemble this code into an initially-empty program memory, starting at program counter 0. The result is a program memory M and a starting location p. Given external state χ, we can then start the stored-program machine in state

$$F(p, -1, N, m_0, h_0^L(\chi))$$

where N is chosen as in Theorem 10. The correctness of this process is summarized by the following theorem.

THEOREM 16 (CORRECTNESS OF THE ENTIRE COMPILER) *For any Pure PreScheme program* P, *there exists a program memory M, a pointer p into M, and an integer N such that for all integers n and external states χ, if $\mathcal{P}[\![\mathrm{P}]\!]\chi = \mathcal{A}[\![\langle \mathbf{ok}, n \rangle]\!]$ then using program memory M,*

$$F(p, -1, N, m_0, h_0^L(\chi)) \stackrel{*}{\Longrightarrow} \langle \mathbf{ok}, n \rangle$$

Proof: Choose N as in Theorem 10. By Theorem 12, we know that in the linear-data machine

$$\langle \mathbf{conc}(\mathbf{cp}\,[\![\mathrm{P}]\!]), -1, N, s_0, h_0^L(\chi)\rangle \stackrel{*}{\Longrightarrow} \langle \mathbf{ok}, n\rangle \tag{4}$$

So we need to find a program memory and stored-program machine state that corresonds to this linear-data machine state.

To do this, let $\langle M, p\rangle = \mathcal{L}[\![\mathbf{conc}(\mathbf{cp}\,[\![\mathrm{P}]\!])]\!]\emptyset 0$, the result of running the linearizer on the linear-data machine program $\mathbf{conc}(\mathbf{cp}\,[\![\mathrm{P}]\!])$ starting with the empty program memory and first free location 0. Since $\mathcal{L}$ satisfies its specifications, we know that $M \models_P p \simeq \mathbf{conc}(\mathbf{cp}\,[\![\mathrm{P}]\!])$. Comparing the other components, we confirm that

$$M \models F(p, -1, N, m_0, h_0^L(\chi)) \simeq \langle \mathbf{conc}(\mathbf{cp}\,[\![\mathrm{P}]\!]), -1, N, s_0, h_0^L(\chi)\rangle$$

This establishes the correspondence between the stored-program and linear-data machine states, and therefore, by Theorem 13, they produce the same asnwers. ∎

As noted after Theorem 12, the conclusion of the theorem could be strengthened to an iff if some more care were taken with errors in primitives.

9. Implementation

The VLISP PreScheme compiler was implemented as two separate programs. The front end translates VLISP PreScheme into Pure PreScheme and the back end translates Pure PreScheme into code for the Motorola 68000.[4] The front end was implemented using about 4300 lines of code and the back end used 2300 lines. To facilitate bootstrapping as described in [7, Section 8], they were both written in the dialect of Scheme accepted by the VLISP Scheme byte-code compiler.

The back end used the 68000 as a target because it was the architecture most readily available to us at the start of the project. Later, the compiler was retargeted to produce SPARC code with very little effort.

Representing our abstract machines with the 68000 requires a mapping similar to the ones just detailed. This section informally describes that mapping and then describes the code generated for the VLISP Byte-Code Interpreter by the compiler.

Immediate data is modeled via a 32 bit quantity (4 bytes). Thus immediate data can be stored directly in any of the 68000 registers (`D0`–`D7` and `A0`–`A7`) or in 4 consecutive bytes of user memory.

The stack s is modeled by the 68000 with the user stack, and its stack pointer, sp, is modeled by the 68000 stack pointer `SP` (address register `A7`). The environment

[4] The front end and the back end were developed at two different sites. The two programs were not merged solely because we did not take the time to resolve conflicting usages of Scheme program variables.

register, up, is modeled by the address register **A1**. For efficiency, the initial environment pointer, N_0, and initial stack pointer, N, are also kept in address registers for quick reset on tail call.

Two details must be noted in using the 68000 user stack as described. First, the 68000 user stack grows downward rather than upward. Furthermore, one unit of immediate data is represented by four bytes of 68000 memory. Therefore the stack pointer manipulations and the linearization algorithm needed to be altered accordingly.

Procedures are represented by their effective addresses. When the initial environment u_0 is being created, these effective addresses (which are 32 bit quantities) are pushed on the stack. On tail-call, the effective address is loaded from the stack into the program counter.

The environment representation is almost completely analogous to that of the stored-program machine, with environment values kept in the first $4 * N$ bytes of the stack. The local stack is handled almost completely analogously as well. The only difference is that for efficiency, the top 8 values of the local stack are cached in in the data registers. The correctness of such caching strategies can be performed as part of the linearization phase; see [18] for details. This simple minded register allocation technique was quite effective. Program execution speed increased by 35% when the technique was implemented.

Representation of the stored-program machine's heap is done differently for the different components of the heap. The first component of the heap, the store for mutable variables, is kept directly in the first $4 * j$ bytes of the user stack (where j is the number of global variables in the program being compiled). The second component of the heap, which tells how many objects are stored in the first component, remains constant during the execution of a given Pure PreScheme program after the initial environment has been established (in particular, it is also j). It is modeled implicitly through the correctness of the instructions manipulating mutable data. The third component of the heap, that which the primitives manipulate, is simulated by the 68000 heap, primarily via operating system calls.

We used a program that computes Fibonacci numbers to give an initial benchmark for the back end of the compiler on an unloaded Sun 3/60. The Pure PreScheme program uses an explicit array to model the recursion stack. It was compared with an implementation written in C and compiled with gcc version 1.37 using the -O switch. In the C version, tail-recursion is replaced by explicit goto's, and arguments are passed using automatic variables, which gcc allocates in machine registers. The C version also uses `malloc` to allocate the array dynamically, just as the Pure PreScheme version does. We found that that our code used about three times as much CPU time as the C version.

A more realistic test of the VLISP software was constructed as follows. One of the authors wrote a C version of the VLISP Byte-Code Interpreter which was designed only for speed and not structured for verification. It was compiled on a Sun 4 using gcc version 2.1 with the -O2 switch, and the generated assembly code was studied. Any inefficiency observed in the code resulted in a modification to the C source.

When the process was completed, all the variables used to describe the state of the byte-code interpreter were placed into machine registers, and the code sequences for the most used byte-code instructions appeared to be optimal.

Tests showed that it took 3.9 times longer to run programs on a Sun 3/60 using the verified PreScheme version of the VLISP Byte-Code Interpreter as compared with the C version compiled with gcc version 1.37 using the -O switch. We consider this a significant accomplishment given the extensive and intricate optimization techniques used by the GNU C compiler.

10. Conclusions

We have presented a verified compiler for PreScheme. Our architecture divided the compiler into three components:

1. A transformational front end that translates source text into a core language called Pure PreScheme.

2. A syntax-directed compiler that translates Pure PreScheme into a combinator-based tree-manipulation language. We call this language *combinator code*.

3. An assembler that translates combinator code into code for an abstract stored-program machine with linear memory for both data and code.

This factorization proved to be a successful decomposition. It allowed us to use both denotational and operational reasoning to their best advantage. Furthermore, each portion of the proof gave us confidence in a different part of the implementation.

The proof of correctness of the run-time structure is operational, rather than denotational, in its structure: that is, it proceeds by induction on the number of steps taken by the machine, rather than on the size of the program. We believe this is a fundamental improvement. Previous proofs of compiler correctness, such as those in [14, 26], were highly complex because they used induction on the construction of reflexive domains as a denotational analog of induction on length of computation. Our proof would likely be just as complex had we adopted this strategy (see [32] for an attempt to do a much smaller problem in a purely denotational style). By using induction on computation length directly, we avoid this indirection. Furthermore, since we deal directly with terms (trees) rather than with their denotations, we avoid the complication of "inclusive predicates," with their attendant complexity.

The implementation experience showed that having a validated compiler and run-time structure eliminated most bugs in the areas covered by the proofs. The various delivered versions of the compilers had a number of bugs, but these were almost entirely in one of two categories:

1. Incompatibilities between the various phases of the compiler, including errors in syntax, etc. These were artifacts of the circumstance that the various portions

of the compiler, including the interface between the front and back ends, were developed concurrently.

2. Problems with the assembly code sequences generated for the stored-program machine instructions. These were mostly minor in nature (registers not being saved across routine calls, etc.), and were below the grain of the proof. Extending the proof to reach this level would require an extremely detailed model of the behavior of the machine and operating system (see, e.g. [17, 4]). In practice, however, the stored-program machine was at a sufficiently low level that implementation of the primitives was easy.

The method of formalizing storage layout relations seems to be flexible enough to model standard representation strategies. More of these are presented in [7, 31].

The proofs of the different stages had rather different styles. The proofs of the transformational front end (Section 3) were most like "traditional" semantics proofs, such as those in [14]. The proofs of the syntax-directed translator (Section 4.7) tended to be more like exercises in λ-calculus. We believe that a fairly simple simplification-based theorem prover could automate most of the cases in this induction. The back-end proofs (Sections 6.6–8) resemble traditional Hoare-style verification proofs, but seem quite stylized and may be amenable to mechanization by systems like the Boyer-Moore theorem prover [3]. Most of the individual proof cases were routine calculations. We believe this is a mark of success for this effort.

Use of a verified compiler need not entail catastrophic performance penalties. On a realistic example, we showed that a verified program compiled by our verified compiler used only about four times more CPU time compared with an unverified version compiled by the optimizing gcc.

We believe that this proof architecture is applicable to other languages as well. There are, however, a number of ways in which this might be done. One might use a modification of the transformational front end to translate the source language into a variant of Pure PreScheme. One could then modify the Pure PreScheme compiler appropriately. Another approach would be to modify the syntax-directed compiler of Sections 4–5 to use the denotational semantics of the source language instead of the semantics of Section 2. In this approach, the front end would be replaced by a source-to-source optimizer.

A key issue in either of these approaches is the incorporation of optimization into the compiler. In real compilers, optimization is performed on many levels. From the point of view of a compiler proof, the job of an optimizer is to derive some non-local invariants that allow the program to be transformed safely. For example, we needed to rely on the invariance of $N_0 \leq |dom(u)| \leq N$, which is not possible to verify locally without additional information. The operational type-soundness of the program is another such invariant. We believe that developing a systematic way of incorporating such information is the most important outstanding problem in semantics-based compiler correctness.

Acknowledgements

Thanks to Greg Sullivan for his careful reading of this manuscript in its final stages.

List of Figures

References

1. Andrew W. Appel. *Compiling with Continuations.* Cambridge University Press, Cambridge and New York, 1992.
2. Henk P. Barendregt. *The Lambda Calculus: Its Syntax and Semantics.* North-Holland, Amsterdam, 1981.
3. Robert S. Boyer and J Strother Moore. *A Computational Logic.* Academic Press, 1979.
4. Robert S. Boyer and Yuan Yu. Automated correctness proofs of machine code programs for a commercial microprocessor. In D. Kapur, editor, *Automated Deduction — CADE-11*, pages 416–430. 11th International Conference on Automated Deduction, Springer Verlag, 1992.
5. William Clinger. The Scheme 311 compiler: An exercise in denotational semantics. In *1984 ACM Symposium on Lisp and Functional Programming*, pages 356–364, New York, August 1984. The Association for Computing Machinery, Inc.
6. Bruno Courcelle. Fundamental properties of infinite trees. *Theoretical Computer Science*, 25:95–169, 1983.
7. Joshua D. Guttman, John D. Ramsdell, and Vipin Swarup. The VLISP verified Scheme system. *Lisp and Symbolic Computation*, 8(1/2):33–110, 1995.
8. Joshua D. Guttman, John D. Ramsdell, and Mitchell Wand. VLISP: A verified implementation of Scheme. *Lisp and Symbolic Computation*, 8(1/2):5–32, 1995.

9. John Hannan. Making abstract machines less abstract. In J. Hughes, editor, *Functional Programming Languages and Computer Architecture, 5th ACM Conference*, volume 523 of *Lecture Notes in Computer Science*, pages 618–635. Springer-Verlag, Berlin, Heidelberg, and New York, 1991.
10. IEEE Std 1178-1990. *IEEE Standard for the Scheme Programming Language.* Institute of Electrical and Electronic Engineers, Inc., New York, NY, 1991.
11. Richard A. Kelsey. Realistic compilation by program transformation. In *Conf. Rec. 16th Ann. ACM Symp. on Principles of Programming Languages.* ACM, 1989.
12. Richard A. Kelsey and Jonathan A. Rees. A tractable Scheme implementation. *Lisp and Symbolic Computation*, 7(4):315–335, 1994.
13. David Kranz, Richard A. Kelsey, Jonathan A. Rees, Paul Hudak, Jim Philbin, and Norman I. Adams. Orbit: An optimizing compiler for Scheme. *SIGPLAN Notices*, 21(7):219–233, June 1986. Proceedings of the '86 Symposium on Compiler Construction.
14. Robert Milne and Christopher Strachey. *A Theory of Programming Language Semantics.* Chapman and Hall, 1976.
15. Robin Milner. A theory of type polymorphism in programming. *Journal of Computer and System Sciences*, 17:348–375, 1978.
16. Robin Milner, Mads Tofte, and Robert Harper. *The Definition of Standard ML.* The MIT Press, Cambridge, MA, 1990.
17. J Strother Moore. Piton: A verified assembly-level language. Technical Report 22, Computational Logic, Inc., Austin, Texas, 1988.
18. Dino P. Oliva. *Advice on Structuring Compiler Back Ends and Proving Them Correct.* PhD thesis, Northeastern University, 1993.
19. Dino P. Oliva and Mitchell Wand. A verified compiler for pure prescheme. Technical Report NU-CCS-92-5, Northeastern University College of Computer Science, February 1992.
20. Dino P. Oliva and Mitchell Wand. A verified run-time structure for pure prescheme. Technical Report NU-CCS-92-27, Northeastern University College of Computer Science, September 1992.
21. Laurence C. Paulson. *ML for the Working Programmer.* Cambridge University Press, Cambridge, Great Britain, 1991.
22. Gordon D. Plotkin. A structural approach to operational semantics. Technical Report DAIMI FN-19, Aarhus University, 1981.
23. John D. Ramsdell. The revised VLISP PreScheme front end. M 93B095, The MITRE Corporation, August 1993.
24. John D. Ramsdell, William M. Farmer, Joshua D. Guttman, Leonard G. Monk, and Vipin Swarup. The VLISP PreScheme front end. M 92B098, The MITRE Corporation, September 1992.
25. Guy L. Steele. Rabbit: A compiler for Scheme. Technical Report 474, MIT AI Laboratory, 1978.
26. Joseph E. Stoy. *Denotational Semantics: The Scott-Strachey Approach to Programming Language Theory.* MIT Press, Cambridge, MA, 1977.
27. Mitchell Wand. Deriving target code as a representation of continuation semantics. *ACM Transactions on Programming Languages and Systems*, 4(3):496–517, July 1982.
28. Mitchell Wand. Semantics-directed machine architecture. In *Conf. Rec. 9th ACM Symposium on Principles of Programming Languages*, pages 234–241, 1982.
29. Mitchell Wand. Loops in combinator-based compilers. *Information and Control*, 57(2–3):148–164, May/June 1983.
30. Mitchell Wand. Correctness of procedure representations in higher-order assembly language. In S. Brookes, editor, *Proceedings Mathematical Foundations of Programming Semantics '91*, volume 598 of *Lecture Notes in Computer Science*, pages 294–311. Springer-Verlag, Berlin, Heidelberg, and New York, 1992.
31. Mitchell Wand and Dino P. Oliva. Proving the correctness of storage representations. In *Proceedings of the 1992 ACM Conference on Lisp and Functional Programming*, pages 151–160, New York, 1992. ACM Press.

32. Mitchell Wand and Zheng-Yu Wang. Conditional lambda-theories and the verification of static properties of programs. *Information and Computation*, 113:253–277, 1994. Preliminary version appeared in *Proc. 5th IEEE Symposium on Logic in Computer Science*, 1990, pp. 321-332.

Index

GPSR Compliance

The European Union's (EU) General Product Safety Regulation (GPSR) is a set of rules that requires consumer products to be safe and our obligations to ensure this.

If you have any concerns about our products, you can contact us on ProductSafety@springernature.com

In case Publisher is established outside the EU, the EU authorized representative is:

Springer Nature Customer Service Center GmbH
Europaplatz 3
69115 Heidelberg, Germany

Batch number: 10755292

Printed by Printforce, the Netherlands